WHO MOVED MY VOTE?

Yugank Goyal teaches public policy at FLAME University in Pune. He is also the director of Centre for Knowledge Alternatives, which documents district-level statistics and cultures of India. He studied law and economics for his masters and doctorate. In addition to psephology, he has written on issues related to law and development, informal markets and knowledge production. He is passionate about education: recently, he co-founded a school in rural western UP.

Arun Kumar Kaushik teaches economics at O.P. Jindal Global University. He is an economist by training and has earned degrees in business economics, law and economics, and development economics. He has authored several papers on electoral politics of India. His other research interests are intellectual property law and its dynamics and distortions. He is most passionate about teaching and especially enjoys quantitative subjects.

'While questions have often been raised about India's flawed democracy despite widely acknowledged credible elections, this book has a critical look at the dependability of the process itself. Through critical analysis of empirical data from several elections it seeks to highlight the intrinsic failures of our electoral system. A thought-provoking book which is a compelling read.'

—**S.Y. Quraishi**, 17th Chief Election Commissioner of India

'This book is an unusual critique of the Indian electoral system that we all take for granted—the first-past-the-post system in common parlance. Interestingly written, it keeps one's attention throughout and asks unusual questions and has apt empirical illustrations of the points it makes from publicly available data. A thought-provoking read.'

— **E. Sridharan**, Academic Director and Chief Executive,
University of Pennsylvania Institute for the
Advanced Study of India

'As Indians, we are proud of the largely bloodless transfer of power that happened in the past seventy years, through democratic electoral means, both at the central and state levels. This is in sharp contrast to often violent transfers and coups, in other postcolonial newly independent nations. That, however, does not mean that our electoral process is flawless. Or whether the elected officials are truly representative. In this book, Yugank Goyal and Arun Kumar Kaushik examine such provocative questions. It is a thoughtful and nuanced take on Indian elections through the lens of a "design" approach. It argues that India's election process has several deficiencies based on a detailed analysis of extensive data. It also extends the debate to include the role of technology and the issue of independence of institutions. This is an important and scholarly contribution based on empirical research, to the study of elections and democracies.'

— **Ajit Ranade**, Vice Chancellor, Gokhale Institute of Politics
and Economics, Pune, and Founding Trustee,
Association for Democratic Reforms

'During the last decade, India is witnessing an increasing engagement of youngsters and professionals with politics. This has also resulted in a more data-driven analysis of elections. While the discourse captures people's choices as a simple yes and no, its sum and summary remains quite complex. This book is a valuable and an inherently democratic effort (pun intended) in making psephology accessible to a larger audience. Further, it studies elections as designs, not just procedure and thus highlights the shortcomings of the present electoral systems. Through astute electoral figures, the book pushes us to think closely about transforming the present system into being more transparent and responsive to the promise of democracy. Dotted with insightful anecdotes across several state elections, it makes a very interesting read, and a must for anyone interested in Indian electoral politics.'

— **Vinesh Chandel**, Cofounder and Director,
I-PAC (Indian Political Action Committee)

YUGANK GOYAL
ARUN KUMAR KAUSHIK

WHO MOVED MY VOTE?

DIGGING THROUGH INDIAN ELECTORAL DATA

WESTLAND NON-FICTION

WESTLAND
NON-FICTION

First published by Westland Non-Fiction, an imprint of Westland Books, a division of Nasadiya Technologies Private Limited, in 2022

No. 269/2B, First Floor, 'Irai Arul', Vimalraj Street, Nethaji Nagar, Allappakkam Main Road, Maduravoyal, Chennai 600095

Westland, the Westland logo, Westland Non-Fiction and the Westland Non-Fiction logo are the trademarks of Nasadiya Technologies Private Limited, or its affiliates.

ISBN: 9789395073707

10 9 8 7 6 5 4 3 2 1

Typeset by Adobe Garamond Pro by Jojy Philip, New Delhi
Printed at Parksons Graphics Pvt Ltd

To
Sheela Devi Goyal
and
Durga Prasad Kaushik, Yogesh Kaushik and Harish Sharma,
who ensured that we don't forget the little worlds
we are all made of

Contents

Prologue

Elections are like motors, guzzling power. In a democracy, authority and power lie with the people—at least on paper. Elections are meant to suck these out of people with the intention of channelling them into select individuals. It is noteworthy that people willingly let these be pumped out, because they realise that the shared power residing within them is too frail and of little use unless collectively vested in some individuals.

This principle of extraction is illustrated in the Constitution of India, which lays down the process by which the country's power-sucking 'assembly' line works.

Something tells us we should call it a rig (like an oil rig) rather than a motor. To use the term 'rigging' to describe this phenomenon is just too ironical, so we will go with the power-sucking motor instead.

The Constitution of India was drafted by members of the Constituent Assembly who were themselves elected. In December 1946, Pandit Jawaharlal Nehru moved the Objectives Resolution of the Constituent Assembly. It had eight resolutions: five of them—Resolutions 1–3, 7 and 8—dealt with the commitments and characteristics that a newly formed nation, namely India, would possess (sovereignty, for instance). The remaining three, Resolutions 4–6, dealt with the people of India.

These three resolutions read as follows:

4. *All powers and authority of sovereign and independent India and its Constitution shall flow from the people*
5. *All people of India shall be guaranteed and secured social, economic and political justice; equality of status and opportunities and equality before law; and fundamental freedoms—of speech, expression, belief, faith, worship, vocation, association and action—subject to law and public morality*
6. *The minorities, backward and tribal areas, depressed and other backward classes shall be provided adequate safeguards*

Resolutions 5 and 6 reflect the cherished ideal of democracy. Yet, they have been mostly ineffective, with the dream of achieving justice and equality seeming distant with each passing day. In fact, Resolution 5 forms the backbone of almost everything our governance discourse is hinged upon. This hinge, however, is creaking, and threatening to give up on us.

The democratic element that survives is Resolution 4. It has stood the test of time, prevailing through the so-called democratic marvel called elections. Scholars and political pundits take pride in the fact that they are instrumental in deriving power and authority from the people, which is then vested into the government. For a long time, we have believed in the electoral process and trusted it blindly. Our faith in the Constitution has been so unwavering that little attention has been paid to the details of the processes involved, or to the accuracy of the assumptions underlying it. India's celebrated image as the 'largest democracy' in the world is a manifestation of its election machinery, not the government. Elections allay the pain of poor governance the country finds itself stuck in; they help us salvage the dream of our predecessors and smoothen out the awkwardness of our disregard for each other as compatriots. Our blind adherence to Resolution 4 helps make up for our complete disregard for Resolutions 5 and 6.

Elections are our saving grace.

But are they indeed?

That is the question that lies at the heart of this book. We think there are several reasons why we must adopt a less enthusiastic view of elections. For our own good. Elections are, by design, distorted. The election machinery draws only *some* power and often pumps it into people who may actually *not* be the intended beneficiaries. The machine's algorithm can be—and is routinely—tweaked, and there is no harm in accepting that.

We show this using numbers. No big words, no rhetoric. We dissect the process of this assembly line and see what has it yielded in the last several decades. Once we have laid it out as it is, you can be the judge of what it means.

THE CENTRAL IDEA OF THE BOOK

Let us put it more succinctly. In very simple terms, we are writing this book to push readers to reconsider putting all their faith in the present electoral machinery as the best way of choosing our leaders. Consider, for instance, how we decide who becomes our leader. It is rather simple, actually. Whoever is preferred by most people takes the crown. But while people's choices are captured as simple ayes or nays, the aggregate results are often more complex. When we dig deeper into how people have actually voted, we realise that the preferred mandate has suffered serious leakages. For instance, in India, people vote for their own constituencies, but New Delhi is taken over by the party (or coalition of parties) that wins the largest number of constituencies (not votes).

This can be explained by another example. If three constituencies, each with a hundred people, vote for A and B in such a way that A wins in two constituencies and B wins the third, the government is formed by A. But what if A won by a ratio of 51–49 in the first two constituencies, and lost 0–100 in the third? In such a situation, A secured 102 (51+51+0) votes, while B got 198 (49+49+100) votes. More people preferred B, but A won the elections.

Political success and distress are actually mathematically decided and one can analyse hundreds of examples on how adding up political preferences of voters is a tricky game. It is quite simple, but the mechanisms within it, and the factors outside it, make it remarkably unpredictable. Through votes, people cast their preference. But there is always a possibility of leakage.

Through the pages of this book, we have attempted to show you just how leaky the Indian electoral process is.

Elections must form the basis of any discourse on democratic polity. Talking about democracy without discussing elections is like talking about aircrafts without engines. But a good part of scholarly and even fictional writing on democracy ignores electoral politics. It is quite a surprise that people dissect several layers of democratic principles and processes without considering the fact that unless electoral processes are reformed, democracy doesn't mean a thing.

In fact, the idea of elections is larger than that of democracy itself. We vote all the time: in corporate boardrooms on whether to invest in the new technology; in families to decide where to go on the next vacation; and even in classrooms to elect prefects. Economists put the idea of aggregating preferences under the field of 'social choice'. Political elections are the most prominent forms of public choice discourse. If one looks at Google Ngram views for the last 200 years—Google Ngram estimates frequency of any string, say, word, used annually in printed texts that form part of Google corpus—one realises that reference to (and therefore interest in) elections was higher than democracy, even though both ideas flourished in a similar fashion. This tipped over sometime in 1915 in favour of democracy, and as of now democracy retains a larger imprint on people's minds when compared to elections.

FIGURE A Relative frequency of the words 'democracy' and 'elections' occurring across printed text in last 200 years

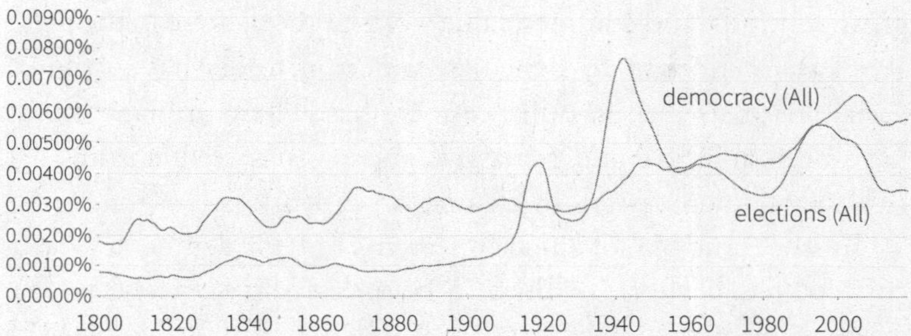

Source: Google Ngram

This book uses elections to shed light on democracy. The underlying assumption for democratic governance is a properly designed electoral process. If the process is designed poorly, democracy as a whole suffers. If the central tenet of democracy is participation, then the first condition it needs to meet is fair participation. We contend that democracy is incomplete unless the electoral system is fair. Surely, no electoral system can be a 100 per cent fair. But the degree to which it is, matters.

The book demonstrates the need to demand a few classes on elections, alongside those on politics, in schools and colleges. As a nation, we have simply set aside any questions on electoral processes, assuming that, like our ancestral village home, it will stand strong forever and won't rust. The book reveals the absurdity of this assumption and exposes that rust.

We are doing two more things along with this. First, we pull out interesting insights from data that go against our dominant thinking and popular narrative. Most of it might actually be fun, especially when readers realise something that they had missed earlier, even after the results were announced. Second, these numbers don't mean much without a story. So, we take the liberty of locating these numbers in the context of political storytelling.

ELECTORAL NARRATIVES AND RESEARCH IN INDIA

Indian politics, as a subject of research, has attracted some of the greatest minds, and commendable work has been done in the field. From Rajni Kothari to Benedict Anderson, India has intrigued social scientists like no other country has. These brilliant minds have been able to build a massive and persuasive literature that richly lays down designs of 'democracy at work'.

In the crucible of such research, Indian democracy as a concept has been crystallised in countless different styles. The celebration of democracy and the project called India, with its surprising cohesion and occasional rifts, has attracted scholarly attention and popular scrutiny from multidisciplinary angles and various schools of thought. At the same time, many deride the heavy-handed state built on the model of oppression to suppress India's pluralism. In many ways, scholars who remain exuberant about progress of Indian democracy sit alongside those who have expressed cautioned frustration about India's trajectory since 1947.

One of the most important of these rugged Petri dishes used to distill Indian democracy is that of elections. As the cornerstone of any democratic polity, electoral studies ought to have a rich tradition of scholarly interest. But for most part, political scientists have not given it the interest it deserves. Many who—while diving into understanding Indian democracy—have ventured deeper, look at it as a procedure followed in letter and celebrate elections as a ritual, *as they are*. Election studies as a separate topic for research and debate has generally been eclipsed by larger questions of democracy and power politics. This, according to us, has been a major oversight.

As a 'mechanism' of democratic governance, election studies must attract some scientific understanding which goes beyond a complex political view.[1] Unfortunately, the emphasis has largely been on politics and not science. Scholarly understanding of Indian elections is woven through a more societal understanding of politics in India, which meanders through the hinges of caste, communal sensitivities, development indicators, (lately) gender and political processes adopted by ruling governments. Elections are looked at as incidents fulfilling procedural democracy and the need to dig deeper into electoral structures of this country is relegated to the background by focusing on a supposedly more imminent issue of substantive understanding of democracy. Therefore, as far as election studies are concerned, social scientists have conveniently tiptoed around the deeper issues of elections by viewing it as a procedure. Focus on procedures alone tends to paint a more buoyant image of Indian democracy.[2] Political imaginations that breed from these conversations rely on opinionated and rhetorical analyses rather than advancing a scientific or technical viewpoint.

The result is that we take people's mandates as the final word. But if it ignores the *process of mandate transfer* in state assemblies and the Parliament, there is a serious trouble in democracy. Let's go back to our analogy of elections being like a motor. The motor is fed an input but that is not the only element determining the output—the design of the machine is equally important. That design (or that algorithm) is what directs the input and treats it. If the design can be manipulated, the input–output relation will behave erratically. That is why it is important that elections be studied as designs and not just as procedures. They build and break their own principles.

Electoral studies, therefore, posit a strange picture. While conversations on elections occupy centre stage in drawing rooms and chai-shop discussions, they have always taken a backseat in university syllabi. In school, we are taught about it through civics textbooks and in colleges as a tiny part in political science courses. In fact, most of us learn about the science of elections through school and college elections. One would be greatly benefitted if one would focus on, say, social history of elections in India,[3] communal determinants of electoral cycles,[4] or perhaps, by taking up social classes and groups, analyse their socio-political location to understand electoral politics.[5] Very little of this actually takes place.

Elections are fascinating experiences. They hold a sensory and emotional appeal for people at large, but they are also an epitome of human imagination. How to aggregate a wide range of preferences? How to design a sieve that screens everything unwanted and allows only that which is desired? How to allow winners and losers in a game that everyone will want to play? Elections are, therefore, excellent sites to study psychology and the ways of the minds of people. One way to do this is to look at them scientifically and quantitatively. A quantitative study would, perhaps, ignore the theatricality of elections, but it will give an accurate glimpse of the backstage. It will scratch the surface and discover patterns. It will build categories and classify events and preferences. It will use some type of numerical lenses to look deeper.

In electoral studies, this numerical science is called psephology, or statistical analysis of election data.

PSEPHOLOGY, SURVEYS AND CASE STUDIES

For most part, psephology has remained at the periphery of political science. Rajni Kothari, the brilliant political scientist who set up the Centre for the Study of Developing Societies (CSDS) in 1963 in Delhi, was possibly one of India's first social scientists to recognise the importance of scientifically analysing elections. During 1967, 1971 and 1980, Kothari and his team at CSDS studied national elections. After a gradual waning of interest in the subject, it was revived again with CSDS's Lokniti in 1996 by

Yogendra Yadav. Lokniti's work may deserve special mention in this context, given the painstaking nature of surveys conducted by them across various parts of India at different points of time and their National Election Studies.

Yogendra Yadav belongs to a rare breed of scholars who navigate across academic silos and speak to people in their language. He built a discourse around psephology through his eloquent discussions and speeches in newsrooms of the late 1990s and 2000s, particularly NDTV. In fact, NDTV's Prannoy Roy was another reason for the interest in psephology in India. His book, co-authored with David Butler and Ashok Lahiri in 1989, *India Decides*,[6] garnered great reviews. A useful first step, the book, however, provided not-so-new takeaways. It claimed, for instance, that the Indian electorate is volatile, that Indians generally vote more for the party than for the candidate, no party has survived the last 40 years without splits and amalgamations, India was never as close to a two-party system as during the 1977 elections, Congress has never obtained more than 49 per cent votes in any general election and so on.[7] Laudable effort, but not as detailed.

During the 1990s, surveys were used as popular methods to peek into the minds of people. This was the time when regional parties were shaking up New Delhi.

Surveys themselves are riddled with several problems. By definition, they can provide only a limited amount of information. When a survey sample suggests or reveals something, it may merely have a statistical correlation with reality. Generalising tendencies of surveys, particularly in the context of a country as huge and diverse as India, can be inaccurate. Think about opinion polls or exit polls. They are an exuberant celebration of *expected* electoral results, with media fever running painfully high and so-called political pundits offering half-baked predictive analyses on the basis of surveys. Often these exit/opinion polls may fail to predict reality. Even though Lokniti experts remain cognizant of this limitation, because of which they spend more efforts in analysing rather than predicting, that is not how the general populace views electoral analysis. People flock to election predictions like students to a college wall displaying admission/final exam lists. These polls become reasons for celebrations and regrets alike, depending on who one is rooting for, at a significant emotional cost. For instance, in one of the studies conducted after the 2009 elections, less than 2 per cent of respondents indicated Narendra Modi as their preferred prime ministerial candidate for the 2014 elections.[8] The results of elections stunned everyone in 2014 and yet again, in 2019.

But practically speaking, nothing can predict reality. Even surveys are inadequate in estimating or explaining the mood of the nation. For them to be close to reality, surveys have to be exhaustive and sampling needs to be scientific. Right now, our survey methods are inspired from American scholarship. While it may be a valuable source of knowledge, its interpretation and design in the Indian context must be alloyed with home-grown survey principles.

Another reason for the relative lack of depth in psephology in Indian intellectual circles is the dominance of a qualitative approach to understanding politics through sociological variables. Western countries have made psephology an integral part of their political science discourses but Indian universities are yet to catch up. This means that even when psephological elements are brought into election studies, they become a form of a 'state of democracy report', lending an impressive image of the 'procedure' of elections.[9] And when they go to mainstream media, the analysis is adorned with hyperboles. In the absence of incisive psephological treatment, Indian elections often attract similar and converging theories, predicated upon leaders, their vote banks, and class and caste dynamics, among other things.

In addition to surveys, another way to carry out election analysis is case studies.[10] Case studies are localised, invaluable glimpses into the minds of Indian voters too. Amongst early commentators, Myron Weiner deserves a special mention. He keenly observed the 1977 elections and built a whole new inventory of knowledge by interviewing stakeholders including campaign workers, civil servants and candidates themselves, by visiting ward offices, campaign rallies and so on.[11] Similarly, Paul Brass' work in this regard has also been exceptional.[12] As an astute observer of Indian politics since the 1960s, Brass has done a critical examination of Hindu–Muslim violence in India.[13] J.M. Lyngdoh, the former chief election commissioner (CEC), had also written a very interesting monograph, *Chronicle of an Impossible Election*, giving an insider account of the 2002 Vidhan Sabha elections in Jammu & Kashmir.[14] These are fascinating insights but constrained by time and space. Also, one would have expected anthropologists and ethnographers to join case-study enthusiasts to study elections, as a ritual,[15] but their interest in electoral processes has remained low.[16]

In this river of survey and case study-based analysis of elections, psephology joins as an important tributary. Numbers tell an independent story, which does not get influenced by changing ideology. So, the conclusions that flow out of examining datasets are immune to categorisation. It doesn't matter what vote share Congress or the Bharatiya Janta Party (BJP) has. Vote shares can be discussed for party A and party B, and yet, the same conclusions can be drawn. The results and associated inferences are sanitised. Further, when we look at numbers, we are looking at the entire picture as revealed preferences. This gives an accurate impression of what people have really thought and considered. Votes are expressions of preferences and, therefore, results are most accurate indicators of what people want. And these days, electoral data is not hard to get. While we collected our data from the Election Commission of India (ECI) publications, these days one can browse through the admirable portals of the Association for Democratic Reforms, Trivedi Centre for Political Data, or even indiavotes.com to understand the numbers behind Indian elections and electoral dynamics.

It must be mentioned that, of late, election pundits have begun to scratch the surface and observe basic numbers in seat share and vote share. Newspapers and data journalism have taken the lead here, which has begun demonstrating the importance of doing electoral studies systematically and numerically. This is indeed welcome, and we hope the book adds to this conversation.

WHAT WE DO IN THIS BOOK

We do not look at poll surveys of any sort. They may contain valuable clues for connecting the dots, but we deliberately try to steer clear of them. The richness of the surveys with tabulations and comparative readings, along with corresponding socio-economic data, is tempting to dwell upon. One can build theories with them. But this temptation is also fuelled from pre-existing notions. It lures us into fitting the data with a theory we already know. It is like when an archaeologist who has dug up something remotely associated with what she was already expecting to find, exults about her findings, and announces the project fulfilled. We would rather dig further to see if we can find something even closer to the truth, however different it is from the expectation we have mapped in our heads before we started digging.

This digging is concentrated in the *declared mandate* of people across all elections, with data pulled out from data published by the ECI. The ECI publishes detailed results after every election. This data is the most reliable source of information in discovering people's preferences. The ECI data on how Indians have voted is our sole source of analysis. This data was appropriately formatted and various calculations were performed on it. We have kept these calculations very basic for ease of understanding. Even simple computations reveal surprising conclusions. In other cases, the data conforms to our existing notions.

Such an exercise, we believe, will be useful for three reasons. First, it will help generate an interest in a hitherto unexplored sub-discipline of psephology for Indian elections. If not today, hard numbers in elections will begin gaining massive importance in the future, as it has already happened in various mature democracies. We hope that, triggered by our findings, interested people will go deeper and unearth far more important insights. Second, it hits a new course for analysing elections, away from emotive subjectivities, far from caste and religious lines, and distant from vote bank-based design of electoral frameworks. Surely, we cannot ignore the hard social realities of this country, but there is merit in an unalloyed study of what people (not groups) have collectively decided and expressed. More importantly, how. Third, using psephology as a key, we hope to resuscitate the conversation on electoral reforms

We must also state here that the book is not a tunnel vision of numbers and numbers alone. The book shall serve a contextual and dialogical purpose. Contextual because we have located these numbers in the historical narrative associated with the particular region and election cycle. In that, we provide summaries and trajectories that electoral politics have taken in particular parts of India. This helps build a relationship with the numbers. The study is, therefore, not in isolation of a host of contextual stories. Indeed, it is crucial to find sense and humour in Indian polity. Consequently, ruling parties or leaders form an important part of our stories too. Dialogical because we leave a number of hypotheses to tickle the reader's imagination. A full-blown account of proofs that these hypotheses require is difficult to work upon in this particular text. Our hope is, in the times to come, some of these ideas will be either disproved or proved. But the sliver of insight that they offer is a ray of hope that the conversation will continue.

We have also made considerable effort in making the book accessible to an audience that is untrained in psephology. In fact, it is written primarily for them. We do not make any grand theoretical designs, and wherever we introduce a concept that may be unusual or new for most readers, we spend a significant space to make it easier, simple and straightforward. The idea is not to focus on the equation but on what it stands for. Wherever possible, we have extensively used graphs and figures to drive home the point. These graphs are a simplified visualisation of how voting patterns have varied across time, and offer a bird's eye view of what happens with our votes. The book is written without assuming any mathematical knowledge on part of the reader.

Finally, it is important to mention that we do not predict anything in this book. We want to take an early stab at Indian elections and see if there are interesting stories to be told. One must realise that predicting winners and losers is a futile exercise and it can never be done with 100 per cent accuracy. What's important is explanations or discovering important patterns in the life of electoral victories and defeats to lend a larger picture of what is going on. In many ways, this book undertakes a journey with your vote, meandering from ballot boxes (and voting machines) to the seat in Parliament or state assemblies. And within that journey, it chronicles the bumps and bottlenecks, delays and incorrect directions that are constant features through the travel.

MOTIVATIONS FOR CHAPTER SELECTION

Our first chapter is a quintessential look at the Lok Sabha elections, from 1952 until now. What has happened, and what voters may have missed, is as important and interesting as it gets. But it also serves another purpose and that is to set the tone for the book.

The tone vibrates with some generic equations without being pedantic. More important than formulae are what the formulae stand for. We simplify the numbers and their force. While the music created by mathematics continues to echo in subsequent chapters, it is in the first chapter where the genre is truly exhibited.

In chapters 2 and 3, we pick up the states of Bihar and Uttar Pradesh (UP), and then Bengal and Kerala in chapter 4. UP and Bihar are two of the largest states in terms of population (a quarter of the country lives in these two states); they are also among India's poorest. With low human development indicators, the two states together are home to more than 36 crore people. Almost equal to the entire population of the United States of America! Located in the Gangetic plains, these provinces are some of the most fertile plains in the world, and unsurprisingly, predominantly inhabited by farmers. Connected by shared history and linguistic traditions, the two geographically identical provinces display similarly located informal economies, low levels of education, endemic poverty, patriarchal set-ups and brutal adherence to caste-based discrimination. The UP–Bihar duo is India's Achilles heel—if you can't fix these two, you can't fix India. When Paul Brass says that north India makes or breaks India, perhaps he is mainly talking about these two states. In 2014, when BJP came to power, how many votes did it get in Hindi-speaking states? Eight-five per cent! Majority of Indian prime ministers have been from UP.

Both states are woven out of a rich tapestry of history over thousands of years. Archaeological records here dating from the fifth to second millennia BCE evolve an idea of India traversing through kingdoms of Kannauj, Magadha, Gupta and Pratihara dynasties from this region. The two states have been the fountainheads of India's religious, linguistic and cultural make-up that continues to this day. Mughals under Babur were already controlling most of present-day UP and Bihar, which continued to be the case at least until Aurangazeb's reign. It was only during the colonial era that the two regions became politically separate. After the Battle of Buxar in 1764, Bihar's revenue rights (along with Bengal and Orissa) came under the control of the British East India Company, but it remained with the Bengal Presidency. It was only in 1912 that it was carved out as a separate political province. During the colonial era, the erstwhile Uttar Pradesh—different from its current form which came to be only in 1957—was tossed from between the north-western provinces (which included Ajmer and Jaipur as well) in the late eighteenth century to the United Province of Agra and Oudh (UP in short) by 1902. While Patna remained Bihar's capital, UP continued shifting its capital from Agra (1857) to Allahabad (1902), and finally settled for Lucknow (1920). The separation between the two regions is, therefore, a colonial accident.

This shared history encourages us to pick them up not just for sheer numbers, but also because they are provinces that have had a distinct impression on the idea of India. Perhaps nothing connects them more than the leader who shook New Delhi in the mid-1970s. Loknayak Jayaprakash Narayan (or JP, as he was fondly called) was born in 1902, in a village called Sitabdiara. Comprised of a few hamlets, the village came under the Saran district of Bihar at the time. Today, it lies at the cusp between Ballia in UP, and Arrah and Chhapra in Bihar. Since Sitabdiara was located in the flood-prone region of the Ghagra river, JP had to frequently move around with his family to nearby villages, to escape flooding, almost akin to moving along the present-day UP–Bihar border.

This human osmosis reflects the naturalness with which the two states can be clubbed together. Decades later, JP was to show India the power of mass revolution, the kind unseen in its independent history, that brought the government to its knees. During the Lok Sabha elections of 1971, Congress had secured 86 per cent seats in UP and 74 per cent in Bihar. After JP (and the Emergency) 'happened', in 1977, Congress got zero seats in these two states. Zero!

This is important. The political imagination of a nation and society as it exists in one's mind is a product of one's own civilisation. The communities are definitively, to invoke Anderson[17], imagined. A shared history of the two regions, therefore, builds a shared sense of the social and the political.[18] And hence, taking them up in our study makes a lot of sense to understand Hindi-speaking voters. Because of the complex historical churnings that the two states have witnessed, the analysis was too vast to be showcased in the same chapter. Hence, we dwell on them separately. But the idiom of political importance continues. Together, they command 22 per cent of India's Lok Sabha seats, and almost 27 per cent of India's population. They are, for lack of a better word, important!

Why did we pick Kerala and Bengal? This is an easy question to respond to. They are exactly what UP–Bihar are not. These two states boast of more equitable societies, with high rates of literacy, political participation, better public service delivery and satisfactory land rights allocation. Their politics is also seemingly very different from other states. The two states have become symbolic of communism in India. The governments are red in hue, and so is the soil. Redness is a mark of iron in the soil. And as communist parties would have us believe, in character as well. Both of them present a somewhat refreshing departure from other major parts of India in their socio-political make-up. Did the similarities of love for football and fish come to mind?

Bengal and Kerala have also tickled political imaginations like no other states have. Bengal is a massive state. It is almost as big as Bihar in terms of population and is the fourth largest in the country in terms of area (after UP, Maharashtra and Bihar).

Poster children of India's culture (Bengal) and tourism (Kerala), the two states have garnered significant scholarly attention from around the world by hosting powerful and democratically elected communist governments. Political participation runs deep in these two states, and as politically charged provinces, they are covered by mainstream media vociferously (think about Sabrimala or Singur). In fact, if you remove Hindi dailies from the list, some of the most widely read newspapers in India are in Malayalam and Bengali (*Malayala Manorama*, *Ananda Bazaar Patrika*, *Mathrubhumi*). Looking at voting in these two states is a treat for someone who has some form of emotional connection with them, or with politics. That would mean a great many Indians.

One can say that UP–Bihar and Kerala–Bengal are two ends of the political spectrum that one may calibrate the entire country within. This statement is a large brushstroke and we know it may sound utterly impatient to some. But there is humorous merit in placing all Indian states between them, either in order of social or political indicators.

There is no special reason for including these four against the rest of the states. The story of Rajasthan could be as important and interesting as Tamil Nadu's and we make no judgments as to why Bihar, UP, Bengal and Kerala may tell more fascinating narratives. We chose them simply because they do tell us fascinating narratives, even if not the *most* fascinating. It is difficult to cover all the states in this book. But the hope is that, encouraged by our work, scholars and writers may pick up other states, dig into their details and possibly tell the world more interesting stories. The idea is to build a discourse, not to cover it in its entirety. And these four states are intellectually sumptuous starters.

Note that for some electoral indices like 'effective number of parties' or 'disproportionality' (explained in Chapter 1), we have not included the 2021 assembly elections in Bengal and Kerala, and 2020 assembly elections in Bihar. For Bengal, the detailed data was yet to come at the time of writing the manuscript, which also obviates Kerala's comparison of 2021 elections there. In Bihar, the 2021 assembly elections were characterised by a number of pre-poll and post-poll coalitions which kept fluctuating. Calculating the indices with changing coalitions before and after the elections may give out spurious results, and hence we avoided it. Again, the purpose is not to analyse a specific election, but to give a flavour of how such analysis can be done, and how it may lead to interesting insights.

In Chapter 5, we excavate silences from the noise in the rise of BJP in the Indian political landscape. The rise of the party has attracted many commentators who have attempted to theorise what we must make of this victory. We offer our two pence here, delving deeper into how votes and seats look, when did BJP's real ascent begin and what we can attribute it to. More importantly, we dissect the recent 2019 Lok Sabha election verdict and analyse the results from a variety of lenses. Numbers surprise us.

Chapter 6 is dedicated to the study of coalition politics in India, which is very important. Indian politics today is strongly characterised by coalition governments. The last four Lok Sabhas have been run by a coalition of parties. The five Lok Sabhas preceding it (during 1989–99) were coalition governments as well. Even the Morarji Desai government in 1977 was a coalition made by a number of non-Congress parties joining forces. More than half of all the Lok Sabhas India has seen have been coalition driven. So powerful has been the force of coalitions that the National Democratic Alliance (NDA), the political association led by BJP, and United Progressive Alliance (UPA), which has Congress at its core, are household names, as much as the two parties themselves have been.

Interestingly, our assumptions about coalition governments too are changing. The idea that coalition governments will always be unstable has been challenged by the consistency and success of the NDA and UPA in running governments for full terms in the last two decades. In fact, it is coalition government politics that encourages regional parties and minority voices to be heard. Let us not forget that it was the coalition government of V.P. Singh which rolled out the recommendations of the Mandal Commission. Kanshiram had famously remarked that a majboor (dependent) sarkar is better than a mazboot (strong) sarkar, since the former has higher likelihood of being sensitive to the disadvantaged.

But coalition governments also have a principled objection. A post-poll alliance disregards political promise. When I vote for political party A, I would like A *and* not B to govern. But if A and B agree to form a post-poll coalition, what happens to the promise that was made to me? I will not be amused by this post-poll bargain. So, while on one side, coalition governments have built a powerful presence, both in terms of reflecting disparate and diverse identities of Indians, they have also weakened the foundational pillars of trust that democracy promises its followers.

In Chapter 7, encouraged by our own findings, we go deeper into the election motor algorithm and open up the guiding principle of elections in India. We lay bare our scepticism with electoral processes here and propose ideas for electoral reforms. Of late, two such debates have attracted popular interest and we find it useful to dwell on them: first, debate on presidential versus parliamentary system of democracy and their relative appropriability for India, and second, the idea of proportional representation. We pry open the black box of electoral politics and attempt to understand these issues. We explain their basic premise and implementation strategy for India, and suggest how, if at all, they could be applied. This chapter adopts a distinct tone from the rest of the book as it proposes why and how we need to radically rethink the way we choose our leaders.

Chapter 8, the concluding chapter, ties the whole book together, with some personal, relevant anecdotes. A constant sentiment reverberating through the book is the fractures in the system that decides the winner based on who has the highest number of votes. The leakage of preferences in this method can only be addressed by replacing it with other systems. This chapter, therefore, helps us view the ease and value that other methods can bring to the system. While by no means new, these methods still elude popular perceptions and understanding of ordinary Indians. We want people to be aware, in a proverbial sense, of some low-hanging fruits.

And that is what we have. If you are looking to find predictions about forthcoming elections amidst the pages of this book, you will be disappointed. If you are thinking of finding political gossip or insider stories about contemporary political leaders who are contesting elections, you will be disappointed. If you are wondering whether the book will favour Congress, BJP or any other party, you will again be disappointed.

But you will enjoy, as John Berger[19] would call it, *new* ways of seeing.

NOTE ON POLITICAL CONSULTING AND GAMING THE SYSTEM

Very briefly, since many readers may be interested in this topic, here is one more reason why numbers are important, and consequently, why we need to watch out for what lies ahead in terms of our democratic futures.

Since 2003-04, when Indian elections have begun taking place through electronic voting machine, an important data has begun appearing for the first time, namely, the booth-level voting statistics. Earlier when ballot papers were used, counting of several booths were done together piling up all the ballot papers in one heap and separating them therefrom. Now, counting is done machine-wise, which means booth-wise. Imagine what the booth-level data can do!

Politicians and their soldiers at booth levels have detailed knowledge about households in a booth-level neighbourhood. Using tools like Google Maps and collecting information about all the voters in that booth through polling lists, it is very easy to ascertain a fairly accurate description of which households would have voted for this person, or not. During the next cycle then, it is only natural that the campaign will use this knowledge to influence households. This analysis will not only optimise campaign costs (spend more on booth neighbourhoods where swing voters lie, and less in those neighbourhoods where chances of winning are low), but more importantly, encourage the contestants to make their constituency-level calculation factor in booth-level numbers. In other words, as a contestant, because now I have booth-level data, I am not interested to woo all the voters in my constituency, but only those who are likely to be influenced. The details don't matter here, but note that contestants, and their political parties, who understand this, carry an edge above the others in elections today. The important point is not about the trick being available to all or not. The important point is that, in this number game, democracy and its laudable goals are shoved out of the window.

EINSTEIN AND HIS QUESTION PAPER

The premise of our work is most accurately located in an (apocryphal) amusing story about Albert Einstein. When Einstein was at the Institute for Advanced Study in Princeton, he set a question paper and handed it over to his teaching assistant. The assistant looked at it and seemed surprised. He asked Einstein, 'Isn't this the same question paper you gave out last year?'

'Yes indeed, it is,' replied Einstein.

'But how can you possibly give the same test to the students two years in a row?' The assistant was curious and baffled.

'Because,' smiled Einstein, 'the answers have changed.'

The questions which the election machinery was designed for, have remained the same, and it is time to see if the manner in which it answers those questions has changed. And in doing so, think about which parts of the machine need repairs. This essentially is what this book is about.

1

Digging through the Lok Sabha

In October 1951, when Princess Elizabeth started her tour of the Commonwealth along with her husband Philip (nephew of Lord Mountbatten), her father, King George VI, was miserably ill. If he died, she was to be pronounced the Queen. But the trip was not to be avoided. So, she flew, but all through her tour, she carried with her the draft declaration of her accession to the throne. George VI died in February 1952. At that time, the royal couple was in Kenya. The draft came in handy—she was immediately proclaimed the Queen of the realms.

Almost exactly during the time that she carried her accession declaration along, independent Indians were carrying ballot boxes! For the English, it was a matter of routine. For Indians, it was a matter of unimaginable transformation, the first-of-its-kind. While the king had died in England, the entire English rule had died in India. An heir had been chosen in England, but a government was to be 'elected' in India. England was calling for the Archbishop of Canterbury to anoint Princess Elizabeth as Queen Elizabeth II while India was calling its 36 crore people to vote.

The ballot boxes were manufactured by Godrej as their first product from the new Vikhroli factory in Mumbai (then Bombay). If you had placed them side by side, some said they would cover 200 miles. More than 2 lakh polling booths were set up, outside which almost 8 crore people stood in queues to vote. Eighty-five per cent of them didn't know how to read and/or write, so they simply chose from the symbols and cast their vote.

Globally these were—in Dicken's immortalised words—'the best of times and the worst of times'. England was welcoming its new ruler. Egypt was overthrowing its monarchy through a violent revolution. Closer home, Pakistan had witnessed the assassination of its Prime Minister Liaquat Ali Khan. And the police forces in East Pakistan were firing on Bengali students protesting against the imposition of Urdu.

We were voting as a nation. And everyone was, including women. Indian women began voting before those in Switzerland!

Almost 3.6 crore people cast their vote on a symbol which looked like a pair of oxen with a yoke driving them. They all knew the party very well, thanks to decades of being the sincere voice of nationalism. The Indian National Congress had churned not just popular but philosophical leaders as well. Today, we know it as the party with the symbol of a human hand. At that time, the symbol was taken up by Forward Bloc, a faction split from Subhash Chandra Bose's Forward Bloc (which couldn't win any seat in 1952). Congress picked up this 'available' symbol of hand, only before the 1980 parliamentary elections.

Fifty-four parties contested in 486 constituencies. Party names were honest and descriptive, a rarity today. Parties called Bolshevik Party of India, Punjab Depressed Class League, Akhil Bharatiya Ram Rajya Parishad, Madras State Muslim League Party, Justice Party, Revolutionary Socialist Party (Uttar Pradesh), Tribal Sangha, Zamindar Party, and others nominated their candidates. Congress won the elections, securing 74 per cent seats with 45 per cent votes. Who was the runner up? The second position was held by independent contestants with 7.5 per cent seats and 16 per cent votes!

It's been a while since Congress got such an overwhelming vote of confidence. In the 2019 parliamentary elections, the party won merely 9.5 per cent seats, with 19.5 per cent votes. The winner this time was BJP, which claimed 56 per cent seats through 37.3 per cent votes. BJP's original face was the Jana Sangh. In 1952, it had just 0.3 per cent seats and 3 per cent votes. Indian voters are not the same indeed. India isn't the same.

Elections are expensive social experiments. They absorb not just the campaign capital, but also state funds. The Election Commission of India (ECI) routinely publishes how much it costs to run Lok Sabha elections. The values have increased significantly over time. From 6 paise per voter in 1952, the 2014 elections claimed ₹46 per voter from the ECI.[1] (This is ten times the inflation adjusted value.) In 2014, the ECI's costs—excluding security—was to be ₹3,500 crores. The most rapid increase in official expenses on elections took place between 2009 and 2014. In 2009, the per voter expense was ₹15.50. In 2014, it tripled. This is perhaps attributed to the awareness campaigns run by the ECI to get more voters to vote. In 2014, India's nominal gross domestic product (GDP) was around ₹2 lakh crores. The 2014 Lok Sabha elections cost the exchequer almost 2 per cent of all the goods and services produced in the country! In comparison, India spent 2.8 per cent of its GDP on education during 2014-15.

These costs don't include the expenses made by political parties on private campaigns. If one looks at these private costs, Indian elections are the most expensive in the world. In 2019, political parties spent ₹700 per voter! This adds up to almost $8 billion or ₹55,000 crores.[2] This is the annual GDP of Tajikistan or Kyrgystan. And in the last 20 years, campaign expenses in India have increased by six times. Even the US presidential elections of 2016 saw lesser money ($6.5 billion, or ₹44,000 crores at the 2016 exchange rate) being spent. It is so bizarre that it doesn't make sense sometimes. Why would a nation which is one-tenth the size of USA (by nominal GDP) have political parties spending more money on elections? Since this money is mostly corporate money, one wonders why businesses fund political parties to such an extent. Perhaps because political power still controls economic power in India. The government still controls much of the resources, and maybe, real liberalisation has not taken place in India yet. We explore this briefly towards the end of this chapter.

The bottom line is simple—elections are important in India, arguably more important than most other national projects. They, in many ways, have come to characterise India as well as democracy. We trust the electoral machinery blindly. We know who we prefer. If they get enough votes, they win and form the government. This edifice rests on the assumption that my vote counts, and in national elections, it influences—in whatever little way it can—what happens in Delhi. But how true is that?

THE MYTH OF REPRESENTATION

When people vote, they express their preferences—for candidates who are contesting to govern them. Citizens are expressing their preference for who their leader should be (the magical words of democracy). In making their choice, they have to select one of the contesting candidates. Let us assume a scenario. I have 20 candidates contesting in my constituency. I will have to select one. I can't rank them in order of preference. I can't give them scores. I have to pick one. One and not more. Far from being a show of pagans with many gods, I have to behave like a devout monotheistic believer. No God but God.

This means the choice architecture is binary in nature. It's either a yes or no.

What does the binary architecture of our choices do? It picks one winner who has been preferred the most (not necessarily by the most). In democratic systems, the winner takes all. Everyone else, no matter how much they were preferred, get nothing. We have to select one leader, and one leader alone. So, whoever is most preferred, gets to be the leader. This system of elections is called the first-past-the-post (FPTP) system.

DEFINING THE WINNER: LOVED BY MOST OR HATED BY LEAST?

There are two interesting complications with this system. Let us try to unbundle the first one first. Voters' preferences are difficult to aggregate. Since there are many people voting, and many people being voted for, opinions will differ. If there are only two contestants, the choice is easy. Whoever gets more than 50 per cent of the votes wins. Simple! If there are more than two contestants, one can find out who is most preferred, surely, but this person may not necessarily be preferred by the majority. Let's say the voting distribution is 34 per cent, 33 per cent and 33 per cent. The first contestant is the winner, but note that 66 per cent voters did not want her to win. This victory is the best outcome we have got. It is fair but it has led to *sadness* in a majority (66 per cent) of voters. One may say, instead of aggregating the preference, this method has segregated it and chosen the recipient of the highest votes. Many people are happy, but many more are sad.

Let's call this preference leakage. Any electoral system, however fair, will lead to a dissatisfied base of voters after the results. This means, unless there is a unanimous choice, leakage must exist. By design, therefore, any democratically elected leader sits on piles of likes and dislikes, and more often than not, majority of dislikes. She may be chosen by, let's say, the largest minority.

The trick is, she was not *preferred by most*, yet she is everyone's leader because she was *disliked by least*.

This means—because likes and dislikes coexist in any democratic result—there may be a better way to define democratic leadership: it is not how much the winner is liked, but how less she is disliked. This idea that least hated (and not most liked) is how we elect our leaders lies at the heart of our democratic processes. For far too long, the world has looked at its leaders as those who have been elected over other contestants, because they were most preferred. But the view that they were elected because they were least disliked introduces a more interesting layer to the perspective.

This adds a new goal that electoral processes must be mindful of. Crudely speaking, the idea is that we cannot make everyone happy with election results. So, let's focus on minimising sadness. If candidate B with 33 per cent votes is given power, the sadness will be 67 per cent (34 per cent+33 per cent), in terms of the share of saddened people. Focusing on minimising sadness as opposed to maximising happiness lends us a useful insight which is closer to reality. Practically speaking, majority of voters are unhappy in the end because it has been rather rare for a party/contestant to get more than 50 per cent of the votes. To say that majority wins, therefore, in the parlance of the FPTP system, is hugely misleading. With 99 contestants in a constituency, if 98 get 1 per cent votes each, then the 99th contestant will win the elections with 2 per cent votes in her favour.

Majority does not win. Plurality does. This is the edifice of our democracy.

Once we flip our viewpoint about the purpose of electoral exercises, we become more grounded and realistic in understanding politics. It suddenly provides us with a vocabulary through which we can access our experiences. So, recognising the sadness of losers is a more accurate depiction of reality. It is closer to the truth and our own lived experiences. Elections yield least unfavourable winners rather than the most favourable.

THE DANCE OF SEATS AND VOTES

The way the FPTP system is deployed raises another (the second) complication. This is peculiar to countries like India. Suppose there are three constituencies with equal number of voters, and two parties are contesting elections. Whoever gets to win two out of the three constituencies will form the government. If, for instance, party X receives 51 per cent votes in two and 1 per cent votes in the third constituency, it forms the government. After all, it won in two of three places. (Party Y lost two seats, securing 49 per cent in each, and won one seat, securing 99 per cent votes.) Now, assuming each constituency had 100 voters, add up the votes the two parties received across the three constituencies.

X received 51+51+1 = 103 votes out of 300.

Y received 49+49+99 = 197 out of 300 votes.

Clearly, more people at an aggregate level preferred Y and wanted her to win. The government, however, is formed not on the basis of total votes, but seats. So, X, who won two out of three seats, forms the government.

Do you see the fallacy here? Despite X being disliked by more people, it forms the government. In other words, since they don't look at the vote share but seat share, it may entirely be possible that the party preferred by fewer number of voters will form the government.

This game, often eluding the layperson's understanding of electoral processes, forms a characteristic feature of voting results in India. We do not follow a presidential system of democracy. As per the plans of the chairman of the Drafting Committee, B.R. Ambedkar, the executive is not exactly separate from the legislature, rather a part of it. People vote for their legislators, who in turn decide on the head of the state, the prime minister. Aggregation of legislators happens at the level of seats, not votes. So what matters is who wins the seat.

Also note that it doesn't matter by how much a person won. The winning margin can be one or one lakh. Both have the same weightage. This gives us another type of leakage. The first leakage is due to plurality (you need highest votes, not 50+ per cent votes to win). The second leakage is that when we aggregate all constituencies, the number of votes doesn't matter at all. All that matters is whether the constituency is won or lost.

The heart of the matter in the electoral process is therefore that of aggregation, or adding up people's preferences. Aggregating preferences, falling broadly under the social choice theory, has been quite an intriguing science. Consider how difficult the exercise is. So many people and so many orders of choices. Yet, everyone is imposed with one choice in the end. For instance, people in the family may have differing desires in terms of where to go for dinner. Ten children and maybe three restaurant options. Yet, only one of them will be chosen and imposed on all. So, leakage is inevitable. To make this aggregation fair, one needs to select a restaurant from this list which induces the least amount of emotional suffering. Unless all of them agree on one location (highly unlikely), they will have to select one spot, even when some would have never wanted to go there. Perhaps that is why parents often act as dictators in such situations. Kenneth Arrow, the winner of Nobel Memorial Prize in economics in 1972, had declared in 1950 why a dictator is the only fair game in any election method (we explore this in the Epilogue). It's called the Impossibility Theorem.

THE 2014 LOK SABHA: THE U-TURN

Let's pick up the 2014 Lok Sabha elections which signify a recent dramatic break from the past in terms of waking up to a massively turned-around Indian electorate. (We dedicate an entire chapter to the 2019 elections, so we don't discuss it here.) Four hundred and sixty-four political parties contested through 8,251 contestants. If parties are consolidated mass of people with distinct ideologies, policy preferences and support bases, imagine 464 such diverse viewpoints getting 55 crore people to coalesce around them!

BJP emerged as the winner, securing an absolute majority with 282 seats, while the incumbent Congress won only 44 seats. The minimum threshold to be able to nominate someone as the leader of the opposition is 10 per cent of the 543 seats in Parliament. Congress could not even attain this figure in 2014. Contrast this with the first elections in independent India when it won 364 out of 489 seats!

This is a massive turnaround, in less than 75 years. Indian voters, therefore, become most fascinating minds to study. But if 75 years is long enough a timeline to change not just the mindset, but also voter base, consider BJP's path. The last time it came to power in 1998, it got 182 seats. This had declined to 116 in 2009. The trajectory would have predicted a further decline. But 2014 brought it 282 seats. It was as if the party was scavenging for leftovers but it was served an eight-course meal. On the other hand, Congress, which won 206 seats in 2009, was reduced to a mere 44 seats in 2014.

What changed the Indian voters' minds suddenly?

Many claim that the rise of BJP was catapulted by the rise of Hindu consciousness. One wonders how true such a claim is. How could these emotions suddenly erupt in a short span of five years? One may also assume that voters were frustrated with the heavy-handedness and corruption of public leaders and, this time, cared for development rather than old loyalties. Further, the crushing defeat of Congress may suggest a disregard for dynasty politics. But scratching beneath the results, our assumptions may not be accurate.

Frankly, we are not sure if Indian voters are indeed gravitating towards economic growth as the voting criterion. Distilling such conclusions can be very difficult. Vaishnav and Swanson's work[3] is instructive in this case. They show that even though during the 1980s and 1990s, which were economically very tumultuous years for India, the economy had not been an important criterion for Indian voters. But it appears as though the last decade somehow was. For instance, seat share and average annual per capita growth rate are positively correlated during 2000–12. While these correlations are indicative, it's not easy to generalise.

But more interesting would be the story of how Indian voters think about dynasty politics. Kanchan Chandra has explored if 2014 indeed marked a death knell to dynasty politics.[4] In 2004 and 2009, Lok Sabha members coming from political families made up 20 per cent and 29 per cent respectively of the strength of the House. In 2014, this figure was 21 per cent—not very different. More than 80 per cent of all Members of Parliament (MPs) under the age of 30 and half of all in the age group of 30–39 years, belong to a political family.[5] The trend decreases slightly with age.

Surely, the election of someone for the top job does not reflect anything about what is going on in the states and other parties. That is why scratching beneath the numbers assumes importance. What the North and South Blocks conceal are the emotions and aspirations of millions of voters. It is like archaeology. The deeper we excavate the layers, the richer our understanding becomes. Sometimes, we unearth evidence to solidify our assumptions. Sometimes, a different artefact to reconfigure our history. And sometimes, a whole new world to rewrite it.

THE VOTE SHARE STORY

Vote share is simply votes won by a party divided by total votes polled. In cricketing parlance, it is the strike rate of a player.

Here's a piece of startling statistic. It was largely agreed that 2004 was a fruitful year for the United Progressive Alliance (UPA) led by Congress. They secured 221 seats, making a democratic claim to New Delhi. Their seat share was 40.7 per cent. The seat share of the National Democratic Alliance (NDA) led by BJP was 34.6 per cent. Simple deal, right? But if you look at the vote share, UPA's was 35.9 per cent and NDA's was 36.2 per cent!

Indeed, the NDA had secured more votes than UPA, but our electoral rules ensured it had no impact on the formation of the government.

Vote shares tell us fascinating stories about competition. Interestingly, the vote share of the winning party has mostly been declining since 1951, from 45 per cent to 31.3 per cent in 2014 and 37.3 per cent in 2019. The highest vote share was secured by Congress in 1984, at 48.1 per cent.

What about the second highest vote share, party-wise? If the highest vote share is reducing in its value, then second highest vote share must surely increase? This is indeed the case, but it is happening at a slower rate. From 3.29 per cent votes in 1951, the party with the second highest vote share in 2019 gathered 19.5 per cent votes. The value of the third-largest vote share has not seen a specific increasing or decreasing pattern. It has been hovering in single digits throughout (an average of 7.3 per cent), except peaking at around 11.5 per cent during the coalition politics of 1989 and 1991. The competition for the second spot hasn't been exciting (not taking into consideration independent candidates).

Figure 1.1 illustrates the point—the real face-off in terms of votes is taking place between the first and the second party, with a real close finish in 1998. The spike of 1977 is Congress' failed attempt to retain its position. However, the most interesting part of this graph lies elsewhere. Until 1971, the votes for the second party had hardly increased. In other words, a profound impact of the Emergency on the electoral landscape of India was to make the runner-up party also important in Indian politics.

FIGURE 1.1 Seats and votes margin between the winner and the runner-up across Lok Sabha elections

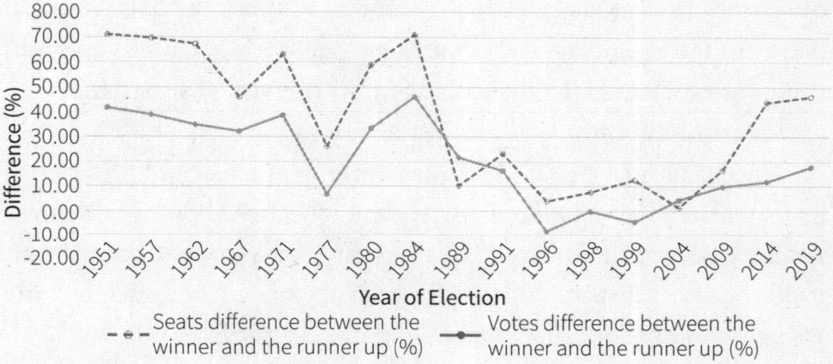

Note two other things here. One, the dominance of Congress has always been seat based, not vote based. Despite the commonly held belief that the 1950s, 1960s and most of the 1970s were Congress-dominated, Congress' position was hinged on seats, not on people's votes. Across all these decades, Congress secured most votes, but never the majority—always remaining in the range of 40–47 per cent.

One must remember here that not having a majority of votes is very common in most democratic environments. Therefore, aggregation is never perfect. And our idea is not to belittle Congress' towering presence in shaping Indian democracy in the early years. There is little doubt that the solid edifice of democracy that we see flourishing today rests on pillars constructed by the Congress leaders of the time. But at the same time, it is important that we recognise that Congress did not have unwavering support across the country, even during its heydays.

So, who did everyone else vote for? Contrary to most perceptions, there were many other popular parties in the early era of independent India. In 1951, during the first general elections, more than 50 parties contested polls. In fact, the second highest votes went to independent candidates—around 16 per cent!

Next was the Socialist Party (10.6 per cent) and Kisan Mazdoor Praja Party (5.8 per cent), led by two of India's most inspirational dissenters in the last century, Acharya Kriplani and Jayprakash Narayan (JP) respectively. Congress secured 45 per cent votes and these two collected 16.4 per cent of all the votes. The remaining got distributed among 50 other parties.

Kriplani and JP joined hands in the next Lok Sabha elections to form the Praja Socialist Party, which secured 10.4 per cent of votes. This was again the third highest. Independent contestants took the second spot, with 19.3 per cent votes. Interestingly, only 16 parties contested the second general elections.

The second thing is that vote share differences have been thinning down. The figure shows that after 1984, the vote share difference between parties receiving the highest and second-highest votes is converging. This difference was negligible in 1998. BJP, with 182 seats, got 25.59 per cent votes, while Congress, at 141 seats, secured 25.82 per cent. The difference was a paltry 8.5 lakhs approximately, of the almost 37 crores votes polled. Such convergence may signify increased levels of political competition. It may also suggest a growing similarity between voters' preferences, or parties' policies and mandates. Further, it also suggests the emergence of other parties who are taking away the vote share of the first party.

Each of these reasons may contribute to the outcome. What's more important to recognise is that we have evolved in our political decision-making. We are more informed, and more conscious of our choices. One can also say that parties have become smarter in their outreach. Strongholds of winning parties had been penetrated by hitherto weaker parties, particularly after the 1970s. The underlying idea that winners are merely those who are least disliked is at play here. It is easier for voters to switch sides to someone they may have disliked a little bit more because the one they disliked least was not as good as they expected.

What is the cost of switching in any election? In simple terms, it is the risk. There is a risk that the new government may betray on its poll promises. With the rise of regional parties in the 1980s, who chimed in with the voters' caste and community base, this risk appears to have minimised. And as the incumbents became more inaccessible, more conscious voters began experimenting with their own choices.

One may also claim that, through vote share convergence, practically speaking, the political spectrum of Left and Right is not divided in a watertight manner between respective political parties, as is often perceived. For most part of our recent political history, the narrative has categorised our votes between the liberal Congress and the conservative BJP. There is merit in recognising that such categorisation is rather vague. Both Congress and BJP trigger different emotions in people's minds, and generalising their character may be ignorance at best, misleading at worst. Both these parties must have displayed similar social goals and policies to reach out to the median voter, and may have been successful in doing so. Both these parties have created massive social welfare schemes and both of them, since the 1980s, have played obvious religious cards to win vote banks. Now, names too do not quite matter as much. That is why, in practice, the Samajwadi Party, despite being named a 'socialist party', does not quite have a commitment towards socialism.

THE SEAT SHARE STORY

Simply put, seats won divided by total number of seats gives the seat share. The number of seats won in the Lok Sabha is the only number you look at to form the government.

Congress has ruled independent India for almost 54 of the total 75 years, lopsided towards the beginning of our independent history. During early Congress-era India, the party's seat share remained massive. It bagged almost three-fourths of the total seats in the first three Lok Sabha elections—in 1952, 1957 and 1962. It was a period of Congress' dominance as the most popular party. In fact, until 1967, the re-election rate of incumbents (that is, the rate at which incumbent governments will be voted back to power) was as high as 85 per cent.[6]

It was in 1967 that trouble started brewing. Congress' seat share plummeted to a mere 54 per cent. It lost in seven states: Gujarat, Madras, Orissa, Rajasthan, Bengal, Kerala and even Delhi. The re-election rate during 1967–79 had come down to 54 per cent. These monumental losses may have horrified Indira Gandhi, who was the lone soldier, with Nehru and Lal Bahadur Shastri dead and Morarji's bitterness increasing by the day. This anxiety eventually led to a split in the party.

Congress' fortunes recovered in 1971, with seat share climbing up to 67 per cent. Indira Gandhi imposed the dreaded Emergency in 1975. She called for fresh elections in 1977. But this time, the party was brought to its knees. Congress could win a mere 28 per cent of seats. By the time Congress tasted defeat, irreparable harm had been done to the democratic institution of political parties. Robert Michels, in his 1911 seminal work, built the idea of '*iron law of oligarchy*'. In a somewhat prophetic fashion, he had claimed that, driven by technical and tactical necessity, any democratic organisation (or a party) would inevitably fall into a situation where a small group of elites—oligarchs—would run and govern it. Indira Gandhi was India's introduction to this law. With leadership voids in parties and in the absence of institutional structures to build a leadership line, dynasty politics was to become the order of the day.

The next two election cycles were in favour of Congress; the party's seat share in 1980 was 67 per cent and in 1984, it was at an all-time high of 76.5 per cent. But it was 1989 that really changed Indian seat share dynamics, altering the look and feel of Parliament which continues to be seen till date.

Until 1989, the highest seat share would lie in the range of 54 per cent to 67 per cent. From 1989 onward, the seat share has fallen to one-third rather consistently (except in 1991, when it was 45 per cent). More interestingly, while earlier the second-largest party would secure a single-digit seat share (except in 1977), the difference between the largest and second-largest parties began shrinking since 1989. Figures 1.1 and 1.2 explain the trends instructively. Figure 1.2 explicitly shows the seat and vote shares of winners through India's electoral history. Note the shrinking distance between the two, and a dramatic convergence in 1989 (and another comparable one in 2004).

FIGURE 1.2 Difference between seat share and vote share of winner across Lok Sabha elections

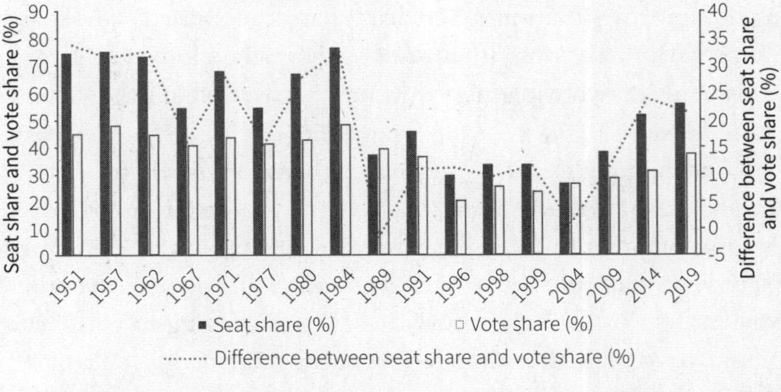

A few things emerge starkly. The real opposition, in terms of contesting parties, actually remained consistent until 1984. From 1989 onward, Indian voters began locating their leaders in regional parties. India had begun shifting its political focus from a single-party to a multi-party democracy. Faith in Congress had wobbled, and events of the 1980s brought to surface the evil underbelly of the political class, divorced from ethics and adopting consequentialist and divisive politics. Voters had become more conscious. Literacy rate in the 1980s had climbed several notches higher, and there was a significant rise in the circulation of regional newspapers. Whenever voters become more conscious, political competition increases.

We now look at the difference between seat share and vote share of the winning party, and try to organise our thoughts around what could this indicate. Refer to Figure 1.2 again. It reveals that the difference between seat share and vote share has been decreasing over time, although it has increased in the last three elections. What does this mean?

Notice that if a government has high seat share and low vote share, it means the preference aggregation did not properly take place. It had a leakage. The higher the difference, the higher the leakage. When parties secure seats and not votes, it explains that victory would have come with smaller margins. It is easy to imagine a situation when seat share can exceed vote share hugely. But it is more important to appreciate how a large gap between the two explains a thin margin over which the victory is decided.

And if margins are thin, one may crudely label the victory as a game of chance, more than a game of substance. Consider in our hypothetical example, where 98 contestants secured 1 per cent votes each and the winner got 2 per cent. If one of the other contestants could have secured just 2 per cent more votes, she could have been the winner. This razor-thin margin tells us an interesting story. Governments are standing on a frail edge, which can dismantle them in the next elections rather easily. If promises remain unfulfilled, or if the perception of failures abound, switching voters may easily turn the tables around. For instance, let's say in a population of 100 voters each in three constituencies, the winner took over two constituencies, A and B, by 1 per cent margin in each. So, she secured 51 votes in each of them, that is, a total of 102 votes. Let's say she did not get a single vote in constituency C. For this winner, it is generally unlikely that all 102 are loyalist voters. What is the smallest number of undecided voters in the two winning constituencies that could topple the government in the next elections if they change their minds? Very small, actually—just 2 votes each in constituencies A and B, which is merely 2 per cent of the votes in those respective constituencies. The government must be able to keep them happy in addition to ensuring the loyalists continue to remain loyal. This also means that if the government does well, it may be able to attract more undecided voters in its favour in the next elections.

Indians, as voters, are not necessarily a complacent lot. Scholars and journalists often liken Indian voters to those who usually look past the deeds of incumbents, or as plainly inert who may simply continue to vote for incumbent leaders. This view may be misguided. Figure 1.2 shows the difference between vote and seat share thinning down from 1951 to 1989. This indicates that the switching population has grown in size, and loyalists have shrunk. People have been changing their ideologies, stances and narratives. The leakage in democratic choices is reducing. People's voting mandate is getting more adequately reflected in seat victory patterns. Parties get seats because they get votes. This could be a result of voters getting politically more conscious, or it may be the emergence of regional parties with whom voters feel a deeper affinity.

Indeed, the emergence of regional parties is a major consideration here. In fact, in 1989, the vote share exceeded the seat share, which is unprecedented. Note that in any democratic election, preference aggregations cannot be perfect. In fact, given the diversity of human thought, a high seat share coupled with low vote share is very common. But this also means that the winner does not need to win over the hearts of everyone. They need just enough votes that puts them above the next highest party in terms of votes in that constituency. After all, it is eventually all a number game.

COMPETITION AND DISPROPORTIONALITY

But how do we assess political competition? One easy measure of political competition is to estimate the 'effective' number of parties in an election. This is not about how difficult the fight between contesting parties was, but about how many contestants are actually fighting. Elections involve many parties, but not all of them are as strong. There must be a measure to tell us how many were 'actually' there. It's not just the number of parties because a vast majority of parties simply do not exert any sizable influence on election outcomes. During the eve of the 2019 Lok Sabha elections, India had almost 2,300 registered political parties, of which seven were recognised as national and 59 were recognised as state parties (parties are 'recognised' based on past election performance criteria). Like universities in India, only a few of them really exist in the minds of people. The others are hardly able to make a mark. Figure 1.3 gives us a rough idea.

FIGURE 1.3 Total number of parties and national parties contesting in Lok Sabha elections

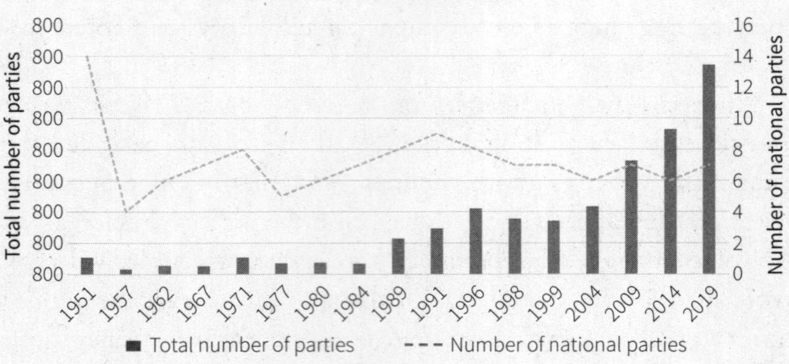

Consider, for instance, security deposits. Every candidate has to deposit some amount of money for contesting elections (it's not much—₹10,000 for assembly elections for 'general' category candidates, for example), which gets forfeited if the candidate is unable to get one-sixth of all votes polled in their constituency. The policy on forfeiture is meant to prevent frivolous candidates from contesting. But, of course, many people still do. In both the 2014 and 2019 Lok Sabha elections, both of which had more than 8,000 candidates contesting, almost 86 per cent candidates lost their deposits. Clearly, therefore, the number of parties will not make any sense for assessing competition. Hence, the increase in number of political parties contesting does not necessarily mean an increase in electoral competition.

We are interested in what we call 'effective' number of parties, or ENP, which is the hypothetical number of parties that took part in an election which are almost equivalent in strength. In other words, looking at election results, how many parties of equivalent strength would have hypothetically competed? We estimate this by looking at how strong the parties are. And indeed, the seat share or vote share is a good proxy for estimating the strength of that political party. Added for all the parties, this gives an impression of how cut-throat or competitive the political parties were. This is, therefore, a measure of the elections, not parties.

ENP is calculated in four steps. First, take party's seat share, second, square it (multiply it by itself), third, add it for all political parties, and finally, reciprocate it (divide 1 by the number).[7]

Squaring in many statistical formulae is done so as to pronounce big numbers much more than small ones. (Small numbers like two or five, when squared, give four and 25 respectively. When we square a big number like 20, we get 400; 100 squared is 10,000. Here, we square to suppress small seat shares (weak parties) and amplify big seat shares (strong parties).

Reciprocating positive numbers smaller than one always yields a number greater than one, which is what we want—to get a sense of how many 'effective' parties there were. The smaller the number, the less competitiveness there was (few teams, let's say), and the bigger the number, there was more competitiveness (many teams).

ENP can be interpreted as the number of hypothetical, equivalently strong parties (how much votes or seats they got) that would have the same total effect on electoral competition as the actual parties (of unequal strength) have had on it. When all seats are won by one party, ENP is the lowest, which is one. On the other extreme, if all the parties win equal number of seats, ENP is equal to the number of parties. Clearly, a higher value of ENP indicates many effective political parties in elections. ENP is, therefore, a reliable measure of electoral competition.

When ENP is estimated using vote share (instead of seat share), we denote it by ENP_v. Note that ENP and ENP_v need not be the same, unless vote share and seat share of all parties are the same. But they should move in the same direction, generally.[8]

In addition to ENP or ENP_v, another metric gives us an even more comprehensive picture of the quality of a certain election, and that is the difference between seat share and vote share. In the preceding section, we highlighted how high seat share can often come from a rather low vote share. If that has happened, we know there has been a leakage of preferences. We call this conceptual estimate used to understand the difference between seat share and vote share as disproportionality, abbreviated as DISP.

Disproportionality index is a measure of how representative a government is, that is, how much does it represent the preference of voters. This is measured using the difference in seat share and vote share, because a perfectly representative government will be one where seat share and vote share are the same. Mathematically, it is done through simple steps. First, find the seat share (number of seats won by a party divided by total seats) and vote share (number of votes won by a party divided by total votes). Second, subtract vote share of that party from the seat share. Third, square this value (to remove negatives). Fourth, do this for all parties and add all of them up. Fifth, divide the value by two. Sixth, find its square root (because we had squared earlier). We can then multiply the value by 100 so that the value, which will be less than one, will now be in a range from one to 100.[9]

DISP is zero, if the political system is perfectly representative. This means that there is no difference between seat and vote share. In this scenario, if a party has got 20 per cent seats, then it has got 20 per cent votes. On the other extreme, if a party has got all the seats without any votes, we are talking about dictatorship and the value of DISP is 100. It is easy to observe that a higher value of DISP indicates poor representation of people.

When we draw the ENP, ENP$_v$ and DISP for India's Lok Sabha, the graph appears as shown in Figure 1.4. Notice that DISP is high in all elections until 1989, except 1967 and 1977. The ENP had remained low during this time as well, which means good competition lowers disproportionality. In 2014, DISP has increased again and ENP has fallen.

FIGURE 1.4 Effective competition and level of disproportional representation across Lok Sabha elections

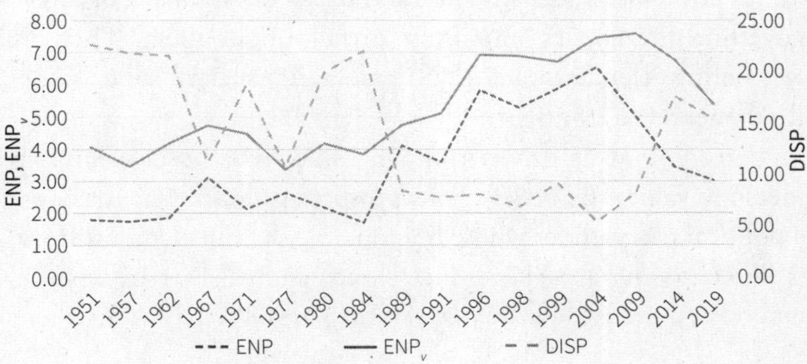

INDEPENDENT CANDIDATES

The result of the Karnataka assembly elections in 2008 was like a football missing the goal by an inch. BJP, for the first time, was very close to forming the government in the state. The trouble was this—it had 110 seats and required 113 to claim majority. Eighty seats had gone to Congress, while 28 went to Janata Dal (Secular) [JD(S)]. Like in 2004, Congress and JD(S) could have joined hands, with a total of 108. The remaining six seats held the key to power. Who was holding these six seats? Independent candidates. Before the Congress–JD(S) marriage could take place again, BJP got these six MLAs into its pavilion, and secured its first-ever power in a south Indian state on its own.

In 2018, when Congress was eyeing the much-needed win in Vidhan Sabha polls in Madhya Pradesh, it fell short of two seats to reach the clear majority mark. There were four independent candidates (they happened to be Congress rebels). These MLAs were absorbed into Congress, which could then form the government with a mere margin of five seats, even when BJP had lost to Congress in seven seats by a margin of mere 1,000 votes. And this is a big state; Madhya Pradesh has more people than the UK, France or Italy. (The Congress government, however, lasted only for a short while. In 2020, several Congress MLAs defected to BJP, and now the state is BJP-governed.)

In any case, independent candidates often make or break governments. So, it's important to talk about them. They are fascinating elements in any democratic society, and rather fundamental to its origins.

Party politics is driven through some shared sets of history, ideology, values and beliefs. For a prospective contender, to choose a political party under whose brand name she must contest from, is like choosing a package. Her choice compels her to espouse, embody or endorse all the views of the party. Partial endorsement means you are not part of it. In party politics, you may want to identify with groups whose value systems appeal to you in totality. But that is only part of it; the party should want to make you its candidate. This is also, therefore, like double coincidence of wants.

If you don't espouse the party's views or when you don't get the endorsement of the party, you can contest on your own. You sell designed dreams to voters by yourself. Voters then vote for you, as an individual, not as part of a collective association of any political party.

Party systems work as brands, helping consumers (voters here) in making a choice. When information is not as transparent, and cannot be transparent, instead of looking for the product (candidate), you look at the brand you trust, and do not worry about the quality of the product. Parties, like brands, can then offer franchises to those interested. Voters are likely to rely on the brand value, regardless of wherever they are. One trusts a party just like one trusts a brand, and therefore, votes for whoever contests from that party. This will be true not just for indifferent societies but also for large societies.

But does one require this 'branding' of a political party when the regions and populations are tiny? Imagine early farming settlement communities. Each hamlet would have its own leader, managing its affairs. They didn't need a party.

Societies that are small, demonstrate parochial loyalty and possess high levels of information about candidates would, therefore, be highly receptive to independent candidates. Also, in such tribal-like societies, people are least bothered with what is happening beyond one's own village or hamlet. The person would matter more than ideas. Surely, the dynamics of independent candidates in elections often reveal what the society is like.

Research shows that independent candidates often end up increasing voter turnout and siphoning off vote share of the winner in many cases.[10] They also add to the choice architecture of voters. But many of these voters who vote for independent candidates could have otherwise voted for national or coalition parties or those parties already in power. In other words, voters may switch from voting for winning parties to independent candidates. This means that independents gobble up votes from incumbents.

Often, they may simply be trying it out for fun, turning into what we call frivolous candidates. In 1996, the ECI increased the deposit requirements for candidates so that only serious candidates could apply. Both participation of independents and voter turnout decreased.

Figure 1.5 is instructive in that regard. Independent candidates have been significant in the first few national elections in India, and their prominence has been dwindling over time. Figure 1.1 was compiled without the independent candidates in question, and hence this was not visible there. But indeed, the second-largest seat and vote shares in the first two elections went to independent candidates! In 1951, independent candidates won on 37 seats with 15.9 per cent vote share. The next cycle had them win a massive 42 seats with 19.3 per cent votes. In 1962,

FIGURE 1.5 Seat share and vote share of independent candidates across Lok Sabha elections

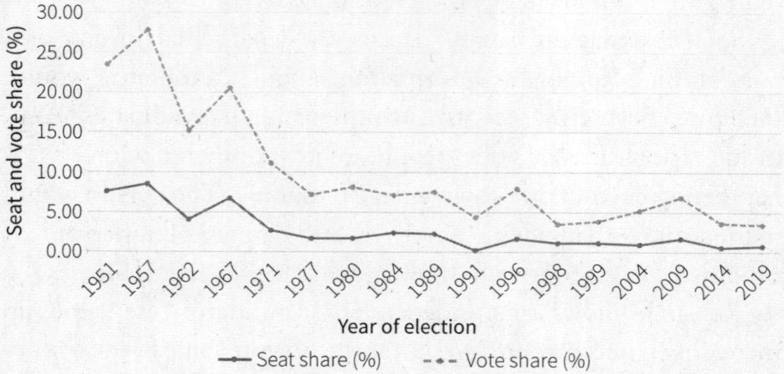

they were the third-largest group with 20 seats and 11 per cent votes. They remained in the third position as a group in 1967, but with 35 seats and 13.8 per cent votes. That is more than 2 crore votes!

The trend moves downward a little bit in subsequent elections, but independent candidates have taken a respectable share each time. Even during the 1996 general elections, despite their victory in a mere nine seats, they secured 6.3 per cent vote share. Even their worst year, in 1991, in which only one seat went to this category, the total votes in their favour exceeded 1 crore. In 2019, of the total 8,000 plus candidates contesting, more than 3,200 were independents. Their winning ratio has been coming down significantly and more than 99 per cent of them lose their deposits of late (compared to only 65–85 per cent in the first four Lok Sabha elections), but they add an interesting colour to the narrative.

And like we said, it tells us more about how we think rather than about the candidates themselves. Francis Fukuyama offers an intriguing account of Melanesian societies.[11] Inhabiting the Pacific Ocean, in several hundreds of tiny islands, Melanesia is one of the most diverse places on the planet. With more than 1,319 languages spoken in these islands, the language density here is one language per 716 sq. km! These islands have been inhabited for thousands of years, giving them a distinct cultural trajectory through history. The socio-political framework has been relational and community-driven. For centuries, the tribes have hunted for their own folk. They had a community leader, with a title that roughly translates to 'Big Man', responsible for gathering and sharing the bounty with his tribe. Without redistribution in his (and only his own) tribe, the Big Man would lose his status.

When the British and French gave up their colonies, they had installed the Westminster style of governments in the newly formed independent nation states. And that was the case with these islands.

The concept of 'electing' a leader that would govern everyone in the islands was alien to the Melanesians. The dramatic differences in the existing social order and newly implanted Western rules resulted in utter disaster there, with huge political turmoil and instances of rent seeking. What the English would call rampant corruption is actually what the Big Men have always been doing there—'to redistribute resources to their kinsmen'; only this time, it was revenue from mining companies instead of meat and shells.

In a similar sense, winning independent candidates would have been like the 'Big Men' of their constituencies. For example, when India became independent, there were around 565 princely states. To think that some new political party will come to these newly independent princely states and win hearts of people suddenly is myopic. Therefore, the dominance of independent candidates in the early phase of India's independent history should not be surprising. The enormous diversity prevalent in our country is also visible in how different our voting preferences have been. But a near convergence in the declining share of independent candidates reflects how far we have come from the mindset of the princely state's subject population. We don't think parochially as much as we used to, perhaps. That is why the brand name of a fighting Indian (or state) party in a battle matters to us, more than an individual soldier. Votes for independent candidates, then, becomes the story of how Indian-hood is being shaped in people's imagination.

TURNOUT

Turnout is a focal point of any electoral festival. Elections don't mean much if people don't participate. How many do anyway in India?

Figure 1.6 shows a somewhat cyclical pattern, with alternating peaks and troughs. The highest levels of turnout so far have been the most recent 2014 and 2019 Lok Sabha elections, at 66.4 per cent and 67.4 per cent respectively; almost 8 percentage points above that in 2004 and 2009. In fact, in 2019, when the poll turnout was even higher than 2014 (marking its record highest in India so far), it was thought to be a result of anti-incumbency. Surely, dissatisfaction levels among people must have been so high that it forced them to come out and vote. At least that's what the feeling among political pundits was. But when BJP won yet again, with a better overall margin in votes and seats, it shook the central narrative of poll turnouts. Note that when high values were witnessed during the 1957 and 1984 Lok Sabha elections, the incumbent returned both times (except that in 1984, it may have been largely out of sympathy towards Rajiv Gandhi who had lost his mother, Indira Gandhi, who was the incumbent).

If we superimpose poll percentages against the total number of registered voters, we realise that the consistency of poll percentage is a remarkable phenomenon. India adds almost 10–20 per cent of voters in every five-year election cycle, which means it adds an average of 4.5 crore voters every time. Figure 1.6 shows the rising trend in electors. This is accompanied by an almost constant rate of poll turnout, which signifies that elections are widely accepted.

FIGURE 1.6 Registered voters and voter turnout (%) across Lok Sabha elections

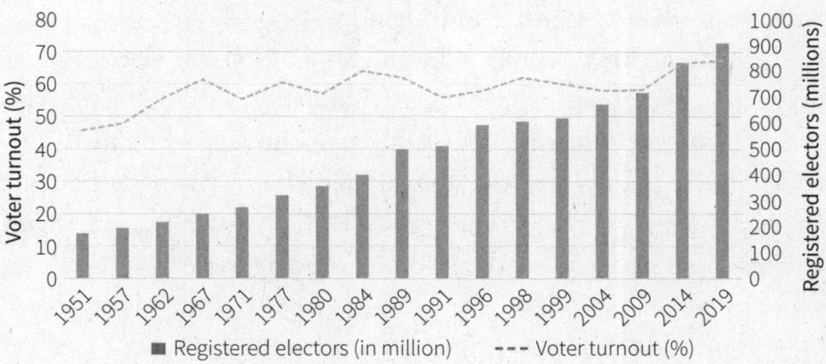

The global average of voter turnouts has been falling (almost 10 per cent in the last 25 years), perhaps due to apathy and decreasing confidence in democratic processes, particularly in Europe.[12] In this regard, Indian values are encouraging. Turnout tells us about trust deficit (it can also tell us how much people enjoy the simple act of voting). How many will vote depends upon how many feel the need to. This will depend upon external as well as internal dynamics. The external would mean disillusionment with elections. The internal would suggest the changing priorities of voters.

In 2019, compared to the 2014 Lok Sabha elections, Madhya Pradesh recorded a massive increase of 9.6 per cent in voting turnout, followed by Himachal Pradesh, Kerala, Jharkhand, Manipur and Rajasthan. The decline between the last two elections was highest in Jammu & Kashmir (J&K), where turnout decreased by 20.3 per cent. In fact, from 1967 until 2014 Lok Sabha elections, J&K has had an average voter turnout of around 45 per cent. In the capital, Srinagar, this value has been as low as 20.4 per cent since 1999. The story of voter turnout in J&K is perhaps the most telling example of distrust in democracy sourced from New Delhi. Turnout figures carry within themselves a practical as well as moral compulsion to participate in the government-making process. This spectre has been rather dismal in J&K. The other noticeable declines in 2019 were observed in small states except Punjab and Delhi.

In general, voter turnout in Indian Lok Sabha elections has averaged at 59.9 per cent. Figure 1.6 illustrates this. A state-wise distribution for the last three elections is shown in Figure 1.7(a). One cannot help but notice the sudden rise in voting behaviour in 2014. But as shown in Figure 1.7(b), 2019 witnessed an interesting surge too—except Bihar, no big state had a fall in voter turnouts.

FIGURE 1.7(a) State-wise voter turnout (%) distribution for the past three elections

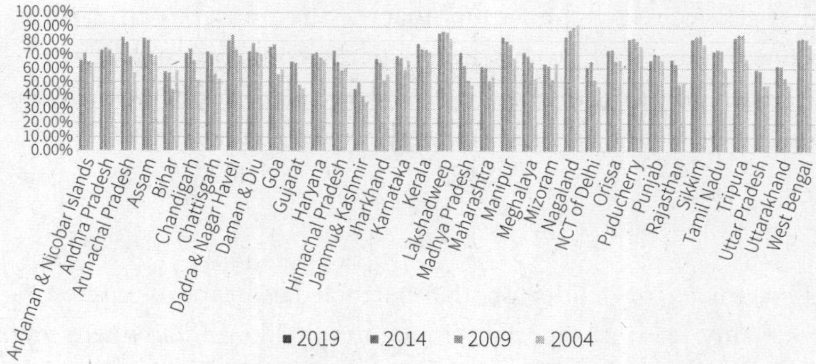

FIGURE 1.7(b) Voter turnout difference across states during 2019 and 2014

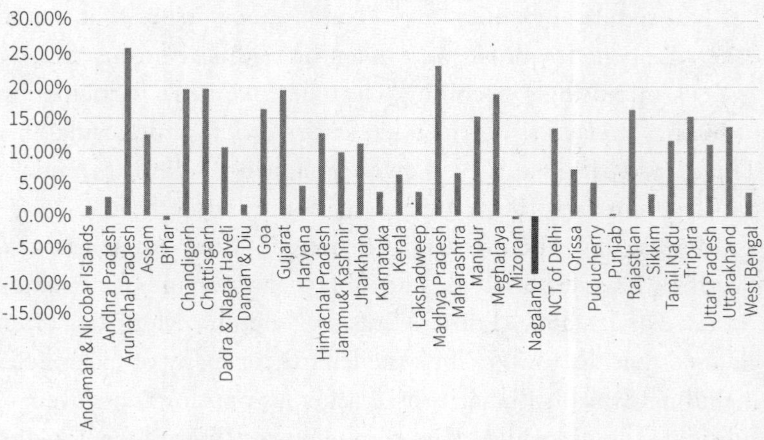

Note: Andhra Pradesh calculation includes Telangana in 2019.

What could have led to the sudden political awakening in 2014 and 2019? As the next section shows, we have had a massive turnout of women voters in 2014 and 2019 as well. One answer is located in demography itself. For the first time, India's young voters, the millennial generation, came out in large numbers to vote. According to an analysis of the 2011 Census data, every month, 16 lakh Indians celebrate their eighteenth birthday. That is the time when they also tacitly tell the country that they have arrived on the voting scene. These young voters are politically conscious and driven by an aspiration to participate in the playground of a democracy like India. Maybe they are the ones inflating these numbers?

GENDER

The impact of gender on the electoral landscape is interesting for many reasons, especially in a country like India, where men dominate politics. They are usually the decision-makers in a family and women often vote for those who the men in the family prefer. This lack of engagement with politics amongst women has had significant policy costs. For instance, issues that would otherwise benefit women were taken up with less enthusiasm.

It is increasingly becoming clear that women's participation in politics leads to a more gender-sensitive view of policymaking. This participation can be viewed as a two-fold effort, namely, participation by voting and participation by contesting.

Increase in women voters has mattered indeed. In the past two elections, it has led to a higher level of recognition in policymaking circles. For instance, Prime Minister Narendra Modi has often claimed that the focal point beneficiaries for many of his policies including Swachh Bharat-related schemes on sanitation, welfare subsidies for girl child education, Ujjwala Yojana for cooking fuel, and even the legislation against triple talaq were women. Similarly, the alcohol prohibition regulation in Bihar in 2015 was motivated by Chief Minister Nitish Kumar's electoral promise to women, who had long advocated such a move since it was hurting their families financially.

With women contestants, and elected leaders, many women-centric policies are likely to be adopted. Despite the prevailing scepticism about women local leaders often acting on behalf of their husbands, studies have shown that even though their election may not change people's preference to vote for them, it definitely breaks down gender stereotypes,[13] even raises aspirations and educational attainments for girls,[14] and leads to an increase in public expenditure in public goods which directly concern women, like water, and on issues such as violence against women, childcare and maternal health.[15] Studies have also shown that women legislators are less likely to be corrupt or criminal, are more efficacious and may also lead to higher growth in economic activity.[16] Overall, there is a huge value in looking at how women have participated in Indian elections.

Let's look at their voting behaviour. Historically, they have voted much less than men, but this gap is reducing over the last few years, and that is encouraging. Look at Figure 1.8 where a convergence is clearly taking place. The poll percentage is estimated by dividing the number of women voters by total number of women eligible to vote (and the same for men). In the latest 2019 elections, male and female voting percentages were almost the same.

FIGURE 1.8 Poll percentage of men and women in Lok Sabha elections in India (%)

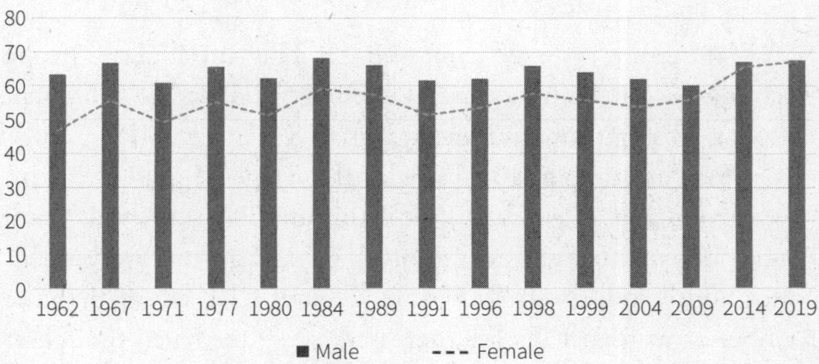

From 1962 until 2009, women's participation hovered in a narrow range. But the sharpest climb was witnessed in 2014, when women's vote participation increased by 18 per cent. It may, therefore, be interesting to dig deeper into state-wise changes during 2009–2014. We can do this by estimating female–male difference. The indicator is essentially the difference between poll ratio of females and males. If positive, it suggests more females as a share of total eligible females went to vote than males. We map this across all the states for 2009 and 2014. The results appear in Figure 1.9.

FIGURE 1.9 (Female–Male) Turnout in 2014 and 2009 Lok Sabha elections across states

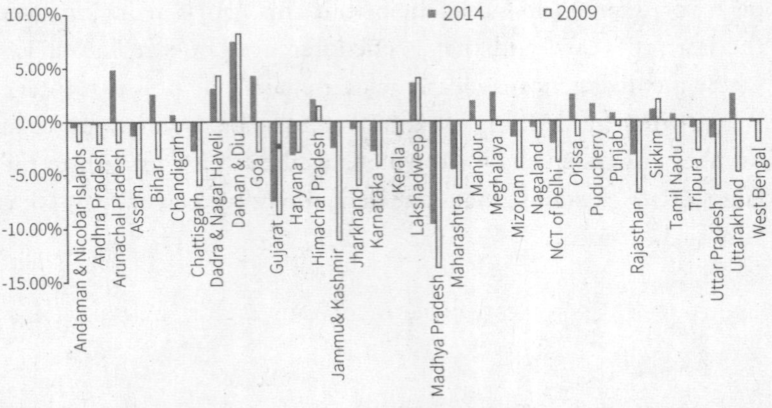

What about women contestants? The 2019 Lok Sabha elections had the highest share of women Members of Parliament (MP), 14.3 per cent, translating into 78 women MPs. This is rather low, as compared to the global average of 22.4 per cent. (Even countries like Sudan, Afghanistan, Pakistan and Saudi Arabia have better representation.)[17] This figure, however, has continuously improved over time. Figure 1.10 shows that the number of women MPs has increased over time, even though at a glacial pace.

FIGURE 1.10 Percentage of women contestants and elected MPs in Lok Sabhas

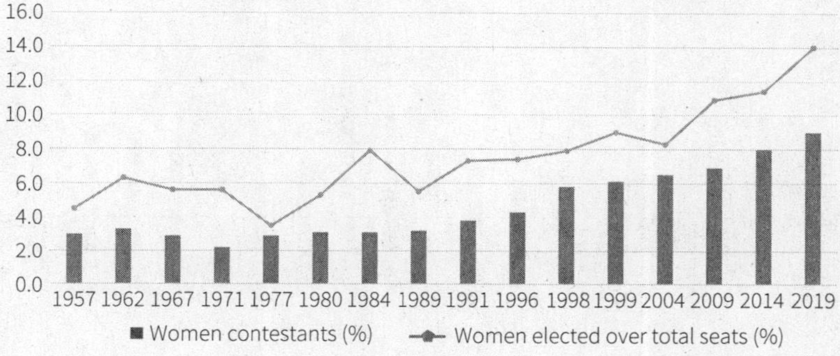

The lesson to be drawn here is more poignantly illustrated in Figure 1.11, in which we plot men and women contestants against two axes. We see that the rate of participation of men and women has changed over time. And this is important because it tells us that the rate of participation of women *with respect to* men has not changed much. It also shows significant increase in women contestants in the last four Lok Sabha elections. In fact, the rate of increase of women contestants is markedly higher than that of MPs, suggesting that the probability of their selection into Parliament has gone down. (Note that the drop during the 1996 Lok Sabha elections was because of an increase in the value of election deposits, when even male contestant figures had dropped to one-third the value.)

A parting food for thought here: research shows that the likelihood of women contesting elections is higher in constituencies where they are more disadvantaged in numbers and more likely to run in constituencies reserved for scheduled castes (SCs) or scheduled tribes (STs). To some extent, both are surprising facts.[18] We can never know who women vote for, but we do know some aggregate results when they vote, or when they contest. Perhaps what would also be interesting to find is the rate at which women contestants perform in terms of vote share. In

FIGURE 1.11 Men and women contestants across Lok Sabha elections

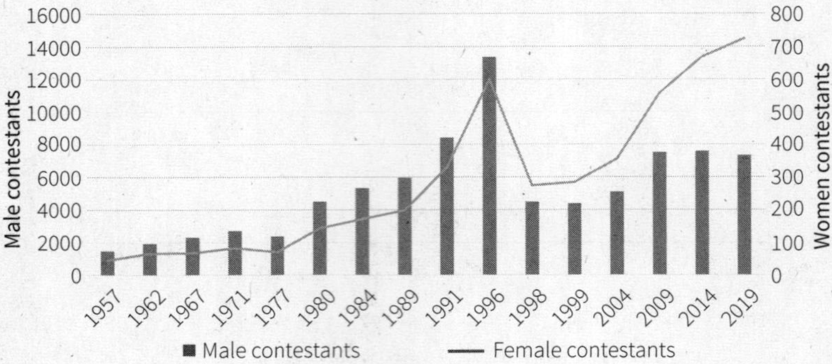

any case, their presence raises fresh interest in studying Indian elections through numbers.

ELECTIONS, MONEY AND CONTRACTS

Consider the top companies in India by market capital—TCS, Reliance, HDFC Bank, HUL, ITC and SBI. Consider the same list in the US—Apple, Alphabet (Google), Microsoft, Facebook, Amazon and Berkshire Hathaway. Is there a pattern in the respective groups?

Here's the difference. Almost each company in the US has made it big without any government contract or service. And almost no company in India is big without government's purchase orders. This stark difference is repeated across developed and developing countries. In the former, you need skills and merit to become big. In poor countries, you need the government's patronage.

Data is revealing. If you take private firms and state-owned enterprises incorporated before 1985, and find out how their share in the total profits of all firms changed before and after liberalisation, the results are striking. During 1988–90, these incumbent firms held more than three-fourths of the profits, assets and sales of all such firms in India. During 2003–05, these values had only gone to 90 per cent.[19] Even the so-called liberalisation did not change resource allocation much!

Couple this piece of information now with what we discussed in terms of how expensive a machinery the elections in India are. Indian political parties spent more than $8 billion in 2019 elections. This is for a country with an annual average per capita GDP of around $2,200. So, in other words, elections gobbled up annual income of 40 lakh Indians. Why such huge spending on campaigns for elections in a country where people continue to die due to inadequate access to safe drinking water?

Because government controls all the resources. So, for rich Indians and corporates, it is totally worth their while to give money to political parties. In fact, a lot of money. Companies in India surely need the government to flourish. This is indeed a matter about public procurement, but perhaps at another time. It is certainly serious food for thought.

Elections are, for lack of a better word, very, very important.

2

Bihar

The 1999 Bollywood flick *Shool*, directed by Ram Gopal Verma, was an edge-of-the-seat thriller. It showcased the links between crime and politics in modern-day Bihar with an acute sense of imagination, and (despite being a box-office flop) went on to win the National Award for Best Hindi Film.

Bihar lends itself to a poetic imagination, much like the movie *Shool*. It has a uniquely rich tapestry of history and culture that adorns almost every history textbook in the country—with the empire of Magadha and one of the most profound ancient centres of learning in the world called Nalanda. Therefore, it has an intellectually envious reputation for having been the hub of the study of arts and humanities. But in reality, and in the practice of politics today, it hardly matches its past glory. For those wondering what the meaning of the Hindi word shool is—it is pain.

Many have claimed that when Paul Appleby, the noted American scholar on public administration, wrote a report on Indian governance at the behest of the Ford Foundation in 1953, he regarded Bihar as the best governed state. Interestingly, some research indicates that Appleby never made such a claim. The point is, we love this anecdote because of the irony it presents us with. It has been mentioned so many times in so many forums that nobody cares about its accuracy anymore. It is like a belief of an incredulous kind—and therefore worth remembering.

When a favourable story about the past becomes popular, one holds, guards and retells it as much as possible, perhaps exactly because it's so distant from the truth of the present. It is like Norma Desmond's character (played by Gloria Swanson) in the Hollywood movie, *The Sunset Boulevard.*

Perhaps Bihar has needed this fiction more than any other place. Almost 89 per cent of its population lives in rural areas, but only 22 per cent of its state GDP comes from agriculture. Bihar performs badly on development indicators, with its per capita income being one-fourth of the national per capita income and a third of its population being illiterate. A third of its population also lives below the poverty line. Not surprisingly, it has one of the largest shares of migrants moving to other states.

All of this inescapably pushes the state into ever-alert political sensitivities. The powerful polity of what was once the epicentre of Magadha Empire became a distressed and ignored principality of Bengal during the colonial era. In 1912, it became a new state. Champaran was the starting point of modern-day Bihar's political consciousness as well as Gandhi's India. It was here that Gandhi replicated his Transvaal's experiment of Satyagraha in 1917. This was a journey that would show the world how a nation can revolt without bloodshed. Jayaprakash Narayan showed it again in the 1970s during the 'Sampoorna Kranti' revolution against Indira Gandhi. Perhaps Bihar is waiting for a third revolution to take place.

Bihar has to be understood as a robust representative sample of whatever we imagine Indian politics to look like. A fertile land chained in feudal and caste hierarchies emblematic of corruption and clientelist politics, it dreams of its glorious past every night and wakes up to a renewed vigour for political engagement. Politics is life in Bihar. And this has to be understood not in terms of the character of its leadership alone, but in the everyday interest and imagination of the Bihari populace.

BIHAR POLITICS: FROM JP TO LALU AND NITISH

The 2015 assembly elections in Bihar were a playground for the coalition of two arch rivals, Janata Dal (United) [JD(U)] led by Nitish Kumar, and Rashtriya Janata Dal (RJD) led by Lalu Prasad Yadav, who also joined hands with Congress and a few other parties. On the other side was BJP and its allies. This was a one-of-a-kind election battle in the history of the state for two interesting reasons. First, the 18-year-old partnership between JD(U) and BJP, which saw them through three assembly elections (of which the previous two were favourable), was broken this time. Second, Nitish and Lalu had joined hands after being arch enemies for 25 years. Election pundits were claiming that given Nitish's empty promises during his incumbency and the continued animosity between the foot soldiers of JD(U) and RJD, an easy election victory for BJP was a foregone conclusion. At the same time, many believed that the power of the unified other backward classes (OBCs) through the union of Yadavs (Lalu), Koeris and Kumris (Nitish) was to greatly diminish BJP's vote share.

BJP lost the elections. In a historic coalition-making, Nitish Kumar formed the government with Lalu Prasad Yadav. In just two years, Nitish was going to expel Lalu and join hands with BJP.

Except for a brief period under Janata Dal and few years interspersed by the president's rule, Bihar was mostly ruled in an unchallenged manner by Congress chief ministers (CM) for 40 years after Independence. Their upper-caste landowners routinely secured votes from landless labourers through a patron–client relationship.[1] This continued until the 1960s when agrarian relations began changing, and upper OBCs (Yadavs, Koeris and Kurmis) began articulating their consolidation.[2] In 1967, the collective opposition against Congress-led Bihar led to the election of the first non-Congress CM. The government didn't last long due to internal rivalry. Fresh elections were called in 1969, which resulted in another hung assembly. After a continuous tug-of-war between Congress and its opposition, peppered with the president's rule, Congress returned to power in the state in 1972.

Post-Emergency elections gave Bihar politics a powerful image. Jayaprakash Narayan, one of the most inspiring political leaders of independent India, triggered the 'Sampoorna Kranti' and the Bihar movement. He mobilised masses of aspirational and bright students in Bihar against Indira Gandhi's politics of corruption and high-handedness, and dictatorial government. Many of these students would go on to become powerful leaders of India in time—Lalu Yadav and Nitish Kumar, for instance.

In the Lok Sabha elections of 1977, Congress lost in each and every constituency of Bihar. In the Vidhan Sabha elections of 1977, Janata Party won more than two-thirds of all seats in Bihar. In many ways, Bihar changed the fabric of India's democracy and became the shining beacon against the darkness of a power-hungry rule that had gone against the ethos of India's founding from 30 years ago.

In 1980, Congress came back to power and remained there until 1989, though with fragmented leadership. But the release of the Mandal Commission Report in 1980 (implemented in 1989), coupled with the already-brewing caste consciousness, began affecting Bihar's politics deeply with mobilisation of the lower castes, marking a clear shift in political dynamics.[3] The Bhagalpur riots in 1989 and the demolition of the Babri Masjid in 1992 changed political equations in Bihar irreversibly. The 1990s witnessed a political transformation with backward castes and Lalu Prasad Yadav emerged as the next towering leader of the masses. Muslims and Dalits united under Lalu Yadav's Janata Dal (JD) while upper-caste loyalties were divided between BJP and Congress. Under Lalu, JD swept the elections in 1990.

However, due to internal rivalry between lower-caste factions, JD got divided and Nitish Kumar carved out another political party—Samata Party—from it. Lalu managed to win again in the 1995 elections, but soon, news of a fodder scam broke out. Crores of rupees were being embezzled for several years for purchase of fodder for vast and fictitious herds of livestock, all under Lalu's watch. He resigned from the party but installed his wife Rabri Devi as the CM. This was quite an unprecedented decision, not because of a dynasty-driven performative, but because Rabri had only been a homemaker all her life, with no political engagement (or acumen, as many would say). Lalu continued to run the government with Rabri as his proxy. He floated a new party called RJD, which won the 2000 assembly elections, although with a poorer performance compared to 1995.

All this while, despite his penchant for corrupt practices, Lalu had been churning a new kind of caste politics in Bihar. He was bringing hitherto marginalised groups into the political mainstream and ensuring communal harmony. All of this worked for a while, but indices related to law and order, health and education, and civic amenities too were falling to deplorably low levels during the 15 years of his rule. Discontentment was seething among non-Yadav castes on the 'Yadavisation' of political elites.

The bitterness between Lalu and Nitish had only grown all this while. Nitish Kumar had been forging an alliance with BJP in the late 1990s, and consolidating his loyalty amongst his own Koeri and Kumri castes along with the upper castes. In 2005, his party, JD(U), in a coalition with BJP, emerged victorious. This show was repeated in 2010 with a stellar performance, where the Nitish-led coalition won 206 of the 243 constituencies.

The year 2015 was different and most interesting. Nitish and Lalu, arch enemies for 25 years, joined hands to defeat the rising wave of BJP, flagged off by the rise of Narendra Modi in

New Delhi in 2014. The grand alliance between JD(U), Congress and RJD (called the Mahagathbandhan) led to a hard-earned victory for the trio, which secured 73.5 per cent seats and almost 42 per cent of votes.

HISTORICAL NARRATIVE ON BIHAR'S ELECTORAL POLITICS

Bihar's excitement with respect to political participation is historic indeed, and part of it may have to do with a strong sense of caste-based identities that have ossified in the region over time. These identities have played crucial roles in elections in recent decades even though their consolidation had begun long before India attained independence. For instance, the All India Kurmi-Kshatriya Sabha was established to protect the interests of the Kurmis as early as 1910. This was even before the formation of the Communist Party of India (CPI). No wonder some of the earliest trade union movements in India came about in the 1920s in the Jharia–Dhanbad coal mine belt in Bihar. One of the earliest peasant movements in India, the All India Kisan Sabha (peasant front of the undivided CPI) was triggered in 1936 in Bihar. These mobilisations had taken place early in Bihar, and it is no wonder that the state became the face of Indian politics, and continues to be so even today.

The importance of political collectives in the state produced inspirational leaders during the freedom movement. Rajendra Prasad, Babu Jagjivan Ram and Jayaprakash Narayan, for instance, came from Bihar. Provincial politics in Patna was too localised to fit the extraordinary leadership talent of these people who soon became national leaders. The political vacuum in the state after Independence was filled by names like Sri Krishna Sinha and Anugrah Narayan Singh. Both were towering leaders in their own right. But soon after Independence, despite their selfless and progressive attitudes, there was a subtle tension with respect to who would take on the role of Bihar's CM. Singh, according to some commentators, relinquished the position of CM to Sinha, and avoided an embarrassing exposure of the internal power play.

Bihar was to see many such power plays in later decades. Crucial to these power plays was the attitude of Bihari voters themselves. Politicians come from amongst the people who they represent. They are indeed a reflection of voters in many ways. Two interesting episodes reveal how Biharis think about politics and vote.

First, the year 1967. It was a watershed year in Indian politics since this was the time when people began to experiment with non-Congress governments (Congress' seat share had gone down from 73 per cent to 54 per cent in 1967). Bihar was the cradle of this change. Congress slid from almost 60 per cent seats in 1962 in the Bihar Assembly elections to 40 per cent in 1967. The ENP (effective number of parties) in the state had almost doubled during this period with the lowest disproportionality index ever (indicating highly representativeness). Congress was forced to take a reality check; the party's slide was big enough to trigger the political tussle that would split the grand old Congress, and would later perhaps institutionalise sycophancy in the party's circles.

Second, the Emergency and its impact, which moulded Indian politics forever, was all cast as much in the sociopolitical refineries of Bihar as in the courtyards of Indian judiciary. The Bihar Movement was the precursor to the Emergency, and the impact of whatever happened in Bihar during the 1977 elections was a turning point in the Indian electoral landscape.[4] While India was distressed in general, it was in Bihar that revolutionary fervour reached a crescendo.

The Indian economy was in shambles. The 1964–67 period reflected negative growth rate. National income grew at 4.3 per cent during 1954–64 but after the recession, it went down to a mere 2.9 per cent during 1967–73. The growth of per capita income had slowed down from 2.1 per cent (1954–64) to a mere 0.6 per cent (1967–73). The employment rate in the organised manufacturing sector had halved in these two decades. The industrial production of the country had slumped to 2–3 per cent during 1965–75, from 7–9 per cent in the previous decade. During 1972-73, the average rate of inflation was above 2 per cent per month! The 1971 war and the oil shock of 1973 only added to the woes.

Delhi was trying to handle all of this. It couldn't, however, handle Bihar's response. Bihar was boiling from frustration for years by then. Between 1967 and 1974, Bihar had 11 governments (both Congress and non-Congress) and three spells of president's rule. The state had a large body of politically active students (many of who went on to become future politicians) who had been clashing with the administration since 1956. The spread of Naxalism in Bihar was no accident, but a result of a receptive populace that would participate in overthrowing governmental orders. In 1974, under JP's leadership, Bihar's population (students, in particular) formed various senas, sabhas and movements to start widespread agitations across Patna and beyond, against the government. For JP, Biharis provided the hope and fodder to inspire and fuel revolutionary sentiments against the Congress government. The demonstrations and gheraos were sights to behold; a real display of mobilised power on the streets with people that shook the country from within. Those were the times when the country saw what Bihar meant for Indian politics.

The roots had, however, come from Gujarat. Drought and crop failures, coupled with a corrupt administration, were ingredients for a violent recipe that stirred a student movement in Gujarat which reached its peak in January 1974. Indira Gandhi took swift action in response to Morarji Desai's fast unto death (he was a veteran Congress leader and her father's close aide) and gave in to the demands, dissolving the Gujarat Assembly. Bihar, too, got inspired. JP even travelled to Ahmedabad lauding the Gujarati efforts, and brought home the idea of a Sampoorna Kranti—total revolution.[5]

The temperature was high, and a spark was needed for revolutionary combustion. June 1975 was an unforgettable month. On 12 June 1975, a judge of the Allahabad High Court, Justice Jagmohan Sinha, convicted Indira Gandhi for violating electoral conduct and declared her election invalid (in the famous Raj Narain case). This sent a new wave of energy in Bihar and nationwide demands for her removal, with their epicentre in Bihar, became loud and clear. The appeal in the Supreme Court, heard by Justice V.R. Krishna Iyer on 24 June, allowed her to continue as the prime minister until the full bench decided the case, but forbade her to vote or draw a salary. This was being construed as her victory, but Bihar sprang into a greater action. Supported by enormous crowds, a collective of five opposition parties, rallied in New Delhi on 25 June, asserting Prime Minister Gandhi's lack of moral authority to rule. Fearing a complete paralysis of administration, Indira Gandhi, in a response that was as quick as it was surprising, declared Emergency on 26 June.

A lot has been mentioned and written on the period of Emergency and the aftermath, but few have noted peculiar details from the polls of 1977 across states. Janata Party's victory in the 1977 Lok Sabha elections was not a surprise, given what had happened in preceding years. It is important to note how Bihar and indeed other Indian states responded during the Lok Sabha elections of 1977. In Bihar, Congress got zero seats! It did not win a single seat in UP, Haryana and Punjab either, and the lowest vote share for Congress, along with Haryana, was in Bihar (23 per cent).

Interestingly, for many of us who consider Congress' demise in the 1977 elections as a uniform phenomenon across India, that was not the case. Congress retained its top position in the southern states of Andhra Pradesh, Karnataka, Kerala, Tamil Nadu and even in Maharashtra in western India. The backlash to the Emergency, therefore, was a defiance from the Hindi-speaking regions of India, dominated by Bihar, UP and Haryana, highlighted in Figure 2.1. Indeed, if you had looked at the electoral outcome map of 1977, you would see a distinct horizontal boundary between two colours, the colour of the Janata Party in the north and Congress' colour in the south.

FIGURE 2.1 Congress seat share (%) and vote share (%) in 1977 Lok Sabha election across states

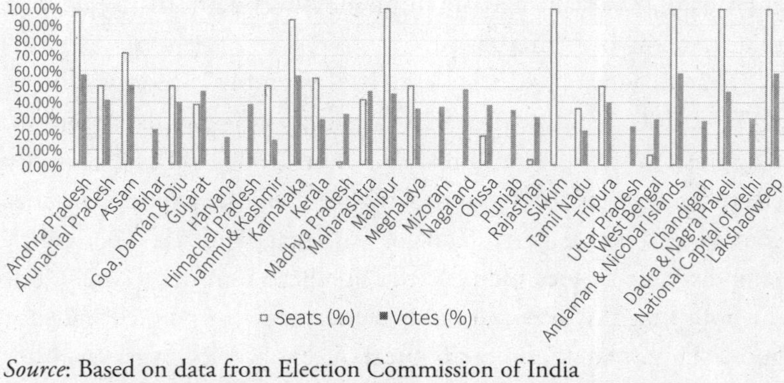

Source: Based on data from Election Commission of India
Note: Vote share for Sikkim was not available in the official ECI report.

Another interesting feature of the 1977 elections—which is much less spoken about—is that Congress may have gotten very few seats, but its vote share didn't remain as suppressed. Janata Party's vote share was 41.3 per cent, and Congress' was 34.5 per cent. This is a smaller difference between the two parties' vote share compared to 2019 (when NDA's vote share was 37.4 per cent and UPA's was 19.01 per cent). In other words, the Congress' defeat in 2019 is worse than its defeat in 1977. In fact, even the defeat in 2014 was worse than 1977. Who would have thought? The real thrust of shifting powers, therefore, does not come with comparing the JP movement in the 1970s with Anna Hazare's in 2010s. Because, as the voting patterns shows, frustration with Congress in 2014 was far deeper than in 1977. Yet, the JP movement captures the minds of Indians much more than that of Anna Hazare. It looks like the more powerful indicator to form public opinion is not the style in which a political party is uprooted, but rather the uprooting of an entrenched political party. In the 1970s, Congress seemed invincible. That was not the case in 2010s. But we must not forget that, despite the suspension of civil liberties in the 1970s, Congress won 189 seats in 1977, and its involvement in corruption cases and anti-incumbency in the 2010s relegated it to a mere 44 seats in 2014.

That is why, if you look at the assembly elections during 1977–79/80, you realise that, contrary to popular opinion, Congress wasn't quite 'finished'. The 1977 Bihar Assembly elections resulted in Congress winning 57 seats and 23.6 per cent votes (Janata Party had got 214 seats and 42.7 per cent). It is difficult to locate any 'pride' in these numbers, surely, but do note that this was the same year in which Congress did not get a single seat in Bihar in the Lok Sabha elections. In other places, Congress had shown tough tenacity. For instance, in the Maharashtra Assembly elections in 1978, Congress (Indira) and the breakout faction Congress (O) together claimed 43.6 per cent votes (131 seats) against Janata Party's 28 per cent (99 seats). In the Karnataka Assembly elections of 1978, Congress had won very comfortably, clinching 149 of 224 seats and 44.25 per cent votes. It also retained highest votes and seats in Meghalaya and won the largest number of seats and votes in the Punjab and Goa Assembly elections in 1980. Perhaps Himachal Pradesh was the only exception during that period where the Lok Sabha results mirrored the Vidhan Sabha's.

The party surely lost its sheen in a few other states, like Tamil Nadu, Kerala, Jammu & Kashmir and West Bengal. But in these provinces, it had already been facing a squeeze because of the rise of regional parties. In fact, under the local political preferences, one may argue that Congress actually performed quite well in these places. So, its decline couldn't be attributed to the Bihar movement. Bihar was relevant, but mostly to Hindi-speaking India.

Even in Bihar, this story was short-lived. In the 1980 general elections, Congress took hold of more than half the seats in Bihar, with 36 per cent votes in its favour. JP had died by then, and throughout the 1980s caste politics had come to be extremely entrenched in the state—something that continues even today.

The Bihar movement was the fountainhead of a young brigade of firebrand leaders who would mobilise masses in the 1990s and beyond, painting the Indian political landscape with the new hue of regional parties. From student revolts in the Bihar of the 1970s came Lalu Prasad Yadav, Nitish Kumar, Mulayam Singh Yadav, Sushil Modi, Ravi Shankar Prasad, and even Arun Jaitley. This was the cultivation of an entire generation of future leaders who would go on, in time, to become ministers/CMs in the state as well as cabinet ministers at the Centre. Interestingly, even Narendra Modi had participated in the Navnirman movement in Gujarat, which had taken place in 1973 in Ahmedabad, and had acted as a spark for the revolution to spread in Bihar. Indeed, Bihar was the furnace where these leaders were getting baked.

The political peace that Bihar was looking for in the 1970s continued to elude it in the 1980s as well. There was no consistent and stable leadership. Even though Congress remained in power through the 1980s, it changed the CM half a dozen times. The general indices on law and order, poverty and vulnerability, or education and health had been unimpressive through the decade. In fact, caste-based cleavages became even more distinct. Arvind

Das reminds us about the character of post-Independence Bihar in which three white-collared professions flourished the most—and eventually became a hallmark of the 1980s—namely, medicine, civil engineering and, most importantly, political power-brokerage, also called as pairvikari, loosely translated as lobbying.[6] Plagued by a poorly implemented abolition of the zamindari system, land became the hotbed of political and social churning, into which caste politics got comfortably folded in. This manifested in pairvikari where feudal patronage was designed entrepreneurially, giving rise to a capital structure of a society where few elites came to run the economy from within their impenetrable circle. Admissions, contracts and other such entitlements became resources for a give-and-take political economy, most despairingly visible in mafia economy and booth capturing. Caste-based politics was a potent spice that helped brew these into ugly bloodbaths.

The 1980s were marked by a rapid rise of caste-based conflicts and violent crimes. What began with the Belchi massacre in 1977 continued with heart-wrenching sagas of communal violence unfolding at Parasbigha and Pipra in 1980, Gaini in 1982, Kaithibigha in 1985, and Arwal, Kansara and Darmia in 1986. These were predominantly rural incidents but urban Bihar was not untouched by it. By some estimates, at least one caste or class carnage was taking place every four months in Bihar during that decade.[7] This is also the period of the emergence of caste-based hate groups called senas. There has been a propagation of Ranvir Sena (Bhumiyars), Bhumi Sena (Kurmis), Brahmarshi Sena (Bhumihars), Kuar Sena (Rajputs) and Lorik Sena (Yadavs), in addition to ultra-left organisations. Violence had reached its heights during the Bhagalpur riots of 1989.

Bihar, in a way, had been paving the way for centralising caste in everyday political equations through the 1980s. Caste had always been important given the unique history of subjugation in the state. But in the 1980s, it took a different turn. During the late 1970s, Bihar's then CM, Karpuri Thakur of the Janata Party, mooted the idea of implementing Mandal Commission's recommendations in the state in 1979, thereby opening the floodgates for a deluge around caste discourse. In 1989, distressed by the caste and communal flare that had engulfed the state, a rather surprising name emerged for an alternate leadership in the state—Lalu Prasad Yadav. Lalu, whose party won the 1990 elections with a sweeping majority, carried a reputation for being a political leader with a sense of humour and a rustic wit. This, in a way, tells us something about Bihar, too.

When Lalu's politics is called as the 'politics of state incapacity',[8] it is, in some sense, declaring Bihar's 'democratically endorsed non-governance',[9] and while old orders were being dismantled, there was nothing new that replaced them.[10] They voted for leadership rather than the party manifesto (after JP's death in 1979, Janata Party's JP faction too could not secure any significant victories in subsequent elections). That is why, even after offering him popular support from 1990 until 2005 (three elections) despite his clear involvement in the fodder scam, it was really the law-and-order problem and arbitrariness of the feudal order that led people to vote out Lalu in 2005. Yadavs form a significant majority of voters in Bihar, and there is tribal loyalty that one sees in many Indian provinces, like Bihar. Lalu's seizure of power during 1990–2005 was symptomatic of a wave of caste mobilisation that was sweeping across a number of regions in India during the time. From 1952 until 2010, the Vidhan Sabha elections have seen a caste convergence of elected representatives. In other words, the share of the upper castes is decreasing and that of the backward castes is increasing over time. This change has been gradual except in 1990 and 1995, when the number of backward caste MPs suddenly jumped, while that of upper castes dropped. See Figure 2.2.

FIGURE 2.2 Share (%) of upper-caste and backward-caste MLAs in Bihar Assembly through the years

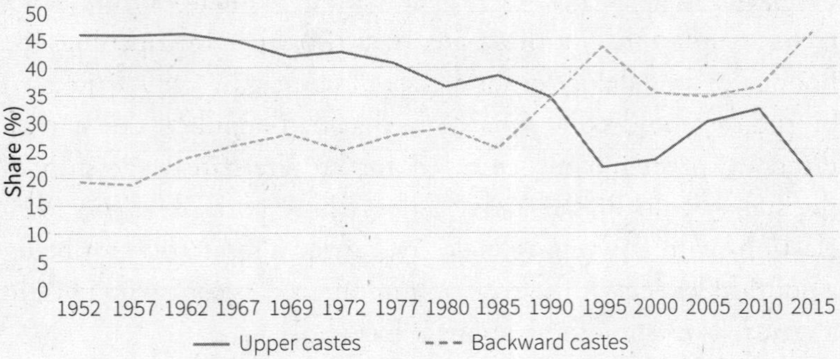

Sources: Manish K. Jha and Pushpendra, 'Governing Caste and Managing Conflicts in Bihar, 1990–2011', TISS (for 1952–2010 data) and *Times of India* report (for 2015 data).

More than a decade of misrule and anarchy was enough. On assuming power in 2005, Nitish Kumar, on the issue of governance, did not quite do away with his caste-based configurations. An interesting insight revealed by numbers, however, is as follows. Between Lalu's last victory in 2000 and Nitish's in 2005, Jharkhand was separated from Bihar and made into a separate state. In 2000, Lalu's party, RJD, received 38 per cent seats through 28 per cent votes while Nitish's newly formed Samata Party received 10 per cent seats and 8.5 per cent votes. In 2005, Nitish's party, now called JD(U), secured 36 per cent seats with merely 20 per cent votes, even though RJD got 22 per cent seats with 23 per cent votes. RJD received more votes than JD(U) and yet lost in seats. Even in 2010, when Nitish won with bigger numbers (23 per cent votes with 47 per cent seats), RJD still bagged 19 per cent votes and merely 9 per cent of seats.

POLITICAL COMPETITION AND DISPROPORTIONALITY IN BIHAR ASSEMBLY ELECTIONS

We look at the seat share and vote share of the parties in the assembly elections in Bihar. Two of the most popular indices, which we will use in this analysis, are that of disproportional representativeness (DISP) and electoral competition (ENP and ENP_v); we discussed the latter in Chapter 1. In this way, we observe the undercurrents of election shifts in Bihar in a rather nuanced estimation of results. Figure 2.3 shows the three important variables of ENP, ENP_v and DISP. While ENP and ENP_v indicate political competition, DISP suggests the degree to which seat share and vote share diverge from each other. To re-emphasise, DISP measures how divergent are vote share and seat share in an election across all the parties. Stated differently, a high DISP means the elections had huge difference between seat and vote shares, indicating the mandate of the seat is not supported by that of the votes as much. Low values of ENP indicate that effectively, it looked like few political parties contested.

FIGURE 2.3 ENP, ENP_v and DISP for Bihar Assembly through the years (winners mentioned against years)

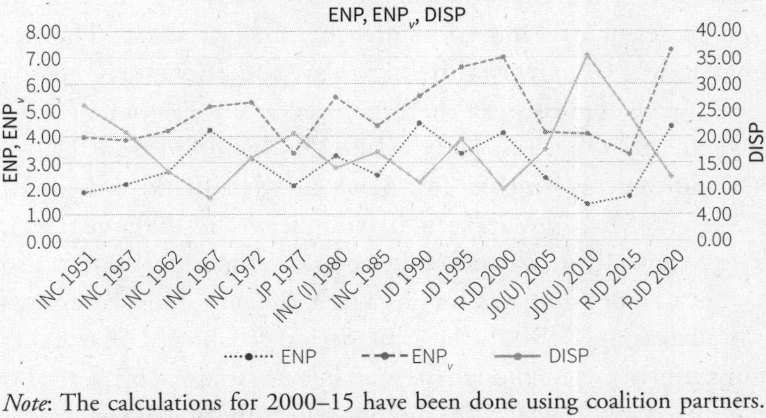

Note: The calculations for 2000–15 have been done using coalition partners. Party with highest seat share is represented with years in the figure.

We notice the electoral competition increasing in 1967 and 1990. Indeed, the 1960s were marked by change in agrarian relations. Upper backward castes (Yadavs, Koeries, Kumris) emerged as new land-owning groups, ready to articulate their political vision.[11] Congress suffered a major setback in 1967, and its seats were absorbed by other parties. But this was perhaps the most representative government, since DISP is the lowest ever in 1967. Even in 1977, when post-Emergency anti-Congress sentiment led Janata Party to sweep Bihar elections, the DISP values remained fairly high.

The 1980s marked a changing political rubric of the state, surfacing the dormant sentiments in assembly elections in 1990. Interestingly, 1990 was characterised by low electoral competition (high ENP) and highly representative government (low DISP). This was Lalu's handiwork. He came with a high level of trust of the voters. Low DISP means rather low leakage of mandate.

In 1995, the statistic reversed. Lalu retained power, but DISP had doubled with an increasing ENP_v. This indicates that representation fell and competition increased. This cannot be explained by Nitish Kumar's exodus from JD (taking the share of Koeris and Kurmis away from the consolidated backward caste votes) since his party had got only seven seats. Nor did the seat shares of BJP and CPI suffer any major setback. The real change was Congress' withering away, and JD's strengthening position. Congress' seat share reduced from 71 (out of 324) seats in 1990 to 29 in 1995, while JD's increased from 122 to 167 during the same period. Also note that Jharkhand Mukti Morcha (JMM) saw its seats halving between 1990 and 1995. Hence, effectively, there were fewer parties in 1995, which also meant competition was tough. The most important thing was the increasing DISP during this period. It showed that Lalu's government, even though it was able to secure 167 seats (as compared to 122 in 1990), did not reflect the will of the people (increase in its vote share was marginal). Clearly, this indicated a dissatisfied electorate.

Surprisingly, in 2000, electoral competition increased. This means Nitish Kumar's consolidation of the Koeri–Kumri base must have been stronger this time. The fodder scam had had an impact on Lalu's reputation and popularity by then. The value of DISP reduced dramatically, going below its 1990 levels. This massive drop in DISP indicates that seat share and vote share somewhat converged. In other words, the leakage was limited and the government was indeed representative. At an aggregate level, victories were genuine and consistent—desired parties were really desired. Hence, the declining number of seats for RJD truly signalled a diminishing support base for Lalu.

This got confirmed in 2005. Most political pundits have argued that the 2005 change in political leadership from Lalu to Nitish was a major discontinuity in Bihar's political narrative. While this may be a surprise on the surface, the story of election numbers does not suggest any unusual break. When we perform the calculations based on two major coalitions that had been formed before elections—Nitish-led JD(U) with BJP, and Lalu-led RJD with Congress—we do not observe any surprises. Political competition had considerably reduced, quite predictably. Disproportionality had increased expectedly, indicating big differences between seat and vote share. This means that the results of 2005 carried high levels of dissatisfaction. For most political commentators, this election was a clear divide between JD(U)+BJP, who were banking on backward castes (Koeris–Kumris) and upper-caste votes, and RJD+Congress, who were relying on backward castes (Yadavs, primarily) and Muslims.

The 2010 assembly elections follow a similar story. The much-touted victory of 206 out of 243 constituencies by the Nitish-led alliance is a story of misplaced euphoria, concealing the reality of vote share. Securing more than seven times the number of seats than the Lalu-led alliance, Nitish and BJP secured mere 50 per cent more votes. The victory margin was very thin. This is reflected in the unprecedented high level of DISP and corresponding low value of ENP. The DISP value is 35.4 in 2010, which is the highest ever. In some ways, one can claim that Nitish's victory in 2010 was established on a strong seat-support but not vote-support. Seen through this lens, the 2015 election results were not surprising. The 2015 elections had not been favourable for JD(U)—it was the alliance that saved it. Sitting on a huge seat share and vote share difference, Nitish could not have performed in the same way. Now that victory has been snatched with a sizable DISP again, the anxiety, if any, is well-founded. Bihari voters are swinging.

The 2010 and 2015 assembly elections in Bihar had the lowest level of electoral competition since Independence, if one measures it using seat share. Interestingly, if one uses vote share, the effective number of parties was considerably high. This discrepancy testifies to the fact that large (and crucial) number of voters have been in a swing mood. Low margins of victory mean winners need to perform well, since shifting of a small group of voters is enough to topple them in subsequent elections. In some ways, the 2010 elections were highly deceptive—they had a very clear majority, and yet, an uncomfortably huge divergence between seat and vote share.

And that is the key fact. For Bihar, DISP has remained significantly high. That is to say, for its entire political history, Bihar has witnessed significant leakages in aggregating the will of its voters. The state—despite the so-called caste consciousness—does not offer a politically cohesive mass. No wonder that even after the separation of Jharkhand from Bihar, regions of Magadha, Mithila and Bhojpur keep asserting their unique identities over each other. The Maithili-speaking region is clamouring for a separate state. These voices get drowned in even louder narratives of caste-based identities. The innumerable castes in Bihar are said to be important factors for sociopolitical organisation of the state.[12] But somehow, the juxtaposition of these communities alongside each other disables a predictively straightforward thinking. Bihar, despite lending a homogenous pattern, remains a political kaleidoscope.

Bihari voters swing. That is the bottom line. They swing slowly, but they do. And with enough efforts, one can make them swing faster. This makes votes more important than seats, and drives home the point that mandates in seat-driven politics will be significantly eroded. A focus on votes is what builds a sustainable edifice of democracy.

For instance, let's look at what happened in 2015 once again. RJD secured 80 seats and JD(U) bagged 71 seats. The third-highest seat grosser was BJP with 53 seats. Now, look at the votes. Guess who received the largest number of votes? It was BJP with 24.4 per cent of all votes. RJD and JD(U) got 18.4 per cent and 16.8 per cent votes respectively. Congress, which had half the seats as that of BJP, got one-fourth the votes as BJP did.

This is a telling story of how mandates get manipulated by design. With 80 seats, RJD was able to woo 69 lakh voters. With merely 53 seats, BJP got more than 92 lakhs. Who got to be the CM? Nitish, whose party attracted 63 lakh voters. He has been running the government for more than 10 crore people. The preference of 63 lakh individuals imposed on a population of 10 crores!

Such wide disparity is possible indeed. Bihar had 6.8 crore eligible voters, out of which merely 57 per cent voted. And then, voters had all kinds of preferences. But the idea of first-past-the-post (FPTP) ensured they got some mandate, however incomplete or dissatisfactory. Numbers don't inspire us much. Sixty-three lakhs in 10 crores constitutes only 6.3 per cent. Perhaps nowhere is the distinction between what people wanted and what they got starker than in Bihar.

BEGUSARAI

Begusarai is not exactly famous. It is a small city with 3 lakh inhabitants, located to the north of the Ganga in central Bihar. It has a tiny, nondescript village called Rachiyari. This village earned huge fame in the 1957 elections. The reason was that it was witness to the first instance of booth capturing in Indian elections. This is where it all started. For several years, the local Begusarai goon, Kamdeo Singh, was hired for booth capturing across the state. It was as if a new specialty was emerging. By the late 1980s, this menace had reached such heights that the Representation of People's Act, 1951, had to be amended to make it an explicitly unlawful activity. Innovated and perfected in Bihar, many Indian states have, since then, learnt this art, UP in particular. When it comes to twisting politics into crime and money, Bihar comes to mind.

Bihar reminds us of our commitments. One wonders what would Rajendra Prasad think, if he were to visit Bihar today. The state of affairs in Bihar politics is one of the most pressing reasons why we need to urgently look at what goes on in the design of electoral politics and voting mandate. Nitish Kumar, who became CM with a much lower number of seats and votes in his favour compared to BJP and RJD in 2015, in a matter of a mere two years conveniently knocked RJD's Lalu out and invited BJP to form a new coalition government. (As this book goes to print, he has done the reverse in 2020 assembly—expelled BJP and invited RJD this time.) Think about what was made out of the will of people who had voted in favour of the Mahagathbandhan and those who had decided not to go with BJP, and had rejoiced at the earlier verdict. Is it based on who people want, or who the leader of the assembly wants?

Rashtrakavi Ramdhari Singh Dinkar was one of the most prolific Hindi poets of the last century. JP had famously recited his poem during the Emergency, attracting lakhs of people to Ramlila Maidan in Patna. The words have been etched in history now: '*Sinhasan khali karo, ke janta aati hai* ....', translating into, 'Vacate the throne, for the people are now coming ...'

Dinkar was born in our very own Begusarai.

3

Uttar Pradesh

Very few would have heard of Justice Mohammad Ismail. A former judge at the Allahabad High Court, he was recruited by Sardar Patel to help build the judicial system of the Eastern States Agency (comprising parts of Chhattisgarh, Orissa and Bengal). He was working out of Raigarh when he received a letter from Pakistan. It was a request from the newly formed neighbouring country to become their High Commissioner in India. During Partition, he had refused to move to Pakistan. But this time, he accepted the offer. Mohammad Ismail was the second Pakistani High Commissioner in India, from 1948 to 1952. And all this while, he remained an Indian citizen!

Justice Ismail hailed from Gorakhpur and even spent his last days there.

This, in many ways, explains the contradictions embedded within UP, particularly its flirtations with religion. UP is perhaps one of the most important provinces in India, for all the right and wrong reasons put together. Scholars have often felt that it was UP where the Pakistan project really took place and was cultivated with vigour. It is the state which is the epicentre of the Hindu–Muslim divide that still smoulders within India. Vazira Zamindar, in her book *The Long Partition*, reminds us that Partition was not a moment in history, but has remained a continuous exercise of displacement through several decades later.[1] This has been particularly true about Muslims in UP leaving for Pakistan through the 1960s and even the 1970s.

One must remember that the Muslim League's base, until the late 1930s, was largely in UP (United Province at that time)[2]—and not in the Muslim-majority states of Punjab, Sindh, North Western Frontier Province (NWFP) or East Bengal. This was both despite and because of Muslims being a minority there. UP provided the desired anxiety of elite Muslim intelligentsia for the Muslim League to flourish and gain a stronghold along with the idea of Pakistan. In 1937, when the provincial elections took place, Congress won with a landslide. It secured 133 out of 228 seats in UP; the Muslim League could only secure 26 seats. Even out of the 482 seats reserved for Muslims across the country, the Muslim League could only secure 109. To make matters worse, Congress—perhaps buoyed by its success—declined the League's offer to form a coalition and forced them to merge into Congress. This made the Muslim League even more anxious. By the 1940s, Project Pakistan had become a major force, and was being heard the loudest in UP.

This is the land of the famously claimed Ganga-Jamuni tehzeeb, where, for instance, a Muslim Lucknowi family sohar song (sung when the lady is pregnant) used to be, '*Allah miyan, hamray bhaiya ko diyo Nandlal* …' (Oh, my Allah, bestow on my brother a son like Krishna …).[3] This is also the land where, according to Paul Brass' revealing work, riots have been systematically orchestrated during elections.[4]

And that is why UP has led the political narratives of India in a depressingly grand manner. Consider Ayodhya. It has been the focus of India's electoral politics and has dominated the Indian political discourse for more than 20 years now. Where else can it be but in UP. With a population of 24 crore, UP contributes 14.7 per cent seats to the Lok Sabha. The closest second is far off—Maharashtra, with 7.3 per cent! UP's size is enough to steer the direction of electoral mandate in favour of a party. Also, it is the state from where eight out of 14 prime ministers of India contested elections (six of them also belonged to UP). This means that UP is important not just because of its sheer numbers, but also holds a figurative significance in Indian political make-up. Further, the fractured and complex nature of the UP political landscape is also reflected in the fact that the state had witnessed a CM-less (president's rule) regime ten times until 2002. In fact, the first time that a CM was able to complete a five-year term since 1967 was not until Mayawati's terms ending in 2012.

What makes UP even more important is that it is also the epicentre of BJP's political avatar. The very first assembly in the state, held in 1952, witnessed the third-highest vote share going to Bharatiya Jana Sangh (BJS), the precursor to BJP. It secured 6.45 per cent votes, although with just two of the 430 seats. As the political wing of the Rashtriya Swayamsevak Sangh (RSS), BJS was started by Syama Prasad Mukherjee, the powerful academic barrister who had a fallout with Nehru while he was the minister of commerce and industry during 1947–50. This led him to quit the Indian National Congress and form the BJS. It merged with the opposition parties for the 1977 Lok Sabha to help form the Janata Party. In 1980, when Janata Party was dissolved, BJS crystallised out of it in the form of BJP.

During the Emergency, UP was another 'shool' (pain) for Indira Gandhi, in addition to Bihar. Congress, an effortless winner in the state since Independence, did not receive a single seat in 1977.

And did we mention that presently Bihar and UP have the country's largest fertility rates. And so, if delimitation happens in a few years, the contribution of UP (and Bihar) to Indian Parliament will increase even further, making them even more significant.

HISTORICAL NARRATIVE OF UP POLITICS

The first assembly elections in UP were held in 1952. Congress won 90 per cent of the seats, with 48 per cent of votes. Socialist Party stood at the second position with 4.6 per cent seats and 12 per cent votes. In 1957, BJS had picked up the second position—almost 10 per cent votes for 4 per cent seats. Congress lost its votes to 42 per cent and seats to 66.5 per cent. The year 1957 also witnessed an increase in voter turnout to 44 per cent; five years earlier, in 1952, it had only been 38 per cent in the state.

Things didn't change much in 1962 in terms of Congress dominance. UP voters perhaps remained content with whatever Congress offered to them, mostly the upper-caste leaders. Here's a quick introduction of these leaders: Pandit Govind Ballabh Pant, the Almora-born Brahmin lawyer, had significantly contributed to the freedom movement. He had been the CM of the United Province during the late 1930s and even at the time of Independence. When he was requested to move to New Delhi to fulfil his expectations of being part of the Union Cabinet, he was replaced by Sampurnanand, the Benarasi Sanskrit scholar, who held the position for the longest uninterrupted span (1954–60). A tiff with Kamlapati Tripathi and Chandra Bhanu Gupta (both towering leaders of the state and its future CMs) led to him being shunted off to Rajasthan as its governor from 1962 to 1967. Many say that his posting was the starting point of a culture that was to become central to Indian politics—removing unwanted but powerful people to positions such as governors of states. He was followed by Chandra Bhanu Gupta, after which Sucheta Kriplani took charge. Except Charan Singh, the powerful 220-day Jat CM from the 1970s, UP voters, who were largely from backward castes, had only witnessed upper-caste leadership until 1989. It was only then that Mulayam Singh Yadav took centre stage.

One may wonder why lower-caste representation and caste politics took so long to take shape in the state. The rise of regional parties focused on cultivating social reforms for oppressed castes in India (and even in UP) had begun almost three decades ago. Perhaps part of the reason for sustenance of upper-caste leaders in the state was because of the broad-minded outlook of leaders of the same times. Indeed, these leaders were difficult to be categorised under some ideological umbrella.

Pandit Govind Ballabh Pant, for instance, despite being a strong supporter of Hindi language and locating it within the central government, was instrumental in abolishing the zamindari system in UP, passing of the Hindu Code Bill, mandating monogamy for Hindu men and giving rights to Hindu women for divorce and to ancestral property. Sampurnanand, known to be a strong advocate of Sanskrit, Hindu astrology and ban on cow slaughter, had no recorded instance of pushing his ideas except in encouraging the building of an astronomical observatory. He was the foremost in promoting the idea of prisons with no bars during his stint as governor of Rajasthan and he championed the idea of treating convicts with an intent of reformation rather than retribution. Chandra Bhanu Gupta set up various educational centres, particularly in Lucknow, ranging from children's museums, libraries to hospitals and even homoeopathic clinics. Sucheta Kriplani, the celebrated Haryana-born Bengali freedom fighter and wife of the socialist Acharya Kriplani, was the first woman CM of any state in India. She drove transparency in her governance and made successful attempts to prevent economic decline in the state during her tenure. Kamalapati Tripathi, the ardent loyalist of the Nehru–Gandhi family, was one of the few who had the courage to challenge the party, particularly in the 1980s, even going as far as declaring that the disputed Babri site be preserved as a national monument.

Upon closer scrutiny we do find that blanket labelling of Indian politicians of the early days with a singular ideological brush may be unwarranted. More research on this aspect would be needed, and surely this is an important point to consider in the politically charged climate of today. To us, it also suggests that voters liked status quo, and that they had not even begun recognising what political voice is.

No wonder, then, that the first major public and violent resentment against the government in UP took place as late as in 1973 during the Provincial Armed Constabulary Revolt for better work and pay conditions in the battalions of Bareilly, Meerut and Agra. The then CM, Kamalapati Tripathi, resigned due to this rebellion. In fact, it was only in 1981 that a major anti-Dalit atrocity in the state post Independence was documented. This was the case of Phoolan Devi, a Dalit from the Mallah community, who was gangraped by upper-caste Thakur men. A year and a half later, she formed a gang of men from her community and avenged the wrong-doing by killing several men from the Thakur community of that village. She surrendered, served her time in prison, and then contested elections, which she went on to win twice. The fact that she was shot in 2001 by an assailant who wanted to avenge the deaths of Thakurs killed by her tells us how deeply entrenched caste consciousness continues to be in the region.

In fact, today, when caste mobilisation is at its highest, caste-based violence is significant (in 2016, more than a quarter of all crimes committed in UP were against lower-caste people). Whether people remained muted earlier or whether reporting was inadequate, one cannot say with certainty. It is also likely that the rates have gone up as an ugly response to political mobilisations of caste. One cannot claim what it may actually be.

But we have gone ahead; let's go back. The 1967 assembly elections in UP were fascinating, when Congress had to vacate their chief ministerial position in the state. By then, new shifts had begun to take place. Congress stood at a mere 46 per cent seats and 32 per cent votes, while BJS climbed up to 23 per cent seats and 22 per cent votes. The proximity of seat and vote share for BJS is interesting. It shows there was little leakage at an aggregate level. People had begun to prefer BJS's imagination. Congress' dominance in UP had been waning by then; there were six other parties, and 18 per cent votes were bagged by independent candidates. UP politics, in that sense, mimicked India's, where local leaders who did not toe a particular party line were exerting their local influence as independent candidates, and they could not have been ignored. Even though several parties came together to field Charan Singh, the Jat leader, as the CM in 1967, the assembly remained hung for most part. In the next four years, UP witnessed four CMs and two presidential rules.

The other interesting thing about the 1967 UP elections is the slight divergence in Lok Sabha and Vidhan Sabha results within the state. This was perhaps the last time that voters were witnessing simultaneous state and central elections. In the Lok Sabha results of UP, 53 per cent seats went to Congress and merely 14 per cent seats to the BJS. BJS also secured much lower (9 per cent) votes in Lok Sabha than in Vidhan Sabha. This indicates that UP voters preferred Congress in New Delhi even though many of them wanted BJS in the state.

BJS, however, began witnessing a decline in its popularity in the phase between 1969 and 1974. In 1969, it secured only 49 seats. Charan Singh, who had formed Bharatiya Kranti Dal, took away 98 seats. He had defected from Congress, but Congress still maintained a tally of 211 seats. This meant that the real casualty of Charan Singh's new party was BJS. The party's vote share had come down from 22 per cent to 18 per cent in two years and Congress was still controlling one-third of votes in the state. ENP in 1969 remained very similar to that in 1967.

Charan Singh was an interesting personality who had far-reaching influence on Indian politics. Let us discuss him briefly here. Paul Brass, the American scholar well-versed in Indian political processes and particularly UP, in his array of excellent accounts on Indian politics, chose to write a biography of only one person—Charan Singh!

Not only did Charan Singh preside over an unusual alliance in UP during 1967 that brought both the so-called far left (CPI) and the far right (BJS) under one umbrella (one of the firsts in India), he was also responsible for fundamentally altering UP politics during the late 1960s and early 1970s with far-reaching consequences in terms of realigning voter preferences. He was also responsible for centralising peasants in the political equation. As the first non-Congress CM of the state, he rejigged political priorities from the earlier focus on big dams and industrialisation that catered to the urban middle-class, to agriculture, rural investments and small-scale industries. He was a Jat peasant leader who understood farmers' emotions, which had been ignored for centuries, and lent them a voice. He gave rousing speeches in public and private spaces on the privileges of urban Indians belonging to upper castes such as Brahmins and Thakurs, and forcefully articulated the interests that directly related to the backward castes in the region. UP voters responded to this, and one can safely claim that his presence was a major precursor to the emergence of Dalit politics in the state. He reminded New Delhi about this massive voter base, particularly in December 1978, after his conflicts with the Morarji Desai government, when he mobilised thousands of 'dhoti' clad farmers from western UP and Haryana to walk to Lutyens, giving elite bureaucrats a first taste of what 'real India' was. It is no wonder, therefore, that the Mandal Commission was established in 1979, while he was the prime minister. In fact, after his death in 1987, non-Congress leaders have often competed to carry his baton, be it Mulayam Singh Yadav, V.P. Singh, Ajit Singh (his son), and even Mahinder Singh Tikait, the Jat leader from western UP. Those who sit on a voter base of lower castes or farmers today, in a state that was otherwise homogeneously governed by upper-caste leaders earlier, enjoy their power to mobilisations and prioritisations brought in the power centres by Charan Singh.

In fact, in the Vidhan Sabha elections of 1974, Charan Singh's party, Bharatiya Kranti Dal (BKD) pulled the second highest number of seats with 106 (21 per cent votes), while BJS remained at 61 (3 per cent votes).

The 1977 assembly elections were unprecedented, both in India and in UP. Congress was able to retain power on mere 11 per cent of seats while Janata Party (which had consolidated many parties, including BJS and BKD) bagged 83 per cent seats with 48 per cent votes. During the power tussle in Lucknow between Chandra Shekhar and Charan Singh, the OBC leader Ram Naresh Yadav took the CM's seat.

Numbers here, though, conceal something more substantive. Congress' seat share in 1974 was 50.7 per cent. In 1977, this had come down to a mere 11 per cent. This is a crushing defeat by any standard. But let's look at the vote share. In 1974, it had 32.3 per cent votes. How many did it have in 1977, the poster-child year of Congress' debacle? At 31.9 per cent, its vote share was almost the same as that of the winner. A 0.4 per cent points reduction in votes meant 95,000 voters. So, mathematically speaking, there was a difference of only 95,000 voters as compared to 1974. This is interesting at another level altogether and raises questions on the merit and heaviness of the victory and loss. The victory of the Janata Party was well-founded. It had 83 per cent seats and 48 per cent votes. This was a solid win. But the loss was viewed only through the lens of seats. Congress bagged 47 seats against Janata Party's 347. Janata Party was the winner. More than 1.1 crore people wanted it to come to power. How many people wanted Congress to come to power? Around 75 lakhs. That's not too wide a gap. This is another example to show what happens in a society where seats, not votes, matter.

No surprises then, that 1980 reversed this trend, mirroring what happened in New Delhi. While BJS had re-emerged from Janata Party as BJP, BKD (Charan Singh's party) emerged as Janata Party (Secular). Interestingly, if you look at only these two parties, BJP's politics was not as appealing to UP voters as BKD's. In 1980, BJP bagged mere 11 seats (with 11 per cent votes) while BKD got 59 seats (22 per cent votes). In fact, even in 1985, Lok Dal (Charan Singh's renamed party) bagged 84 seats while BJP secured only 16 seats, even though both almost maintained their vote shares. Many Indian voters today think that BJP's slow and steady rise took place in the 1980s. The fact is that compared to its predecessor, BJS, BJP had hardly begun to make any significant impact until late 1980s. Congress, in both 1980 and 1985, was the top party with (very roughly speaking) two-third seats and one-third votes. The 1980s were marked by power tussles between Delhi and Lucknow rather frequently, igniting an era of coalition politics. During that decade, UP had seven CMs. The political confusion was so high during the decade that 1989 witnessed one of the highest jumps in both the number of parties contesting and the number of independent contestants winning elections. While in 1985, 13 parties contested; in 1989, 42 parties took part. In 1989, 10 per cent of seats and 15 per cent of votes went to independent candidates.

Surely, as we now know, in 1989, the landscape changed unrecognisably. Janata Dal, led by V.P. Singh and Mulayam Singh Yadav, took half the seats and one-third the votes in UP. BJP had still remained at 11 per cent votes, but won respectably high (57) number of seats compared to their previous performance. A watershed moment for Congress in terms of votes occurred in 1989. Most people believe Congress really started losing votes in 1977, but it was indeed in 1989 that the vote share plummeted dramatically, sliding down from 40 per cent votes in 1985 to 28 per cent in 1989 (in 1977, Congress' vote share was around 35 per cent).

Scholars contend that this was the turning point where corruption and religious sentiments were making their way into the politics of India. The highlight of the 1980s and 1990s was the emergence of powerful caste-mobilisation in politics, both under Mayawati and Mulayam Singh Yadav (Bahujan Samaj Party's [BSP] debut in UP swept off almost 10 per cent of votes in 1989). The era beginning 1991 marked the emergence of fractured mandates in the state, and until 2003, UP had seen ten CMs and three presidential rules. The fire that spread through the 1992 Babri Masjid demolition in Ayodhya had plunged the country into the abyss of communal hatred that plagues us to this day. Thanks to religious schisms like the Shah Bano case in the Supreme Court, the Ayodhya mosque–temple divide and even the Bofors scam during Rajiv Gandhi's tenure, the shock waves through Congress' vote base were felt heavily. Congress had 63 per cent seats and 39 per cent votes in 1985, but it got reduced to a rubble—22 per cent seats and 28 per cent votes in 1989 in UP.

During this time (1985–89), BJP had increased its seat share from 4 per cent to 13 per cent in UP, even though votes increased only from 9.8 per cent to 11.6 per cent. However, the year 1991 saw BJP's seat share rise to an unprecedented 52 per cent and vote share to 31 per cent. How did the opinion suddenly change in a short span of two years? The 1990s in UP were turbulent times. Some research has shown the complicated birth of coalition politics in the state but we will skip the details here. If we look at the numbers, however, new things come to light.

Figure 3.1 helps us compare Congress and BJS/BJP. Let's look at Congress first. This is the grand old party which had managed a solid 65 per cent seats and almost 40 per cent votes in UP during 1985. From the previous elections, this was a decline in seat share but increase in vote share. Next came 1989, and many claim that Congress' decline started in this year. This must be revised. The year 1989 was definitely disappointing for Congress—its seat share plummeted to an astounding low of 22 per cent (loss of 43 percentage points). But note that the vote share did not quite fall. It fell only to 28 per cent, which is a loss of 12 percentage points. (Even in 1977, the defeated Congress had still managed to win 32 per cent of votes, so the party's loss in both 1977 and 1989 was of seats). Crudely speaking, this means the margins of victory of the other parties were not as much as the margins which Congress claimed in its heydays. Both seat shares and vote shares of Congress had continued to fall steadily until 1995, but the rate of seat share decline was far more than that of vote share. Even later, when Congress was continuing to lose seats, it maintained a respectable vote share of around 15–17 per cent. In 1996, its vote share had plummeted to 8 per cent. Congress' real threat of elimination occurred in 2017, when it managed just a measly 1.7

FIGURE 3.1 Seat and vote share of Congress and BJS/BJP in UP Vidhan Sabha

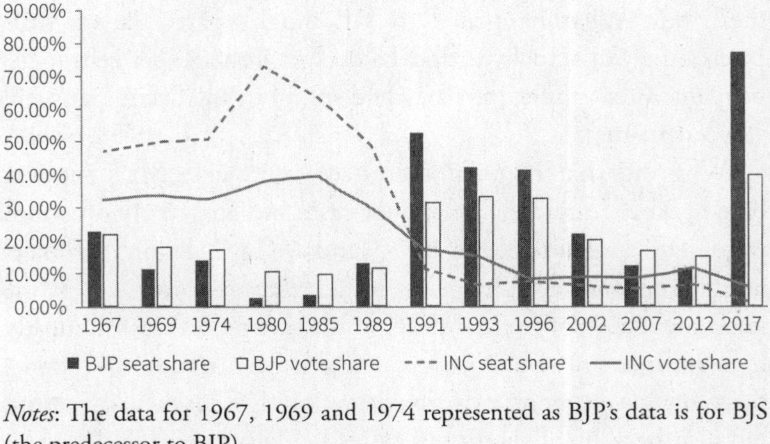

Notes: The data for 1967, 1969 and 1974 represented as BJP's data is for BJS (the predecessor to BJP).

The year 1977 is not included because BJS didn't contest election.

per cent seats although with 6.2 per cent votes. (This 6.2 per cent should be put into context. In 1989, when BJP secured 12 per cent votes, it had 57 seats. Congress, in 2017, had almost half the votes but managed only 7 seats.)

Speaking of BJP, UP had been particularly kind to the party. When L.K. Advani's rath yatra was intercepted by Bihar's CM Lalu Prasad Yadav in Samastipur in October 1990, BJP made a calculated and strategic move to pull out of the government (both in Delhi and Lucknow), calling for fresh elections. It paid off. BJP had been surviving with 4 per cent and 13 per cent seats in 1985 and 1989 respectively and vote shares hovering in the 10 per cent range. In 1991, the party secured 53 per cent seats and 31 per cent votes! This was a jackpot.

We often forget that something else too happened in 1990. The V.P. Singh government in Delhi implemented the Mandal Commission in August that year, which enabled caste-based reservations for other backward classes (OBCs). This led to widespread demonstrations among students—reports mention around 200 self-immolations of students nationwide. It is common to think that reservations benefit the parties who roll them out. What happened to V.P. Singh's party, Janata Dal? Interestingly, it actually suffered a decline from 30 per cent to 18 per cent votes (surely, the party had split, but the decline was still very surprising).

Why did that happen? Here's an argument. BJP's support base had been middle class, upper-caste Indians, many of whom were left disgruntled by the Mandal Commission. Scholars like Ramchandra Guha have noted that the impact of the implementation of the Mandal Commission report was felt mostly in north India, not only because of the heavier reliance of students there on government jobs given low levels of industrialisation, but also because of the upper castes being numerically larger in the north. They did not vote for Janata Dal that year.

BJP's vote base, for long, has been Hindi-speaking north Indian voters. So, when BJP pulled out its plug from Janata Dal party, it appealed to its north Indian voter base heavily. Sounds sensible then that BJP was looking at a lucky 1991. From 11 per cent voters favouring BJP in 1989, it suddenly lifted to almost 33 per cent in 1991, and remained there for the next two elections (1993 and 1996). The year 1991 was really when people came out in large numbers to vote for BJP. (But only within UP. As we show in Chapter 5, BJP's rise in India had taken place earlier, in 1989 itself.)

And what was the impact of the mosque demolition which took place in December 1992? In the 1993 elections, BJP's seat share dropped from 53 per cent to 42 per cent. But the vote share increased, from 31 per cent to 33 per cent. Interesting, isn't it? Many more people voted for BJP. But many voted against it as well. Those who voted against were more widely spread, so the number of BJP's seats declined. Those who voted for the party were perhaps voting in the existing stronghold constituencies of BJP. From the numbers, it looks like the Mandal Commission secured more votes than the rath yatra for BJP. Also, the *promise* of a Ram Mandir rather than the actual demolition of the mosque was more positive for BJP. This is, of course, one view. The other view is the rise of BSP. While in 1991, the party had merely 12 seats, in a matter of two years, it had bagged 67 seats.

One must be aware that even though BJP was the largest party in the state in 1991, 1993 and 1996, it got to make its own government only in 1991. The travesty of democracy lies in coalition politics, which we will discuss in Chapter 6, but UP offers a compelling image in which BJP remained in political wilderness, even though it had a strong home base there. That is perhaps why BJP supported BSP in 1995 as the latter made a Dalit woman the CM in UP. Mayawati was a phenomenon in a state which had been ruled by upper-caste men for most part of independent India's history.

BJP had given its support to the BSP on the condition that the two parties would have the opportunity to alternately appoint CMs in six-month intervals. Mayawati reneged on her promise. Circus ensued in the Vidhan Sabha in the months to come. Such suspended animation of BJP had been continuing in New Delhi as well (see Chapter 6 on coalitions).

Consider a few numbers. From 1996 to 2002, BJP's seats were halved and voters reduced from 33 per cent to 20 per cent. UP voters had rewarded BJP in both 1993 and 1996. Thirty-two per cent voted for BJP in 1996, while in 2002, only 20 per cent did. This fall cannot be looked in isolation from other parties. This becomes evident when we look at the results of 2002, 2007 and 2012. It was the reign of the Samajwadi Party and BSP.

POLITICAL COMPETITION AND DISPROPORTIONALITY IN UP ASSEMBLY ELECTIONS

The 1980s and 1990s changed UP, and in doing so, changed Indian politics. The emergence of regional parties shifted the power balance. This led to higher levels of effective political competition, and better representativeness reflected in lower disproportionality. See Figure 3.2.

The ENP and ENP_v declined till 1977, and rose up until 2002 and then declined again. Of particular interest are 1977 and 2017. Based on seat share, the effective number of parties were the lowest in these years—1.43 and 1.62. This means that despite having a large number of parties contesting, effectively, the competition was between very few parties (there were hardly one-and-a-half parties in UP, of equivalent power). So, 1977 and 2002 were similar contests. The year 2002, in this regard, lies at the other end of the spectrum. BJP, BSP and SP took 88, 98 and

FIGURE 3.2 ENP, ENP_v and DISPR across Uttar Pradesh assemblies (Winners are mentioned against the years)

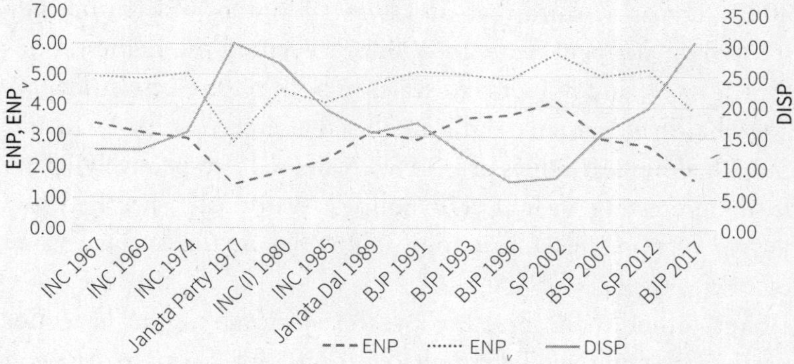

143 seats overall—clearly not very solid wins for any. The topper in 1996 (BJP) had taken 174 seats, and that in 2007 (BSP) took 206 seats. The year 2002 was among the most indecisive ones.

What about effective number of parties with respect to votes (the ENP_v value)? If ENP and ENP_v diverge, it reflects voter preference leakage. Stated differently, if the effective number of parties based on seat share is smaller compared to the same value based on vote share, it means a big number of votes did not translate into the mandate and there was a significant leakage. So, when ENP was lowest in 1977 (1.43), the ENP_v was also the lowest (2.8). This means, for most part, votes did get translated into seats. Notice that the other occasion for low ENP was the 2017 elections, when ENP was at 1.62 but ENP_v was at 3.85, which was relatively higher. So, compared to 1977, in 2017, there was significant leakage.

This is well represented in disproportionality (DISP). As discussed in Chapter 1, DISP reflects how representative an electoral result is. A high DISP indicates high leakage and that the winner does not carry the mandate strongly. The winner is indeed a winner, but only because the seats somehow managed to be on her side even though the votes were not. The average disproportionality in UP has been at around 17. The lowest, single-digit disproportionality was recorded in 1996 (7.7) and 2002 (8.3). One-third votes in UP in 1996 went to BJP and they secured 41 per cent seats. In 2002, SP secured the highest, one-fourth votes, and 35 per cent seats. In both these elections, voters got what they wanted. And note that the same years of 1996 and 2002 had highest values of ENP (3.7 and 4.17 respectively). This is an interesting insight. UP politics, historically, has had low degree of political competition compared to the average value of 2.83.

Yet, other than these two years, electoral results have not been representative. Take 2012 elections, for example. SP won 55 per cent of the seats but it had received just 29 per cent of votes. The previous BSP government (2007–12) was also highly disproportionately represented, with a victory in 51 per cent of seats but just 30 per cent of votes in the state. Compare it with the 2002 elections, where the largest party, SP, won 35 per cent seats with 25 per cent votes; BSP won 24 per cent seats with 23 per cent votes; and BJP won 21 per cent seats with 20 per cent votes—a much more closely tied-up seat and vote share proportion indicating much better representation of the three major parties with good competition. (The representation was similar in 1993 and 1996 elections.) But the historically high disproportionality was evident in 1977 with Janata Party winning 83 per cent seats with just 48 per cent votes. Congress had 32 per cent vote share while its seat share was just 11 per cent. This aspect of disproportional representation largely remains a point of discussion. Notice, in 2017, when BJP swept off 77 per cent seats and 40 per cent votes, the SP and BSP combined secured more votes than BJP; no wonder the disproportionality recorded was the highest.

Perhaps these intuitions will appear by simply estimating the difference in seat and vote share between the winning party and the runner-up. See Figure 3.3. This simple calculation yields interesting insights. The seat share margin was highest in 1977, followed by 2017, 1980 and 1985. Winners during these elections came to the top with massive mandates. It was the lowest during 1991, 1993 and 2002, and one would suggest that the winners were simply lucky with just 10–15 per cent additional seats compared to the runner-up.

Now notice these figures for vote shares. The highest vote share margin was during 2017, 1985 and 1993 and the lowest was during 1989, 2002, 2007 and 2012. The small difference in vote share is crucial because this means that the mandate was not as strong as one would have expected. Janata Dal in 1989, SP in 2002 and 2012, and BSP in 2007 secured merely 2–5 percentage points higher votes than the runners-up. Put differently, the only two periods in which UP CMs completed their five-year terms had victories which could be termed more appropriately as winner's luck rather than as aggregated preferences. The winning voters just happened to be really dispersed across the constituency.

FIGURE 3.3 Seats and votes margin between the winner and the runner-up (%)

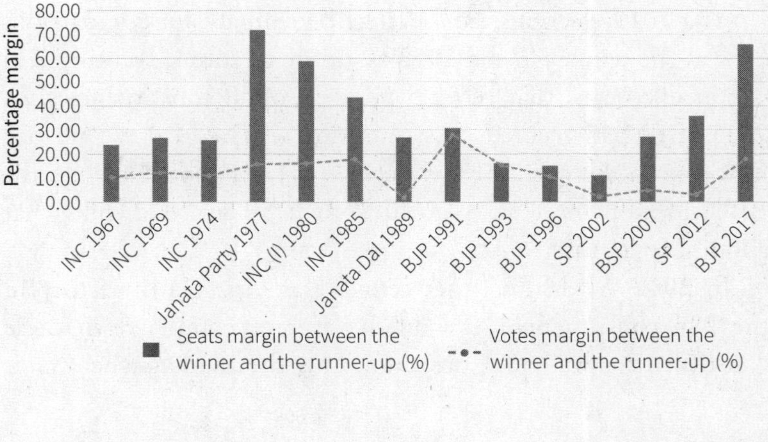

THE 2017 ELECTIONS: QUALITY OF BJP'S VICTORY IN 2017 vs SP'S 2012 WIN

With UP elections round the corner as we write the book, let's look at the last 2017 Vidhan Sabha elections. BJP's victory in the 2017 UP assembly elections was unprecedented. It attracted two types of responses. For BJP lovers, this was like rainfall on parched earth. But notice that this victory of 77.4 per cent of seats stood on the foundation of 39.7 per cent of votes. More strangely, the BSP had only managed 4.7 per cent of the seats with a vote share of 23 per cent. The concentration of power with BJP, therefore, doesn't reflect people's true preferences at the aggregate level. We then wonder whether the party was just a lucky winner.

A fairly basic and reliable indicator of the quality of an electoral win is the margin of victory. As a rule, if the party wins majority of the constituencies, it wins the elections. However, if the margin of win is thin in these places, it means the party could be ousted the next time with a tiny number of swing voters. As a corollary, if the runner-up has won its constituencies (wherever it has won) by a huge margin, then we assume it has a good stronghold in those constituencies. The other variable that indicates the strength of the victory is the vote share. If the value is large, then we know the party's victory is of high quality.

The 2012 elections are a perfect benchmark for comparison. SP was the winner in the 2012 assembly elections, securing 224 out of 403 seats, that is, 55.5 per cent of all constituencies. In 2017, BJP had secured 312 seats (for neat results, we are not factoring in the coalition), which is 77.4 per cent. Now clearly, BJP had won more seats in 2017 than SP in 2012, but what about its margins?

In 2012, SP had a 9 per cent average margin of victory in the 224 constituencies it won. Its average vote share in these constituencies was 36.3 per cent. This meant that wherever it won, it defeated the runner-up by an average of 9 per cent votes and had an average of 36.3 per cent votes in its favour. For the whole state, the vote share value was 29.9 per cent. Contrast this with BJP in 2017. The party's average margin in the 312 constituencies that it won was 15.04 per cent and the average vote share was 44.1 per cent (39.7 per cent for the whole state). Both margin and vote share were significantly higher for BJP in 2017 than those of SP in 2012. BJP, in 2017, was, thus, unequivocally a worthier winner than SP in 2012.

However, these average values could be deceptive if the distributions are highly skewed, that is, the presence of extreme values on the higher side could lead to a higher overall average. Thus, if the winner gets 40 per cent margin in many of the constituencies, the average might go up. So, if the margins are spread out widely in the winning constituencies, it doesn't tell us much. It could well be the case that in many places, BJP's margins in 2017 were low, but they were very high in some, pulling the average a little higher than SP's in 2012. Mathematically speaking, only if the margins and vote share in the winning constituencies are 'normally distributed' like a bell curve, would BJP's high vote margin values in winning constituencies during 2017 be comparable to SP's in 2012.

When we evaluated the results, we found the median values close to normal distribution. The median value shows the point until where half the elements are covered. The median winning margin in the SP's 224 seats of 2012 was 8 per cent and median vote share was 35.4 per cent. Remember, the average values are very close to these figures—9 per cent margin and 36.3 per cent vote share. For BJP in 2017, the 312 winning seats yielded a median margin of 14 per cent (average of 15 per cent) and median vote share of 43.6 per cent (average 44.1 per cent). This means the average values are indeed a real representation of election results which show the superiority of BJP's victory.

So here is the quick lesson from this exercise. In an otherwise imperfect system based on first-past-the-post (FPTP), with huge vote-seat share differences, there are other ways to compare quality of victories between two parties or elections. In 2017, the difference between BJP's seat share and its vote share was much larger than that of SP in 2012. Yet, if one looks at margins, one recognises why BJP is a more 'appropriate' winner than SP. Figure 3.4 shows these values.

FIGURE 3.4 Comparison of parties' victories in 2017 and 2012

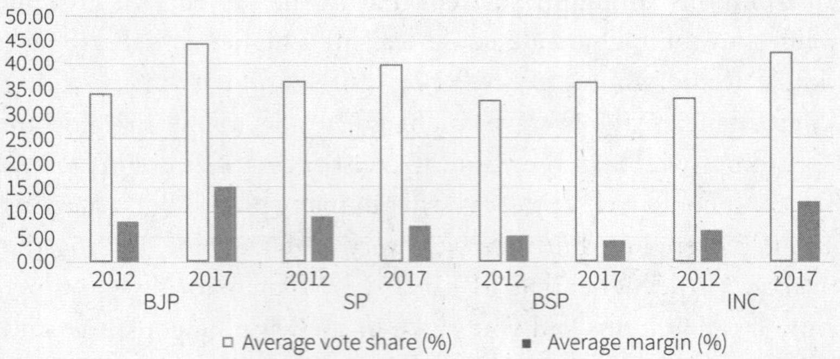

Note: This data shows the values for all the constituencies in which these parties had won. It just shows each party's quality of victory. The number of seats won does not matter here.

We also see that the wins of the poorest quality have been those of the BSP, both in 2012 and 2017. It had the lowest average margin of victory in the seats it had won and lowest vote share in those winning seats. When commentators lament the BSP's low seat share and high vote share, they must also factor in how weak the foundations of the BSP's victories had been anyway.

This is but part of the story. We go back to our drawing board. Look at the DISP figures. UP had witnessed highest DISP in 2017, a staggering figure of 32.75. Crudely stated, one-third of the mandate was lost.

How do we reconcile better margins for BJP (15.04 per cent) with high levels of disproportionality? Well, in our estimate of BJP's margin, we only looked at the winning constituencies. The disproportionality is a better estimate for an aggregate result. In other words, while BJP is winning comfortably wherever it is winning, it is losing disastrously on average wherever it lost. These things become important when one has to assign political funds to constituencies. Should I invest more in constituencies where I need a larger swing or smaller? If I do the former, which is what most election strategists do, I secure a victory which is democratically unfulfilling. With ballot boxes spelling out booth-level results, the decision can be highly targeted.

THE UNFINISHED-NESS OF UP

In 2008, Raghuram Rajan, in his speech at the Bombay Chambers of Commerce said, 'The poor need the savvy politicians to help them navigate through rotten public services. The politician needs the corrupt businessman to provide the funds that allow him to supply patronage to the poor and fight elections. The corrupt businessman needs the politician to get natural resources cheaply. And the politician needs the votes of the poor, who are numerous enough to assure him reelection ....'[5]

This is a spot-on understanding of politics, especially in UP, and has now come to become characteristic of Indian politics.

We say that if Latin America had not existed, one could construct it simply from the works of Gabriel García Márquez. One could say the same thing about constructing UP from Premchand's stories. Premchand, the celebrated writer of India who created magic with Urdu and Hindi, wrote a story in 1936, just before he passed away. The story was called *Kafan* (The Shroud). Premchand told the story of an impoverished family with a man, his wife and his father. When the wife dies, the father–

son duo seek money to buy a kafan for the dead body. With some difficulty, they borrow some money from the local landlord. But when they get it, they end up wasting it all on drinking.

This is a short tale poignantly reminding us of the anxieties and humour that is characteristic of the UP that was, and continues to be. In 2002, Kanshi Ram, the architect of the Dalit movement in UP (and in India), and Mayawati's political mentor, announced his decision to convert to Buddhism on 14 October 2006, on the same day when 50 years ago Ambedkar had converted to Buddhism. He wanted to do that with 5 crore of his supporters converting along with him. Four years later, that October arrived, but just a week before the event, Kanshi Ram had passed away.

The cycle continues. The unfinished businesses in UP carry on.

4

Bengal and Kerala

Bengal and Kerala love football. Santosh Trophy, the premier football competition in India for 77 years, can colloquially be called the Bengal Trophy. West Bengal has won the tournament 32 times, far more than the trailing Punjab (eight times) or Kerala (seven times). Kerala has its own Kerala Premier League in football, and Kerala Blasters FC is co-owned by none other than Sachin Tendulkar. In Bengal, the fervour during a football match between two local clubs, Mohun Bagan and East Bengal, can easily outweigh an English Premier League match in London!

There is another reason to put them together. And that is the political leanings of the states—they both lean towards the left. Consistently communist provinces, the two states have been at the forefront of, and often lone survivors from, communist camps of Indian (and even global) politics. In this chapter, we'll go deeper into the second reason.

Discourse on the politics of Bengal and Kerala is varied and rich, attracting an interdisciplinary set of scholars to opine on issues of social importance. Seminal work has been done on Bengal and Kerala separately, but the tendency to study the two states jointly is predictably frequent. In fact, it is rare to witness a social science scholar present their findings on Kerala in a conference and not be asked a question about Bengal, or vice versa. People across the world have often viewed the two states with some sort of intellectual homogeneity. In many ways, Bengal and Kerala are two sides of the same coin in social science research—if you talk about one, the other will follow, implicitly or explicitly.

This does not mean that the two states are regarded as similar in all important sociopolitical aspects. Many are, of course, mindful of the underlying differences between the two states, and literature is persuasive enough to point out the significant differences between the two. Yet, the policy obsession to view the two states together remains.

This fixation may be useful. Indeed, if there are valuable parallels that can be drawn, it is a great policy exercise. But it may be worthwhile to examine the reasons that lie at the heart of this 'stately' academic partnership. The reason for placing the two states together is the long stretch of communist governments witnessed post Independence. Widely regarded as the two—the only two—communist states in the country, they are (in particular Kerala is, given its early adherence to the communist mandate) often considered as unique and celebratory experiments in the history of Marxism, where communist governments were elected democratically and continued to hold power for a long and sustained period. It is in Bengal and Kerala that some of the most widely acknowledged land and social reforms in the country took place. These two states offered unique crucibles in the global laboratory of ideologies, in which communism and democracy were fused together. Indeed, both the states have embellished the grammar of studies in communist governance order.

This is an important view. Where the world has observed horrors of communist governments in post-War USSR and Mao's China, Kerala and Bengal offered refreshing views of democratically elected communist governments in India. Retention of communist power through democracy showed the world that people respect the ideals and governance of communist parties and, therefore, communist philosophy has a powerful acceptance in the minds of people.

This view, however, is hinged on focusing on the outcomes of elections by looking at what type of governments took power. In this chapter, we go deeper into the numbers of election results and examine whether the claim that people prefer communist governments in these states is actually true. We try to show why the broad stroke of painting the two states with the same 'communist' brush needs to be reconsidered.

We come to this conclusion by looking at constituency and party-level data collected from every assembly election that has taken place in the two states since 1967. This allows us to observe the preferences of people as revealed by their votes. By looking at who they voted for, we can categorise people's preferences beyond what they just may say here and there. This exercise will illuminate the importance of people's political preferences, and not just their alleged ideology.

At the outset, let us recognise that the rise of communist parties in the political landscape of Bengal and Kerala had very different beginnings and motivations.[1] In Kerala, the emergence of a socialist party (in the form of Congress Socialist Party) took place earlier as an alternative identity to nationalistic Congress with an unsympathetic view towards the British.[2] In Bengal, communist tendencies erupted not only under the umbrella of Congress through the elite bhadralok but also in communist parties' tacit acceptance of British rule.[3] The social movement in Kerala not only predated the one in Bengal but also superseded the latter in scope and size. In fact, even during Independence, Bengal's CPI had limited political power as compared to its counterparts in Kerala. Where Kerala's first elected communist leadership, during as early as 1957, created headlines around the world,[4] in Bengal, this was to happen only in 1977. Let's start with Bengal.

BENGAL

Even though Bengal had ousted Congress from political dominance as early as during the 1967 assembly elections (Congress was the largest party, but proved its majority in the assembly only through a coalition with the United Front), the stronghold of the Communist Party of India (Marxist), or CPI(M), emerged in 1977 when it won and even retained power until 2011. Congress did come to power in the sixth and seventh assembly (1971 and 1972), but it was clear that Bengal wasn't its playground because even in 1971, CPI(M) secured the highest number of seats. By 1977, CPI(M) had become a powerful force in state politics by securing more than 60 per cent of seats and one-third votes. Jyoti Basu would go on to become one of the longest serving CMs of any state in India (five times: 1977, 1982, 1987, 1991, 1996). In all these five elections, CPI(M)'s seat share remained within an impressive range of 54–64 per cent. The party came to power again in 2001 and 2006, but this time, Buddhadeb Bhattacharya was appointed as the CM.

A few electoral points deserve special mention. In the first Vidhan Sabha in 1952, even though Congress led the tally with 39 per cent votes, the second-highest proportion of votes—22 per cent—went to independent candidates. This astounding figure for independent candidates signifies a hyperlocal political preference, an attitude that continued across decades, given the political make-up of rural politics in Bengal. This may be viewed as a decentralised ideal, but as we discuss later, it is equally likely to have occurred because of rebellious tendencies of armed peasants as well as violent leadership within local party cadres. This trend was repeated in the 1957 Vidhan Sabha elections, with independent candidates bagging 19 per cent votes (again, the second-highest, with Congress leading the list). In 1967, even though the tally of independent candidates fell (they secured

11 per cent votes), it still remained the third highest. This time, CPI had taken the second position.

Two years later, CPI was split due to diverging attitudes towards China after the Sino-Indian war of 1962. The result was a new party, CPI(M). Around that time, Congress had also split creating the Bangla Congress, which sided with the CPI(M) to erect the first non-Congress government there. Congress' vote share hadn't dwindled much, but the Left Front's (coalition of various left-wing parties) vote share rose significantly. Interestingly, independents still claimed the third highest vote share, at around 14 per cent.

The next four years were a political tug-of-war. While parties were claiming their stake in Calcutta through internal and external churning of support in the assembly, the power never remained with one party or person. It kept changing hands between Congress and the Left Front until 1972.

Congress swept the 1972 elections. Everyone was startled, for it got an unprecedented 77 per cent seats and almost 50 per cent votes. CPI(M) won only 5 per cent seats even as it got a respectable 27 per cent votes. Independent candidates had given way this time. The then Congress Chief Minister Sidharth Shankar Ray ruled Bengal with an iron fist and violence. So much so that people speculate if it was really the 1975–77 Emergency by Indira Gandhi or the heavy-handed rule of the West Bengal Congress in the state during the 1970s that led to the wiping out of Congress in the state during the 1977 elections. Congress has never returned to power since then.

Ray was a smooth-talking self-proclaimed liberal, who had written a letter to Indira Gandhi six months before the Emergency was imposed, ideating on the stage-setting required for the Emergency to be imposed.[5] Bengal may have witnessed an extended Emergency under Ray's administration. And, therefore, 1977 was, unsurprisingly, a watershed political moment for the state.

And it was in Bengal that the Janata Party, which had been riding on the Lok Sabha success lion in Delhi, could not form a coalition with the powerful Left Front against Congress. So, it was a tripartite tussle between Congress, Janata Party and the Left Front. The left parties won with an overwhelming majority, much to their own surprise. CPI(M) received 35 per cent votes and 61 per cent seats while Janata Party and Congress got around 20–23 per cent votes. This was the beginning of Jyoti Basu's rule, which would continue until the turn of the century.

Take a few moments to imagine a populace which gave power to the same party for seven elections straight. From 1977 until 2011—seven elections and the same party coming to power after each! What happened, and how did Bengalis decide not to let Janata Party (and its offspring) or Congress touch the magnificent walls of Writers' Building in Calcutta?

What do the numbers from these seven elections tell us? CPI(M)'s seat share showed the following pattern for all the Vidhan Sabha elections held during 1977–2006: 61 per cent, 59 per cent, 64 per cent, 64 per cent, 53 per cent, 48 per cent and 59 per cent. Pretty consistent, one would say. The vote share was even more consistent: 35 per cent, 38 per cent, 39 per cent, 36 per cent, 37 per cent, 36 per cent and 37 per cent. In some sense, to have such consistency across three decades remains unheard of anywhere else.

Let's read these figures with the prime contender, Congress. Its figures during the same period (1977–2006) for seat shares were 7 per cent, 17 per cent, 14 per cent, 15 per cent, 28 per cent, 9 per cent and 7 per cent, while vote share proportions were 23 per cent, 36 per cent, 42 per cent, 35 per cent, 39 per cent, 8 per cent and 15 per cent. If you ignore the last two counts for the moment, we get a pretty consistent picture of vote share for Congress. (We can ignore the last two counts because that was the time when Mamata Banerjee's Trinamool Congress had taken away Congress' share, and right now, we are concerned with Congress' battle against CPI(M).) Also note that the 1977 election was a bad phase for Congress in general. But after that, the party was able to gather close to 40 per cent votes during the next two decades—almost the same as CPI(M). Despite the close fight on votes, Congress could never take up enough seats. In order to make sense of this, we will need to unbundle these numbers across the state. We come to that in the next section.

Meanwhile, it will be interesting to dwell on the political David of the state, Mamata Banerjee, who brought the CPI(M) Goliath, in manners unimaginable, to its knees. The All India Trinamool Congress (TMC), which was formed after Mamata split from Congress in 1998, was able to topple one of the world's most stable and powerful parties in a matter of a few years. Unlike Bangla Congress, which had been formed after prominent leaders like Ajoy Mukherjee, Pranab Mukherjee (the prominent Congress leader of later decades) and Sidharth Shankar Ray (who was the CM of Bengal during 1972–77) split from Congress in the mid-1960s, TMC did not really have such towering leaders to wage a war against the powerful structure of CPI(M) throughout the state. Bangla Congress had sided with CPI(M) and later, fearing massive decline, merged itself back with Congress. Mamata, however, never acquiesced. Within three years of forming TMC in 2001, she secured 20 per cent seats and 30 per cent votes. The seat share fell to 10 per cent in 2006, although votes remained at 27 per cent. In 2011, these numbers increased impressively to 63 per cent seats with 39 per cent votes! Despite a mid-career setback in the Lok Sabha in 2004, when TMC could manage only one seat, Mamata remained undaunted. In the 2009 Lok Sabha, even before taking over the Vidhan Sabha in 2011, she had secured 45 per cent seats and 20 per cent votes.

Mamata has been an unusual leader and Bengal may have been an ideal laboratory for such an experiment. Most politicians have one or more 'political Godfathers' in their careers who they may choose to declare or not. This is particularly true of women politicians in India, who have had a senior mentor (often male), guiding them into politics and backing them up across stages. Whether it was Kanshi Ram for Mayawati, MGR for Jayalalithaa or family mentors for Indira Gandhi, Vasundhara Raje, Mehbooba Mufti and Harsimrat Kaur, women leaders in India generally have had the towering presence of a male member behind them. This definitely does not belittle their own contributions, but there is a point to that. And yet, Mamata Banerjee has been exceptional in this regard.

The 2011 assembly elections were ground-breaking. TMC emerged as the largest party in Bengal, crushing CPI(M), and marking an end to the world's longest-elected communist government (or so they say). Individually, the seat share count of TMC and CPI(M) was practically reversed in 2011 as compared to 2006—TMC's numbers rose from 30 to 184, while CPI(M)'s fell from 176 to 40. This was, in many ways, a repetition of the 2009 Lok Sabha elections in Bengal. Political commentaries likened the Singur protests in 2008—the TMC-led protests against the land acquisition by the CPI(M)'s state government for Tata Nano's industrial project—as the death knell for CPI(M),[6] which also attracted widespread media attention.

But it could not have been Singur alone. Because even in the 2016 assembly elections, people of Bengal overwhelmingly voted in favour of TMC again. CPI(M) was reduced to merely 26 seats while TMC secured 211 seats. In fact, in 2011 and 2016, seat share of CPI(M) slid to embarrassing levels—13 per cent and 8 per cent and vote share to 30 per cent and 19 per cent respectively. In fact, the 2021 assembly election was a battleground between TMC and BJP. CPI(M) was not even in the competition. The 2021 elections were interesting at another level. BJP, the runner up, could not gather as many seats (77, as against 215 of TMC), but had secured a massive 38 per cent votes (as against TMC's 48 per cent). How many seats had CPI(M) secured in 2021? Nil. The story of Bengal is not the story of communism alone. It is the story of their growth and fall. In the later part of the chapter, numbers will reveal the dynamics of Bengal, its politics and its voters.

KERALA

When the CPI won the first elections held in 1957 in the three-year-old state of Kerala, it was a world event.[7] Kerala was the first region in the world to accord democratic victory to a communist party (San Marino had achieved this earlier, but it is a tiny nation of 30,000 people. So often, it's Kerala that steals this record).[8] Think about the 1950s in the context of history. It was the beginning of the Cold War, violent spates of decolonisation of European colonies in Africa, conflicts in the Middle East between the Arab states and Israel, and the unprecedented events of the Cuban revolution. A new world order was being mediated through armed conflicts and violence. Kerala's peaceful elections catapulting a communist government at the helm of political affairs in a newly independent Third World nation sent shockwaves in the capitalist world. This was done by the CPI, built on anti-feudal principles, and the peasant consolidation and welfare state models. And it was a model that people elected.

Kerala itself was a new state, formed by amalgamating Travancore–Cochin with Malabar districts of the region. CPI had been active nationally (it was the biggest contender to Congress in the first Lok Sabha in 1952), but in Kerala, it was banned from taking part in the 1952 Travancore–Cochin assembly elections. By 1957, CPI had emerged as the largest opposition party in the Lok Sabha, and the largest party in the Vidhan Sabha. In fact, for a good part during the first Lok Sabha, Kerala was the only state with a non-Congress party ruling it.

So, in 1957, E.M.S. Namboodiripad became Kerala's first non-Congress CM. CPI had more seats than Congress, but interestingly, Congress had more votes. CPI had 47 per cent seats and Congress, 34 per cent; CPI secured 35 per cent votes while Congress, 37 per cent. Also, independent candidates came third with 11 per cent seats and 13 per cent votes. Again, a first-past-the-post (FPTP) leakage.

The government soon initiated the passage of education and land reforms that aimed to bring schools and colleges under the government, and agrarian bills aimed to distribute land titles to tenant cultivators. This led to what came to be known as Vimochana Samarama (Liberation Struggle), an anti-communist protest against the elected government, led by the Catholic Church, the Indian Union Muslim League, Nair Service Society and apparently, as speculation goes, by the American CIA. The protest resulted in the government being toppled in three years, and Nehru then imposed the president's rule in the state.

In 1960, Congress came to power. This time, even though the party came to power with 50 per cent seats, as a winner it had lower vote share (34 per cent) as opposed to CPI's (39 per cent). The story of seat–vote divergence continued.

In 1965, by when both CPI and Congress had split further into CPI(M) and the Kerala Congress respectively, the assembly elections resulted in a hung assembly. The highest seats and votes went to different parties, yet again. CPI(M), the biggest party securing 30 per cent seats, was not able to secure the highest votes. Its vote share was 20 per cent while that of Congress was 34 per cent (Kerala Congress secured 13 per cent votes). Interestingly, many CPI(M) leaders contested the elections from behind the bars. They had been imprisoned after the split because of their sympathies for China (the Sino-Indian war took place in 1962). President's rule was imposed again, for lack of a clear majority.

Kerala went to elections again in 1967. Guess what happened this time with respect to seat and vote share? The same! CPI(M) was the winning party this time with a clear majority. But again, it secured just 24 per cent of votes while the losing party—Congress—topped the voters' preference with 35 per cent vote share. Note that the difference in seat share of the two parties was huge—32 percentage points! Namboodiripad became the CM for the second time. This time again, he couldn't complete the term, thanks to the party's internal problem. Formed through a coalition of seven parties, it was difficult to maintain trust. In 1969, Namboodiripad resigned for loss of majority and C. Achutha Menon from the CPI, with outside support from Congress, became the new CM. In 1970, his government fell as well, and fresh elections were conducted.

These elections, yet again, witnessed the puzzling phenomenon of the highest seat grossing party failing to get the highest number of votes. Congress, this time, emerged as a party possessing the leading seat share, yet managed to secure merely 18 per cent votes as opposed to 24 per cent of the CPI(M). The Left Front coalition formed the government under C. Achutha Menon again. This time, thanks to the Emergency, he could govern the state until 1977.

When elections were held again in 1977, Congress came to power. This was surprising given the general mood of the nation in 1977. But like we have discussed in previous chapters, Congress was not 'decimated' in 1977. In fact, the party's decline was worse in 2014 and 2019. Kerala was one of the few places where Congress continued its dominance in 1977. In the Kerala Vidhan Sabha, Congress got 27 per cent seats. With an ironically excellent consistency, the winner was, again, not the highest vote share grosser. It secured 20 per cent votes while CPI(M) with just 12 per cent seats was able to secure 22 per cent votes. The assembly was a distressed one, lasting two years with four CMs from three political parties, only to end in an impasse resolved by the president's rule.

It was only in the sixth assembly in 1980 that the winner—the Left Front—won with the highest seat and vote shares. However, political kabaddi did not quite let them manage it well and president's rule was imposed again in 1982. The era of stable governments in Kerala began in 1982. But the interesting thing is that the highest grossers in the assembly elections of 1982 were independent candidates. They bagged a quarter of seats and a quarter of Kerala's votes, as against the trailing CPI(M) which had to be satisfied with 18 per cent seats and votes. The politics in Kerala is very localised, no surprise for a state with high scores in participatory democracy and powerful panchayats.

The 1982 elections also saw something unprecedented. It was the first time ever that electronic voting machines (EVM) were used in India. A radical idea that perhaps found befitting receptivity in Kerala. The Paravoor Assembly seat in Ernakulum district was chosen for this experiment. Merely 50 out of 123 booths were employed for the purpose. Anxieties were natural too, particularly in the camps of Congress and CPI(M) who had their contestants battling head-on. Indeed, there was high-voltage drama in Ernakulum, albeit with an interesting ending.[9] Everyone cheered at the ease and swiftness with which elections were conducted and results declared. The CPI(M) candidate won by a margin of 2,000 votes. Congress raised doubts over the authenticity of EVMs; their candidate A.C. Jose was the former Speaker in the Kerala Assembly, and was expected to register an easy win. The High Court dismissed the plea, but the matter was lent a patient hearing in the Supreme Court of India. The Supreme Court ordered repolling in the 50 booths. Guess what the results were this time? Jose, who was earlier declared to have lost the elections, won the seat with a 2,000-vote margin in the recount.

This event perhaps gave a major blow to the use of EVMs in Indian elections. So much so that despite some experimental usage of EVMs in certain states, it was only in 1999 that they were brought back for general elections, in Goa. Now, they are everywhere. Remember BJP's massive victory in the UP Assembly polls in 2016, and the huge outcry against voting machines with Mayawati calling for re-elections in UP? The ECI disregarded all such pleas. Much to the annoyance of many, it looks like EVMs are here to stay. But while all this scepticism continues, let us not forget what happened in Paravoor in 1982. The EVM and ballot paper results were exactly the opposite!

Since 1982, the story in Kerala is remarkably consistent. The United Democratic Front (UDF), led by Congress, and the Left Democratic Front (LDF), led by CPI(M), have been grabbing power alternately. UDF has led the state during the assembly years of 1982–87, 1991–96, 2001–06 and 2011–16. LDF has secured alternate power spots—1987–91, 1996–2001, 2006–11, and interestingly, won the last two elections in 2016 and 2021. What is remarkable is that even the 1987 and 1996 Vidhan Sabha elections witnessed the uniquely Kerala characteristic of the seat winner not being the vote winner.

Kerala has a fascinating electoral tale. Almost every winner in the elections held until the 1980s had lost on account of vote share. The winning party had never managed to secure the highest votes. And then, post the 1980s, LDF and UDF have been alternating in the state. What does all this tell us about Kerala as a voting machine? Two things stand out neatly. First, voters do not really prefer one against the other as strongly. As a result, the frustration of loss and celebration of victory is more a matter of chance than a matter of some overwhelming mandate.

Second, it looks like both the fronts, LDF and UDF, are possibly ideologically and structurally similar outfits. Even though LDF is categorically left, the UDF also sells people 'leftist' ideas and imaginations. People can't be switching ideologies every few years like their cars. Both LDF and UDF must predicate their promises on similar ideas to explain this alternative power exchange. It is also likely that the LDF and UDF have their respective stronghold constituencies in place. Competition takes place only in select spaces with fringe/margin voters who switch. But otherwise, each party's vote base is established strongly. Parties have dominant hamlets, and most Kerala constituencies are party strongholds. Those that are not are very few in number, but they matter in voting results. We will discuss the idea of party stronghold later in this chapter.

We also note that, the voters of the state are politically very conscious. Its poll percentage in 1957, the first elections, was 65.5 per cent, and in 1960, an astounding 85.7 per cent. The poll percentage in the first Lok Sabha elections was 45.7 per cent. An ordinary tour of 'God's Own Country' reveals how the working class of the region is glued to news channels during elections rather than a soap opera. The poll percentage has always been significantly high and tensions typically heighten during poll season. It is a sight to behold. With high levels of literacy, very prominent panchayat programmes, high human development indices and a tradition of peaceful protests against governments, the state is politically very active. It is no surprise then that the voters in the region are great punishers as well.

A QUICK NOTE ON PRESIDENT'S RULE

President's rule is a funny insertion in the Indian Constitution. Under Article 356 of the Constitution, New Delhi can take away the powers of the state government machinery if the latter does not function according to constitutional provisions. The experience of this article has been rather less simple. The central government can make use of its features whenever it wants to unseat a state government ruled by opposition parties, should conditions turn adverse. The idea of adverse conditions, however, leaves a lot of room for interpretation. The President of India or governors of states are almost always people loyal to the ruling party in Delhi. They are rarely likely to object to signing a document sent to them from the Prime Minister's Office (PMO). As a matter of practice, president's rule was generally understood to be imposed when state governments had lost their majorities in their respective assemblies. This power, though, was abused 'right, left and centre', across almost all the states until the 1990s. Indira Gandhi was particularly notorious for misusing the article. Within a span of ten years from 1966, she has been known to clamp down on state governments almost as many as 40 times. That's an average of one imposition every quarter! The Janata Party, in its short life of three years, did this nine times. As of now, there is hardly any state left where the president's rule has not been imposed (Chhattisgarh and Telangana are the only exceptions). In 1994, after the Bommai trial, the Supreme Court laid down strict guidelines to impose president's rule sparingly. It is only since then that its rampant use has slowed down.

Like many other administrative provisions, Article 356 is also inspired by the Government of India Act, 1935, which allowed British governors to take over provincial governments. In 1949, during the Constituent Assembly debates, Ambedkar, who is credited with bringing this article into the Constitution, expressed his intention of its usage, '… [o]nly when the government is not carried on in consonance with the provisions laid down for the constitutional governance of the Provinces. Whether there is good government or not in the Province is not for the Centre to determine. I am quite clear on the point. ... I share the sentiments expressed by my honourable friend, Mr. Gupta, yesterday that the proper thing we ought to expect is that such Articles will never be called into operation and that they would remain a dead letter.'

If alive, Ambedkar would have been disheartened to see the 'rational' interpretation of our constitutional principles buried in the silences of articles and sections, replacing the life of values enshrined with the carcass of words. We must, however, not forget that the real pain is not about making a mockery of constitutional principles, but of the breach of trust that people have reposed in the electorate. When the president's rule is imposed, it dries up people's trust in democratic values, erodes faith in the electoral process and kills the hope of participatory citizenship. On the other hand, one may also say they are a response to the mess an FPTP system creates.

VOTE AND SEAT SHARE DIFFERENCES: AN ANALYSIS

Vote share is actually never manifested in power but it is important to understand how much a candidate/party is liked or disliked. Now parties can have huge number of votes and, consequently, a high vote share, but it is important that these votes are leading them to winning seats. In other words, victory is important, not the margin. All your supporters being concentrated in some constituencies doesn't help. They should be scattered enough across several constituencies so that they can get you at least a few more votes than the others in each. The margin of your victory can be wafer thin, but all it takes is to get more seats with whatever margin.

Margin is an important but an oft-ignored reason for an election. Margins tell you about the quality of your win. And a poor-quality win is a 'baggage' one must carry into the future. While in the present Lok Sabha or Vidhan Sabha your margin may not matter, it matters hugely in the next election cycle. If your victory is on a thin margin, it means there is a high proportion of disgruntlement in your electoral constituency. There is a huge tipping crowd sitting on the dividing line, and it will take very little for the new elections to turn the other way. In fact, it is in the vote share data that we find what voters have really chosen. A small margin of victory essentially means that almost as many voters prefer the winning candidate as ones who prefer the losing one. A small margin of victory conceals a high level of disagreement with the result. This is something we have seen in most election cycles, if we go deeper into the vote share matrix. Vote shares, therefore, carry a powerful message for the future. Vote share is the detail where the devil lies.

Indeed a handful of voters have changed the course of Indian elections several times. Think about it: the vote share of Congress in the 2014 Lok Sabha elections, when it was the runner-up, was 19.3 per cent; that is, of the total votes polled, 19.3 per cent went to Congress and it secured 44 seats. In the 2009 Lok Sabha elections, BJP had secured 18.5 per cent votes. Guess how many seats did it get with those many votes? 116! There shouldn't have been any major surprise with BJP's rise in 2014 and Congress' decline in 2019.

The seat and vote shares, in any representational democracy where people's preference are aggregated well, should move together. But that may not happen because aggregation is never perfect. This may well mean that whenever seat and vote share diverge, a deeper look is necessary. We must reflect on victories and losses with a more nuanced understanding.

What kind of nuanced understanding can be brought for Bengal and Kerala? We take seat-wise winners and runners-up. We then calculate their respective vote shares. Our intuition is that in a system where preference aggregation is good, total votes of the runner-up should be less than those of the winner. If the difference between seat share and vote share is huge, it needs particular attention. But the most important data to look at is when the vote share of the loser is greater than that of the winner. This showcases a high degree of dissatisfaction.

FIGURE 4.1 Seat share (%) and vote share (%) of the winner and the runner-up in West Bengal assemblies since 1967

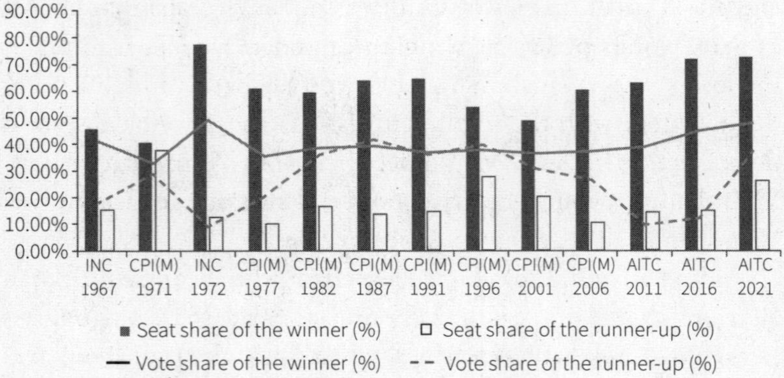

Note: Winners are mentioned against the years.

We notice a rather surprising insight in Figure 4.1. For Bengal, the runner-up had more votes than the winner in 1986 and 1996, and almost as much as the winner in 1982 and 1991. (One may also notice how the difference between the winner and the runner-up in Bengal is beginning to follow the late-1970s' pattern in vote share!) For Kerala, this happened in 1972, 1987, 1996 and 2011. This essentially means that in the Vidhan Sabha elections held during these years, the runner-up was preferred more than (or almost as much as) the winner, at an aggregate level. In individual constituencies, the winner did marginally better, but in those places where she lost, she lost massively. So, her victories were insignificant, but her losses were huge. In other words, the loser lost by a thin margin wherever she lost, but won with massive support wherever she won.

This is a startling insight. This means that there is sufficient reason to believe that the loser was preferred by more than half (or almost half) of the voters in several of the assembly elections in both the states (and in Bengal, more so during the height of communist rule in the state).

Let us compare this with seat share as well. We would be interested to find out how many more seats did the winner get anyway, even when the loser got more votes than the winner. This will also tell us by how many seats did a winning party win, even when it lost in the vote count.

FIGURE 4.2 Seat share (%) and vote share (%) of the winner and the runner-up in Kerala assemblies since 1967

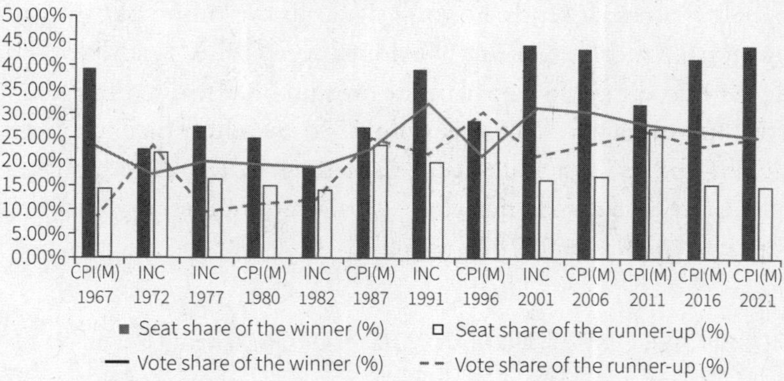

Note: Winners mentioned against the years.

The results are striking. In Kerala, during those Vidhan Sabha elections, when the loser got more votes than the winner, the winning party got a relatively small number of seats overall. The winning seat margin was not very high. This means that the seat share was trying to mimic the vote share pattern. In Bengal, however, this difference is surprisingly huge. Even when the loser had secured more votes (overall) than the winner in the state, it has been decimated when it came to seats.

This is a valuable discovery. In an FPTP system of electoral choice, how much a candidate is liked or disliked, then, doesn't matter. However, this degree of likeability is extremely meaningful in understanding the political opinion of the people. In effect, vote share may be a more accurate measure of desirability of a party, even if winners and losers are decided by seat share. The vote–seat share proportion hides within it the mirror to the voters' minds and holds crucial information on electoral mindset.

Securing a low vote share along with a high seat share confirms the massive leakage in the mandate. The vote share and seat share difference in Bengal is very high, as much as three–four times more than in Kerala. For most politicians, focus on vote share has been rather blurry. Therefore, when seat shares fail to capture people's intent, it sends a wrong signal to the ruling party—just like it happened in Kolkata. We doubt even CPI(M) cadres would have noticed this. If they had, they would have realised that their crushing defeat in 2011 was simply a time bomb that had been ticking for the last four decades, leading to the 2011 political explosion that shred the party into tatters, something that got repeated in 2016 and 2021 as well.

POLITICAL COMPETITION AND DISPROPORTIONALITY

Table 4.1 spells out the disproportionality and political competition in Bengal and Kerala. The latter is expressed for both seat share and vote share, but our focus is on seat share in this case, denoted by ENP. Interestingly, since 1982, assembly elections have been taking place in both the states in the same year. We observe that electoral competition is considerably higher in Kerala than Bengal. Kerala also has fairly low levels of disproportionality in representation.

The graphs indicate strong divergence of the two states in their respective political landscape and mandates. Political competition in Kerala has always been significantly higher than in Bengal. High effective number of political parties in Kerala—even though in decreasing trend—suggest that people in Kerala have a more diverse choice architecture. In Bengal, on the contrary, the value of ENP has remained consistently between two and three,

FIGURE 4.3 Disproportionality and political competition in West Bengal since 1982

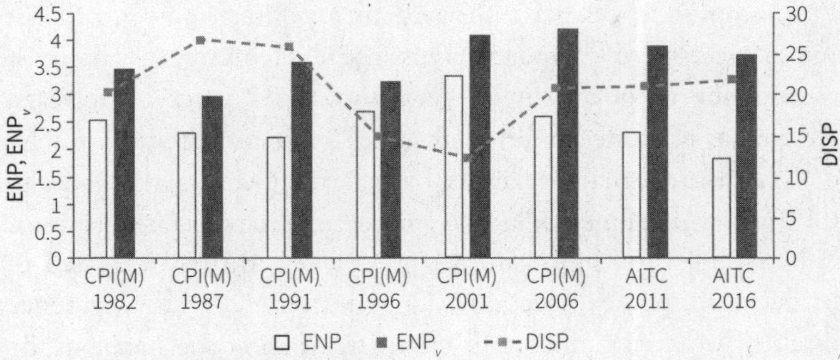

Note: Winners mentioned against the years.

FIGURE 4.4 Disproportionality and political competition in Kerala since 1980

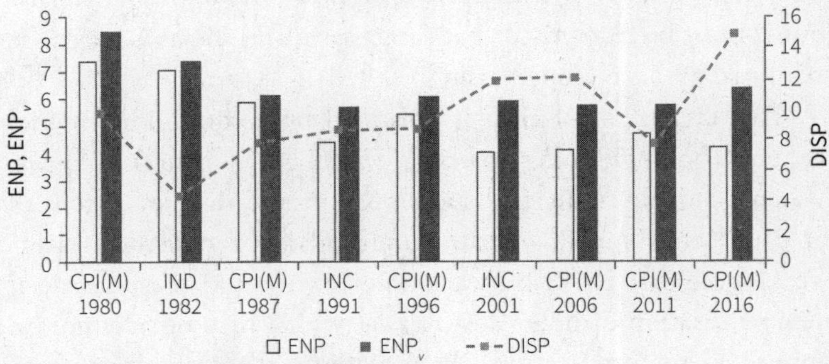

Note: Winners mentioned against the years.

indicating a duopoly-type structure in the electoral market. And even in Bengal, trends suggest that competition levels came down over time. Further, if we notice disproportionality, it is much more in Bengal.

It appears that Kerala's democracy is more mature and healthier, whereas Bengal suffered from a vegetative and unresponsive leadership. The states are far apart in how ideals of political representation and people's choice architecture are reflected in government formation. In Kerala, the high values of ENP and low values of DISP indicate an advanced democracy. People's preferences get translated into political power without much 'leakage' of mandate. This also explains the alternativist ascendancy to power in Kerala. Since 1982, every five years, Kerala has witnessed political switches fairly consistently.

This means that Malayalis have never given a free hand to CPI(M), which emerged as the winner only in alternate elections. Whenever CPI(M) has assumed power, it had been relegated to its defeat in the next elections. The question is, can this evidence disable the leftist claim to the government and governance in the Kerala model?[10]

If we look at people's preferences, and the alternating periods in which the CPI(M) comes to power in the state, it doesn't look like people are overwhelmingly in support of communist Kerala. But it must be recognised that progressive and socialist ideals are exhibited by both Congress and CPI(M).

This means that Kerala is governed by a communist model because both winning parties belong to leftist ideologies. When scholars credit the success of progressive state politics of the 'Kerala model' to the communist governance model,[11] we suggest that it is political awareness leading to such social democratisation of politics in Kerala (which may or may not be connected to communism). Left parties are not able to sustain their victories beyond one election cycle and people rout them out every election to bring Congress back. This alternating show of political preference reflects volatility. But it also keeps the winner on their toes. No wonder that in terms of political promises, both CPI(M) and Congress in Kerala are fairly indistinguishable. This also means that people in Kerala must be well-informed to be able to think (and voice) their change of opinions if the party in power hasn't delivered—a fact corroborated by the available literature.[12] Indeed, Kerala's participatory democracy has been established in literature extensively.[13] At the same time, the sizeable literature criticising Kerala's caste dynamics and politics of exclusion, orchestrated by the left politics of the state, compels us to think deeper.[14] Our findings indicate then that the celebration of socially progressive politics in the state is mainly due to the participatory and decentralised governance of the people, rather than any communist strategy.

In Bengal, the story is fairly different. Except in 2001, the disproportionality index has remained at very high levels. Taken together with a low ENP value, it indicates that power has remained entrenched within the hands of a select party having a stronghold over the position. This explains CPI(M)'s characteristic presence in the state. Bengal's low levels of social development indicators compared to Kerala, despite being lauded as a socially progressive state,[15] can be explained by the monopolistic tendencies of CPI(M) during its rule when political competition had remained low.

In fact, direct interpretations of results support the view that Bengal and Kerala—even though commonly identified as communist states—have significantly diverging 'party formations' with stronger roots in civil society in Kerala and weaker ones in Bengal.[16] Decentralised development in Kerala[17] can be explained by low DISP and high ENP just like a low level of political incorporation of people in Bengal[18] is evident from its high DISP and low ENP.

AVERAGE MARGIN OF SUPERIORITY

Now, we construct another set of variables to dig deeper. We map the winning margins of top three parties in their respective winning seats. We pick up the political parties that emerged as top three in each assembly election in the last five decades (1967–2016) in Bengal as well as Kerala. (Of course, these are parties with highest seat shares.) We take the party with the highest number of seats in a constituency and measure the average margin between that party and the second highest party in that constituency. So, in other words, we observe the winning margins of these parties in their winning constituencies only. We call this average margin of superiority (AMS).[19]

AMS can be a very important indicator of how 'heavy' is the victory of the party. If the first party's margins are smaller than the second party's, then we infer that the second party is in a more 'comfortable' position in terms of greater number of loyal voters in its constituency. In other words, AMS values can be useful tools for parties to understand the degree of their superiority, wherever they are superior. With a high value of AMS, in some sense, the party can afford to be politically complacent in the constituencies of its victory. Note that AMS does not help us compare a given set of parties because it is not an inter-party variable. It selects a party and looks at its relative position with respect to the party just beneath it, in the seat tally of the state. Therefore, AMS is an important indicator of the extent to which the party wields power and confidence in constituencies it has won. With such an indicator, we can analyse how monopolistically a party may behave (wherever it has won). Smaller values of AMS would signify volatility in political preferences amongst people and encourage parties with low AMS to work harder if they are to retain/secure their power in forthcoming elections.

Consider the AMS in the following way. Let's say party A and B contested in 20 constituencies. A won in 15, while B won in five. Clearly, A will form the government. But what was the margin of victory of these parties in their respective constituencies? If the average margin of B is, say 99 per cent, while for A it is 1 per cent, then we know that the winning constituencies of B are really B's strongholds. But A cannot claim such a thing about its victory. It had gotten lucky in the 15 constituencies where it had won, and cannot remain complacent about them in the next election cycle.

Note that this is an aggregate variable. So, this does not tell us anything about the constituency and what is going on in these places specifically. But that's not the purpose of our work anyway. We think what's more interesting is how, overall, the winning party is superior to the losing party. If the average margins (AMS values) are tiny, then we know that the winning party has *just managed* to win, and has not really emerged as powerful and victorious.

In the case of Bengal (Figure 4.5), the AMS for the top three parties in respective years since 1982 has remained consistent at respective levels. The year 1977 was peculiar with high AMS for all the top three parties. During the 34 years of communist rule, when CPI(M)'s power was unchallenged (1977–2006), its margin hovered within the approximate range of 14–17 per cent, which is significant. Another valuable insight in the figure is the substantial difference between AMS values for the first and the second party during left's rule.

With high values of AMS, the party would be in a psychologically complacent position. Bengal has considerably high values of AMS compared to Kerala. This is reflective of the highly entrenched left party dominance in Bengal. Scholars call Bengal a case of left-party-society resting in permanent incumbency.[20] By the early 1990s, it was clear that Bengal was suffering from huge rural inequality and dismal economic realities in all sectors, including agriculture.[21] Yet, the leadership lacked any will or imagination for social services to the poor.[22] Scholars have also shown how deeply entrenched clientelist and patronage politics in Bengal is, which also glues leaders to their seats in power.[23] Panchayats in Bengal came under partisan control[24] and party cadres would adopt mafia-type extortion for the party, with 'CPM goons' becoming a menace.[25] We discuss this in detail in a later section.

FIGURE 4.5 Average margin of superiority of top three parties (in terms of performace) across West Bengal assemblies

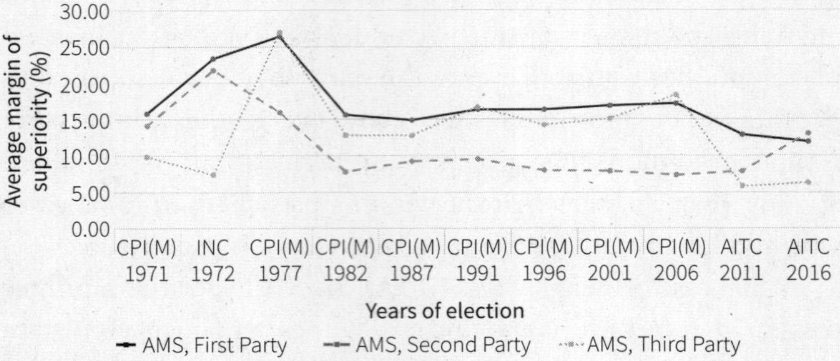

Note: Winners mentioned against the years.

In Kerala (Figure 4.6), the picture is very different. We observe that the values of AMS for the top two parties in Kerala is very small. This means that both the winning party and the runner-up had never been in a comfortable position. Even the difference in AMS values for the first and second parties has not been as big as in Bengal. This somehow also explains the fact that the winner's

FIGURE 4.6 Average margin of superiority of top three parties (in terms of performance) across Kerala assemblies

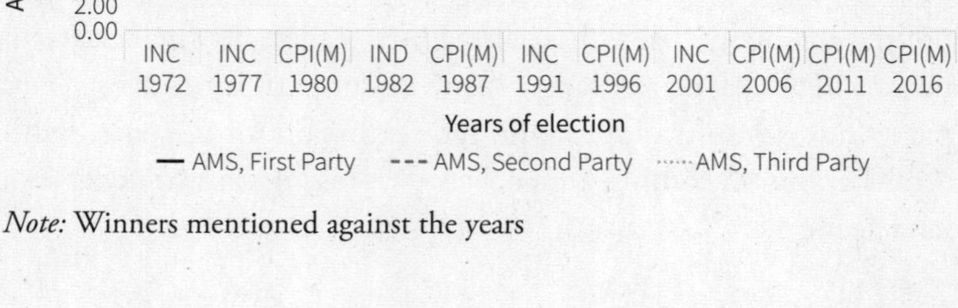

Note: Winners mentioned against the years

AMS has an alternating character. Also note, the AMS of the party securing the third spot is often much higher than that of the first and second parties. This point may not be as useful for us (the third party has often been the Muslim League or CPI) much like in Bengal since a vast majority of seats were distributed between the first two parties; but the other points offer useful insights.

If AMS values of the first party (winning party) are high, we know that in winning constituencies, the party was highly superior to the next best party in those very constituencies, compared to if the value is not as high. Also, since the AMS measures strength on average, it is biased in favour of fewer victories but with high margins. This means that the results for Kerala reflect a very different electorate. Most commentators and scholars believe that the communist strategy works because people demand it,[26] but it is really the supply side (political parties) that offer it. The democratic decentralisation infused in the social fabric of Kerala since Independence[27] was so deeply ingrained that no party could dare shift its policy axis away from communist principles. This also explains the tight competition and similar levels of superiority of parties in almost all the Vidhan Sabha elections.

But the most important result is this: Bengal does not appear to be even remotely close to Kerala in its *choice* of communism as a preferred mode of governance from the perspective of the mandate of the people.

An interesting irony builds up now. If the vote share of the winner in Bengal is low, how can it have high superiority? Well, it can happen, and it is all basically mathematics. This is because AMS does not factor in losses. It contains information on how strong (on an average) the party is *only* in its winning constituencies. It does not tell us how strongly the party has lost in the constituencies that it has lost.

Consider, for example, a province with 100 seats, with 100 people voting and two parties contesting. Party A has won in 51 seats, and B has got 49 seats. Now, in the 51 seats, it is possible that A has secured 90 votes while the rest have gone to B. But in the 49 seats it has lost, let's say it got zero votes. A's total votes will be 530, while B's will be 470. The margins of A's victory are very high (almost 88 per cent), but vote share is pretty low (53 per cent). So, overall, it has won the elections with high superiority, but still has very low vote share. In reality, ENP is always more than two, so superiority is what makes the party feel confident, even though its high value, coupled with low vote share, should set the alarm bells ringing.

RECONNECTING BENGAL'S POLITICS

Narratives on Bengal's politics have been punctuated by repeated episodes of political violence. And there are a lot of such punctuations. Bengal offers India a political reality that no other place does—the first decisive British battle in India (Plassey), the epicentre of the Naxal movement, the land reforms that have taken place in the state, or, for that matter, the importance of village-level politics that have characterised the region.

There is a romantic association of party politics with violence, often connected with Frantz Fanon's use of the term 'violence' to signify cleaning, a self-transformation.[28] Even though post-Independence India has mostly seen Bengal as a communist state, there has also been an emphasis on political violence. While identity politics in various other parts of India is constructed on caste, communal or even linguistic lines, in Bengal it is based on party identity. The party is the Holy Grail in a sharply political climate of voting. The anti-government sensitivity plastered on the walls of Calcutta/Kolkata, the adulation of revolutionary tendencies in the fiery imaginations of people, or even the manifestation of blood in the loving mother Kali have as much fervour as the electoral violence in Bengal's villages.

Right after India attained independence, this anti-establishment structure was visible in an anti-Congress provincial colour. The first three Vidhan Sabha elections in the state led to a sizeable and increasing share of votes for communist parties. There were several communist parties in the state already, and witnessing them coalesce to form a joint collective before the elections was not unusual. In fact, as early as 1962, the CPI (which was to break into CPI and CPI[M] in 1964), All India Forward Bloc, Marxist Forward Bloc, Revolutionary Communist Party of India, Bolshevik Party of India and Revolutionary Socialist Party (notice their heavyweight names!) had formed a joint electoral alliance called United Left Front. The political and intellectual force of this alliance continues till this day. In 1967, they had already defeated Congress to form the first non-Congress government in the state.

This anti-Congress force was so powerful that in 1972, when Congress won the elections in a landslide victory (from 37 per cent seats in 1971 to 77 per cent seats in 1972), there were serious allegations of poll rigging. In fact, even attributing the 1972 victory of Congress in Bengal to the 1971 Bangladeshi war could not be conclusively made because scholars contended that such a war may have encouraged other states to vote for Congress, but not Bengalis.[29] Be that as it may, Congress took over. CPI(M), during this time, got a mere 5 per cent seats with a sizeable 27 per cent votes (a rather rare event). People thought CPI(M) would be finished. But as always, their focus was on seats alone. A high vote share like 27 per cent meant that the party was still very much in power. This is an important lesson in general: whenever a party loses elections by a small seat-share margin, one should not be quick to judge and declare the party's decline, without reading vote-share numbers.

The next time, in 1977, when CPI(M) came to power, it was with a massive 60 per cent seat share, and 35 per cent votes. It formed the government, and was to rule for a good 34 years. But by then, a major cultural shift of political violence had already become embedded in the state. The food movement of 1966, militant industrial worker strikes, and land reforms right after Independence (tebhaga) that continued during the 1960s and 1970s had become part of Bengal's political vocabulary.

Congress, during 1972–77, used the muscle power of its men and the police to establish complete control over the state. It drew new contours of violence by incarcerating tens of thousands of Naxals and killing thousands. The government used goons to silence everyone. That is why, when the Left Front came to power with a massive majority in 1977, the cult of the bomb continued. During 1969-70, with one year of the Left Front rule left, there were about 70 political murders.

Amitav Ghosh's *The Hungry Tide* is a poetic description of the Marichjhapi massacre, orchestrated by CPI(M) and its men. The 'party' built a violent fiefdom in Bengal during the next three decades, and scholars have noted how the party maintained everyday control over people by select deployment of violence through its party cadres at village levels. In various instances, panchayat elections were being held uncontested. Even the panchayat funds had been used to organise party activities. This type of clientelist politics is also explained by poll figures.

If one looks at the uncontested seats in panchayat elections in Bengal, there is a worrying trend all through the reign of the Left Front government (see Table 4.1).[30] Indeed, this 'unnatural' increase in seats which were uncontested by any other party against CPI(M) signifies the presence of loyal constituencies of the party. This could have also been a result of fear. CPI(M)'s fate was most uncertain during 2003. It was in that year that pre-election violence claimed 80 lives and led to a massive increase in uncontested seats.

TABLE 4.1 Uncontested seats in panchayat elections in West Bengal

Panchayat election year	*Number of seats Left Front won uncontested*	*Number of seats won by Left Front uncontested as a share of the total Panchayat seats*
1978	338	0.73%
1983	332	0.74%
1988	4,200	8.00%
1993	1,716	2.81%
1998	600	1.36%
2003	6,800	11.00%
2008	2,240	4.39%

Source: Partha Sarathi Banerjee, 'Party, Power and Political Violence in West Bengal', *Economic and Political Weekly*, vol. 46, no. 6 (February 2011).

Kidnapping and killing of opposition candidates has been common but what is the extent of violence in the state anyway? In 1997, Buddhadeb Bhattacharya, the CM from the party that ruled the state during 2001–11, had said that in the last 20 years of CPI(M) rule, 28,000 political murders had been committed in the state. A left-wing weekly, *Mainstream*, recorded that overall, during the CPI(M) rule, some 55,000 people had been murdered for political reasons.[31] In fact, the nexus between goons, politicians and police has given Bengal the dubious distinction of being a violent and lawless '*Mastanocracy*' (rule of *mastans*, gangs).[32] In Bengal, power has flown from—quite literally—the barrel of the gun. In fact, Partha Chatterjee paints the following picture:[33]

> *The key term is 'party'. It is indeed the elementary institution of rural life in the state—not family, not kinship, not caste, not religion, not market, but party. It is the institution that mediates every single sphere of social activity, with few exceptions, if any. This is indeed the true significance of the shift from the old days. Every other social institution, such as the landlord's house,*

> *the caste council, the religious assembly, sectarian foundations, schools, sporting clubs, traders' associations, and so on, have been eliminated, marginalised or subordinated to the 'party'. Rural life is literally inconceivable without the party ... the party and its local functionaries are the principal arbitrators in all social, family and personal disputes and principal facilitators when individual villagers need help in matters of health, education, finances, employment or travel.*

A low vote share coupled with high superiority of the left parties in Bengal indicate that the ruling Left Front had strongholds and 'weakholds' (where the party was not able to win or it won with a thin margin) rather than a broad sweep of medium-scale strength across the state. In such a scenario, it is likely that the party was just about able to keep a minimum and sufficient number of people satisfied.

This means that there was considerable political rivalry in rural Bengal all through. What still led the Left Front to continue to win without sufficient votes was perhaps a calculated strategy of which places to retain their stronghold in and which places to let go. Frankly, looking at the numbers, one can say that the front would have possessed some mathematical alacrity with which it maintained its loyal supporters so as to be able to just manage a majority in those hamlets.

But they could only do it for so long. The opposition had begun controlling more than a third of gram panchayats by 2003 and half by 2008.[34] Even without looking at panchayat-level data, one can see from our figures that the decline must have begun in the late 1990s or early 2000s. The rise of Mamata Banerjee's Trinamool Congress in 1998 reflects the growing opposition among village-level party cadres, particularly in those places where the front did not have a stronghold; the same places where vote share was low.

The protests against land acquisition under the Tata Nano project in Singur and Nandigram in 2008 reflect the same type of political negotiation as had always been in the region for decades. Except that CPI(M) may have overestimated its urban base, which it tried to woo in its approval of the Tata project, alienating the same populace which it had suppressed for decades through its local party leaders and goons. Indeed, rural elites taking up political positions was uniquely Bengali and had begun as early as in the 1950s. Myron Weiner, the renowned American political scientist and an expert on Indian politics, undertook extensive research to prove this, taking cues from legislative assembly members in Bengal during that period.[35] He had expected rural politics to take centre stage in India over time. That did not happen in the same way as predicted, although it got exacerbated in Bengal.

There is another layer of Bengal politics that reminds us of its rural elites, as well as the nature of party society. And that is the vast amount of illegality that permeates the social fabric of Bengal.[36] Political bargaining and not regulatory mechanisms decide property titles, minimum wages, trade customs, and even the establishment of rice mills. Party, and not bureaucracy, manages this illegality. The vast swathe of dubiously managed entitlements in the state has hardly passed adequate scrutiny. This may be a tall claim, but one thing is clear: when local political intermediaries end up building their own fiefdoms, including adoption of instruments of fear and violence, the trust can easily wane off someday. And when it did in 2011, the verdicts of 2016 and 2021 were expected.

Data provides sufficient evidence to show that people did not *really* like the left. They were simply adhering to an established loyalty because all they cared for was their own entitlement that came through clientelism. For all the claims of land reforms and equality, there is nothing in poll data that shows any overwhelming preference for left parties. The culture of what left parties may have stood for was long dead with the ideals of the

1950s and 1960s, leaving in its place only a mask behind which the dreaded Social-Siamese-Twins of patronage and exploitation were cultivated (invoking Jan Breman here[37]).

Kerala, on the other hand, had been building its party base through intense competition between the UDF and LDF with similar promises made across party lines based, broadly speaking, on left ideologies. The power in Kerala rests with an active voter base which keeps switching its mandate, keeping parties 'on their toes' so to speak. Kerala also has had its fair share of political violence between left parties and those with Congress,[38] but located in different dimensions.

THE TWO STATES ARE NOT THE SAME INDEED

There are three striking features of the political mandates in the two states now. First, Bengal's high DISP and low ENP compared to Kerala shows centralised politics in Bengal, and politically decentralised governments in Kerala. Second, lower vote share in Bengal compared to Kerala indicates strong dissatisfaction against CPI(M) amongst the people in Bengal, compelling us to revise our notions of CPI(M)'s stronghold in Bengal. Third, superiority values in Bengal and Kerala indicate higher levels of political complacency and capture within CPI(M) in Bengal than the ruling parties in Kerala.

Overall, neither do the two states look similar at any level in terms of political processes, nor do we find an overwhelming desirability of communism in Bengal from the perspective of people's preferences. In our view, the differences in the two states from the point of view of the demand side of the political market (what people prefer)[39] is so massive that putting both the states in the same communist basket is unwise.

Elections are sensory experiences, inventories of preferences and expressions of political desires. Their variables cannot be stripped off from any serious political examination, for it is in election figures that much of the truth about society's aggregate value system emerges. In fact, by passing the mighty literature on democracy, political freedom, and civil and political rights through a litmus test of meaningful numerical analysis of election data, we are able to discover alternative visions of political maturity with little effort.

The extent to which our findings support the literature on Kerala's democratic development and decentralised polity on one hand, and patronage politics in Bengal on the other, is important. There is some merit in viewing the policy in Bengal and Kerala through a 'what people prefer' lens. Representative democracy converts an analogue preference of people into a binary 'winning or losing' divide. This is not necessarily the ideal way to aggregate preferences. These shortcomings of the FPTP system are commonly acknowledged in previous chapters and we do not intend to re-emphasise this fact. Our aim is to locate the blind spots in our imagination of politics in Bengal and Kerala.

Bengal and Kerala have another interesting distinction. The states are some of India's largest Muslim homelands. As a share of total population, Muslims comprise almost 27 per cent in each of these two states. Assam (34.2 per cent) and Jammu & Kashmir (68.3 per cent) are the only other two states to have a higher proportion of Muslims among their populace.

And yet, the vote bank politics in the two states is not as religiously vicious as one would have imagined. Communists hate religion and perhaps they were able to ensure, with varying success, that religious harmony is not unsettled. This needs to be recognised.

These states have bundles of contradictions within them. Hemchandra Kanungo, an Indian independence movement nationalist and member of Anushilan Samiti in Bengal (independence revolutionary with commitment towards physical fitness), was the first Indian to learn and master the art of making bombs in Paris from Russian revolutionaries. He was caught in 1908 in the Alipore bomb case. His co-accused at the time was Aurobindo Ghose. Aurobindo later went to Pondicherry and set up an ashram. Hemchandra was sent to the Andamans. Both revolution and peace continued. At one level, according to some reports, underground CPI cadres formed a political organisation called 'League Against Gandhism' in 1934 (formerly known as Gandhi Boycott Committee) and at another level, Kerala has arguably India's highest readership of Gandhi's *My Experiments with Truth*.[40]

5

The Rise of BJP

By some accounts, Kewalram Ratanmal Malkani was perhaps one of the first ones to be imprisoned during Emergency. It was just after midnight of 25 June 1975, the date when Emergency was imposed. He was also one of the last to be released—post the election results in 1977. Otherwise known to be associated with BJS (the precursor to BJP) and RSS, he must have been someone rather important.

Back in the day, RSS was hardly interested in politics and, until 1950, had desired to remain a cultural organisation. In fact, Christophe Jefferlot[1] suggests that despite Vinayak Savarkar trying to persuade Keshavram Hedgewar, the founder of RSS who headed it from 1925 to 1940, the RSS remained rooted to its resolve of keeping away from active politics. Savarkar popularised the idea of Hindutva, and led the Hindu Mahasabha, the earliest political party to be founded to protect Hindu interests. He also tried convincing M.S. Golwalkar (Hedgewar's successor) that RSS must become political.

Golwalkar changed his mind after Gandhi's assassination and a consequent ban on the RSS. One of the chief architects of RSS' path to politics was none other than Malkani. Arguably, the first person to be arrested during the Emergency, Malkani was instrumental in converting RSS into a political force that the world could not ignore.

Golwalkar brought RSS into politics with the help of Syama Prasad Mukherjee. At the age of 33, Mukherjee had become the youngest ever vice chancellor of Calcutta University. He was a member of the Hindu Mahasabha, and a minister in Nehru's first interim cabinet. But after Gandhi's assassination, he left the Mahasabha, and later, due to his differences with Nehru, quit the cabinet as well. Golwalkar met Mukherjee, and they founded the BJS in 1951. They then began inducting senior RSS members into the BJS, which included Atal Bihari Vajpayee.

BJS won three seats in the first general elections in 1951 (see Figure 5.1). In 1977, it got amalgamated into the Janata Party. In 1980, BJS came out of the splintered Janata Party in a new avatar—BJP. This party was soon going to become one of the largest political forces the world would ever see. This chapter belongs to this party and, in many ways, traces both the emergence of the party and that of India during the last three decades.

FIGURE 5.1 BJS–BJP's rise through history

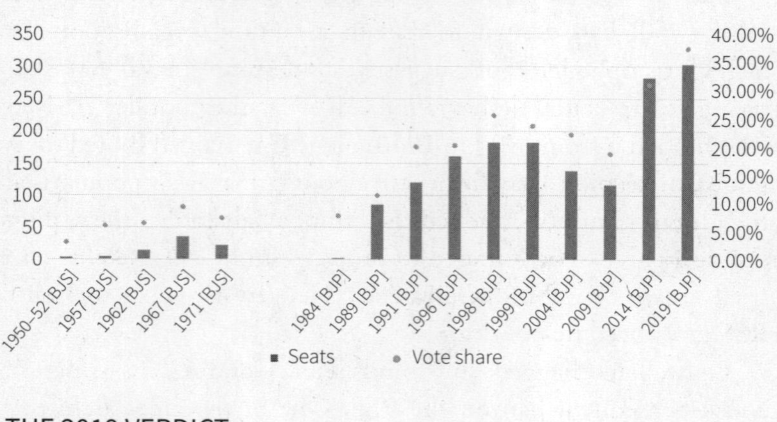

THE 2019 VERDICT

Let's first get out of our way some basic statistics that may have become household knowledge. The NDA increased its tally from 336 seats in 2014 to 350 in 2019 (see Figure 5.2). UPA's tally went up from 60 to 93. 'Other' parties lost badly. In terms of vote share, NDA's performance was even better—it went up from 38.4 per cent to 44.2 per cent. UPA's vote share got pushed up slightly from 23 per cent to 26.4 per cent (see Figure 5.2). This was the biggest election for BJP, with their largest ever vote share of 37.4 per cent; Congress' vote share, on the other hand, remained almost the same. Rarely had a consolidation of votes taken place under only two banners in such a big way, unlike the fragmented mandate as always. This was the first time after Congress' victory in 1957 that a single party has been re-elected with an increase in vote share (which is also larger). Modi is the first PM after Nehru to return to power with a single party winning full majority for both terms. In fact, in terms of vote share victory margins, Modi did with BJP what Congress achieved only under Nehru (see Figure 5.3).

FIGURE 5.2 Seat share and vote share of NDA and UPA, 2004–19

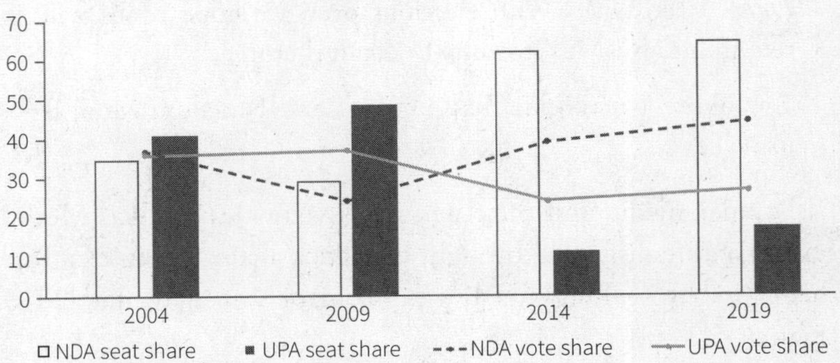

Journalists called it a 'Tsunamo' and 'NaMoMent', and commentators predominantly saw the 'Hindutva' nationalist ideology of BJP being instrumental in carrying the party this far. In doing so, the 2019 Lok Sabha elections were, for most part, a judgment on India, rather than on Modi or BJP. Here's how global headlines chronicled the event:

Scroll.in: 'Saffron Wave propels ...'

Telegraph: 'HE is back' (with a full front page bearing HE in bold and orange!)

Mid-Day: 'The GoT Finale all of India loved'

The Economist: 'The BJP's win is down to Prime Minister, not the Party'

Guardian: 'Narendra Modi's landslide: Bad for India's soul'

Los Angeles Times: 'Narendra Modi's landslide re-election in India is another win for religious nationalism'

BBC: 'Narendra Modi has reinvented Indian politics'

New York Times: 'How Narendra Modi seduced India with envy and hate'

Washington Post: 'India's Modi wins resounding election victory with potent appeal to nationalism'

Dawn (Pakistan): 'With elections over, we hope Modi will rein in his anti-Muslim; anti-Pakistan rhetoric'

The Wire: 'A new India has emerged and Narendra Modi is its voice'

Popular media and their narratives were clear. It was Modi's Hindu nationalism that brought him back again. Let us examine this claim by looking at BJP's performance in 2014 and 2019 (Figures 5.3 and 5.4).[2]

There are around 15 seats out of 543 which have more than 40 per cent Muslim population in India. BJP won four of these, while Congress won five. More interestingly, BJP's vote share in these districts was highest, 22 per cent, even though it was Congress which had the highest vote share in those districts in 2014. The story is the same for districts having 20–40 per cent Muslim population. BJP's vote share increased from 35.3 per cent

FIGURE 5.3 Seats distribution and constituencies' characteristics of INC and BJP in 2014 and 2019 elections

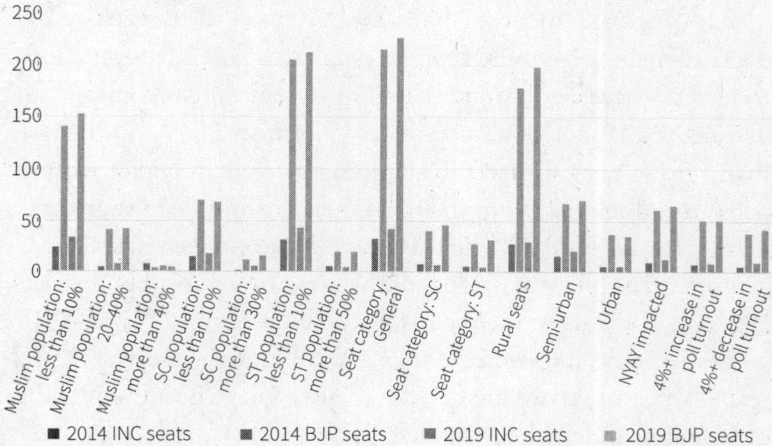

FIGURE 5.4 Votes distribution and constituencies' characteristics of INC and BJP in 2014 and 2019 elections

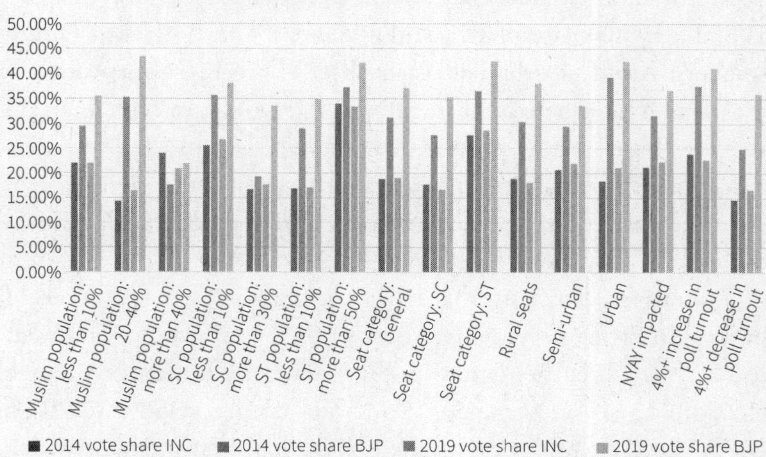

to 43.4 per cent, while Congress' went up merely by 2 percentage points (from 14.3 per cent to 16.4). One cannot say with certainty

that Muslims also voted for BJP. But increase in vote share for BJP in these districts means the reality may be more nuanced.

The increase in vote share for BJP was also registered in constituencies with more than 30 per cent SC or ST populations. In fact, in places with more than 30 per cent SC population, BJP had merely 19 per cent votes in 2014, but in 2019, it was more than 33 per cent. In fact, if one looks at constituencies with 40 per cent population comprising either Muslims, Christians, SCs or STs, the rise in BJP's vote share was 8 percentage points, which is more than the increase during the same time for other districts. BJP got 135 seats in these constituencies as against 117 in 2014, while Congress fell from 32 to 31. Even among reserved SC/ST seats, BJP's vote share increased by 7 percentage points while that of Congress didn't change much.

So, where did BJP lose? Interestingly, in urban India! BJP secured 37 seats in 2014 in urban constituencies, but 35 in 2019. In rural constituencies, however, it went up from 178 to 198! The vote share of BJP surely increased in both, but with a smaller margin in urban areas. In fact, in the 116 constituencies that would have benefited from NYAY (Nyunatam Aay Yojana, a social welfare scheme proposed by Congress in its 2019 election manifesto that promised direct cash transfers to 20 per cent of India's poor), BJP's vote share increased by 5 percentage points as opposed to Congress' 1 percentage point.

Narratives also claim that BJP benefitted from record levels of polling in 2019. Over 67 per cent of 91.1 crore voters came out to vote, which is the highest polling share the Indian Lok Sabha elections have ever seen. But if one digs deeper, relative to 2014, BJP's highest gains in vote share were in constituencies which witnessed greatest falls in polling turnouts. There was an increase of 12 percentage points in BJP's vote share in constituencies where poll turnout had decreased by more than 4 per cent. In comparison, in constituencies where the poll turnout had increased by 4 per cent, BJP's vote share increased only by 2.5 percentage points.

Overall, therefore, the data stands in stark contrast against the-nationalist-wave-driving-2019-elections argument. The rise of BJP's vote share in rural areas tells us something. Rural population, one would think, is affected less by the rhetoric of nationalism but far more by welfare schemes. The NDA had worked out a range of schemes to particularly benefit rural folk; Ujjwala or Jan Dhan, for example. We can't be certain that they worked (BJP's performance in rural areas of Bihar and UP, for instance, suffered), but we can't be certain the other way either.

Another popular argument is that BJP's victory rests in Hindi-speaking states of India. And that is indeed true, if you look at BJP's victory pattern in 2014. But this was not the case in 2019. In 2019, BJP secured most remarkable gains in many non-Hindi-speaking states, unlike what many would believe. In fact, for most of the Hindi-speaking provinces, its performance did not increase significantly. If we keep Himachal Pradesh and Haryana aside—where BJP's vote share went up by 1.3 and 1.6 times respectively—the other states where BJP's victory had a noticeable rise was in J&K, Karnataka, Manipur, Orissa, Tripura, Telangana and West Bengal. States where BJP did not make as impressive a rise when compared with 2014 were Assam, Bihar, Delhi, Chhattisgarh, Gujarat, Maharashtra, Punjab, Tamil Nadu and UP! One may claim that a significant proportion of these states had already been captured in 2014, but it is telling that they did not help BJP relatively more in 2019.

In J&K, without the same number of seats, its vote share went up by 1.4 times. In Kashmir, BJP's vote share doubled, although it was still as low as 3 per cent. Interestingly, here, the vote share of People's Democratic Party (PDP) plummeted from 46.3 per cent to 15.7 per cent. Congress was the biggest beneficiary in the state, recording an 8.9 percentage point increase in vote share.

It looks like people may have been unhappy with PDP's post-poll coalition with BJP. And BJP pulling out of the coalition in 2018—a year before the Lok Sabha elections—made the anxiety against PDP even more distinct.

In Karnataka, BJP's seats increased by 1.5 times and its votes by 1.2 times. These gains were largely felt in Old Mysore, the southern part which had been dominated mainly by Congress. BJP had a significant rise in both votes and seats in constituencies with large SC, ST, Muslim or Christian populations. In fact, all the seats in Karnataka reserved for SC or ST category candidates went to BJP; previously, these had been with Congress.

In Manipur, BJP got one seat while Congress got two. But BJP's vote share went up thrice its previous performance while Congress' fell by 17 percentage points. In Orissa, BJP got eight seats, up from one in 2014, and its vote share rose 1.8 times. This was again mostly felt from districts dominated by SC, ST, Muslims/Christians, as well as in rural parts. Interestingly, Biju Janata Dal (BJD) suffered massive decline in seats (not in votes though). Mathematically, it looks like BJP pulled votes from Congress, and seats from BJD. (This does not mean that supporters of Congress voted for BJP—that can never be known with certainty, unless one looks at booth-level data.)

BJP also swept Tripura, taking both its seats (in 2014 it conceded both), with a rise in vote share from 6 per cent to 49 per cent! Interestingly, here, BJP pulled votes from CPI(M), and not Congress, again numerically speaking. In Telangana, where BJP had a minor presence in 2014, it witnessed doubling of its votes, and quadrupling of seats. Adilabad, with a very high ST population, came to BJP. The other three were Secunderabad, Nizamabad and Karimnagar. The former two have significant Muslim populations. Karimnagar is mostly dominated by Hindus, but vastly rural.

Bengal, they say, was BJP's real battle, and it shocked everyone there. Its vote share increased by more than twice, and it secured

18 seats as against merely two in 2014. Interestingly, in districts with more than 40 per cent Muslim population and more than 30 per cent SC population, BJP's vote share more than doubled and it secured two and five seats respectively, where it had gotten nothing in 2014. In rural Bengal, it secured 12 seats (up from zero in 2014), almost tripling its vote share. In urban constituencies, it retained one seat and got another. But even in urban areas, its vote share went up by 1.5 times.

Unlike the dominant perception, BJP's losses were in their own strongholds. It suffered badly in Bihar—both seat and vote shares declined considerably. This was most acutely felt in Bhojpur and Magadh regions. In Patna, vote share increased, but in the rest of Bihar, which is rural with high share of SCs or Muslims, BJP suffered. In UP too, the number of seats declined, even though vote share increased by a small amount. The party lost Moradabad and Rampur, cities with more than 40 per cent Muslim populations (both of them were BJP's seats in 2014). Overall, most losses took place in rural areas, and in constituencies with significant population of SCs, Muslims or Christians. In that sense, rural voters from UP and Bihar did not contribute to BJP as much as those in other states. Was it because of high expectations going unfulfilled?

In other places, like Assam, Chhattisgarh, Goa, Gujarat and Maharashtra, BJP's victory did not come with a significant increase in its voter base. It was also unable to impress voters in Punjab and Tamil Nadu.

Overall, its losses were less remarkable than victories. It came to power not because it increased its existing voter base in the regions of its stronghold, but by capturing unchartered territories. More interestingly, its new voters were not found in places which would typically be identified as Hindu nationalist bastions, but really, anywhere. It, therefore, appears that the attribution of saffron colour to their victory is somewhat inflated.

Much of our understanding of political ideologies comes from Western experiences. So, when we talk about conservatives and liberals in the US or UK, we broadly mean the rightists and the leftists. This categorisation is not as neat in India. A number of policies of Congress have historically been conservative and that of BJP been liberal, contrary to what one may think. Think about, for instance, how Congress initiated regulations on cow slaughter, and restored the Somnath temple. On the other hand, BJP has continued the tradition of welfare-based policies, which are understood to stem from liberal and socialist ideologies. In the cacophony of political voices, it is only human to create categories and make it easy for the brain to comprehend. But reality may not be that linear.

Can you guess the third and fourth highest vote shares in 2019? Trinamool Congress secured 4.1 per cent votes in the 63 seats it contested elections in. The ever-interesting BSP scored 3.7 per cent votes, as it contested in 383 seats of 543!

BJP'S PERFORMANCE IN CENTRE vs STATES

A striking feature of the 2019 Lok Sabha elections was its surprising mandate when compared with the state elections that took place before and after. The Vidhan Sabha elections held in 2018, 2019 and 2020 showed remarkable divergence from the Lok Sabha elections in 2019, in terms of people's preference for the political party in power. How is it possible that people's preference for political parties differs so much when they vote for their legislative assembly as compared to when they are voting in parliamentary elections? Why should people decide to change their voting behaviour when their expectations and priority of election winners remain the same, particularly when provincial and central elections are not held in distant time. Well, while one ingredient (voters) remains the same, the other—namely the contesting candidates—changes.

In other words, voters may not make a pure choice of a political party. The choice of political party is mixed up with the choice of the candidate. And it may well be said, Indians are very clear about which factor outweighs the other, depending on which elections they are voting in. So, for instance, they are perfectly capable of knocking out the same party which is in power in the state, and then bringing it back to power at the centre in subsequent months. This is what happened with BJP in and around 2019.

Note that this would also mean that people hardly voted for BJP in 2019. They voted for Modi. While BJP suffered losses (relative or absolute) in all the state elections around the 2019 Lok Sabha elections, it won with a landslide in 2019.

BJP's winning chariot began decelerating during the December 2017 legislative assembly elections in Gujarat, Modi's home turf. It lost 16 seats and was barely able to retain control of the state. It captured almost half the votes, but Congress trailed it closely with 41 per cent votes.

The 2018 elections signalled alarm bells for BJP. It suffered defeats in the by-elections held in several constituencies in the year, notably in Alwar and Ajmer in Rajasthan, Gorakhpur, Phulpur and Kairana in UP, and Bellary in Karnataka. In 2014, BJP had won in each of these constituencies. In Vidhan Sabha elections, BJP failed to win Karnataka again. But more importantly, it gave away big states like Chhattisgarh, Madhya Pradesh and Rajasthan to Congress. In 2019, after the Lok Sabha election frenzy was over, states like Maharashtra and Jharkhand also slipped away from BJP's hands, and it could barely manage to retain Haryana. Andhra Pradesh—anyway far away from being BJP's stronghold—witnessed a decline in their vote share too. (Andhra is, incidentally, a state where BJP had one of the lowest vote shares in the country in the 2019 Lok Sabha elections.) The 2020 Delhi elections also thwarted BJP's hopes mercilessly.

Let us scrutinise this aspect more minutely. Consider Figures 6.5 and 6.6 showing the relative performance of BJP in Vidhan Sabha and Lok Sabha in the same states, when the elections took place within a gap of a year from each other.

FIGURE 5.5 Vote share of BJP in the Vidhan Sabha and Lok Sabha in 2019 in selected states

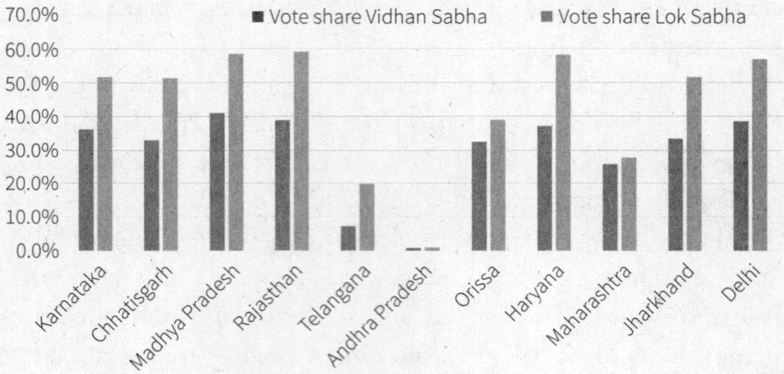

FIGURE 5.6 Seat share of BJP in the Vidhan Sabha and Lok Sabha in 2019 in selected states

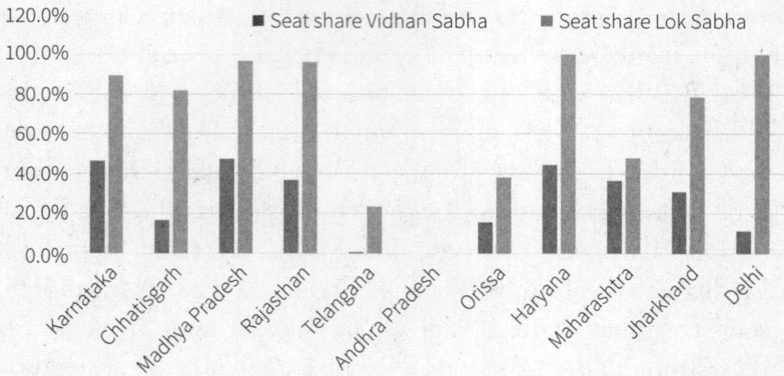

Notice the surprisingly dismal performance in Vidhan Sabha elections, jutted against the 2019 Lok Sabha elections for BJP. The seat shares had almost halved in the legislative assembly elections

in Karnataka, MP and Haryana, and more than halved in the rest. While Maharashtra was somewhat respectable, the party's seat share had reduced there too. In the 2020 Delhi elections, BJP won eight Vidhan Sabha seats while it had secured all the Lok Sabha seats there! The divergence story continues in vote share as well, where around one-third BJP votes were sliced off in the Vidhan Sabha for most states.

It is possible to attribute BJP's Lok Sabha victory against surrounding Vidhan Sabha losses to the Pulwama attack and the subsequent Balakot strikes that took place with barely two months to go for national elections. One view is that these incidents fanned nationalistic sentiments and helped BJP gain the much-needed support which had been waning in the last two years. A closer reading of numbers and electoral data of 2019, however, reveals that gains of BJP really took place in non-north Indian states, which are not 'as concerned' with the Kashmir and Indo-Pak issue as north Indians are.[3] This is a broad brushstroke here, but the Kashmir narrative has strong currency in urban areas of India, where BJP, in fact, did not quite shine relatively. The rural areas, where folks are less concerned about what's happening on the Pakistan-occupied Kashmir (PoK) border, are the places where BJP secured bigger gains. The nationalist fervour as the sole explanatory variable for BJP's victory in 2019 may be overemphasised.

Post-2019 elections, the Indian political landscape became dotted with policies of Amit Shah, the home minister in Modi's cabinet in the second term. He led the revocation of Article 370 in Kashmir in August 2019, which had given the state a special status, and promulgated the Citizenship Amendment Act (CAA) in December 2019, which disallows Indian citizenship to Muslim political refugees from India's neighbouring countries.

To what extent would these two major incidents have affected BJP's fortunes post the 2019 Lok Sabha elections? Andhra

Pradesh, Orissa, Haryana, Maharashtra, Jharkhand and Delhi were the big states that went for elections. In almost all of them, BJP lost.

In Andhra Pradesh, where the party had four seats in 2014, it could not secure a single seat. In Orissa, BJP performed better than the previous Vidhan Sabha elections, but poorly compared to the 2019 Lok Sabha elections. In Haryana, it lost seven seats. In Jharkhand, it lost 12 seats, and in Maharashtra, it lost 37 seats. These were disappointing losses. Delhi's elections took place after the massive protests the city saw against the CAA. The Aam Aadmi Party (AAP) took away 62 out of 70 seats. But despite winning eight out of 70 seats, BJP's vote share was 38 per cent, and this was a increase of 6 percentage point. In the 2019 Lok Sabha elections, in which BJP took away all the seats, BJP's vote share was higher than that of AAP in the 2020 Vidhan Sabha elections.

Be as that may, BJP's anxiety in provincial elections is natural. Indians are not voting on party lines, but are strongly inclined towards looking at the human face of the party in question. In that sense, leadership crises in a post-Modi BJP, and presently in Congress, will be among the most challenging situations that Indian politicians are facing/will face in the times to come.

STATE-WISE RISE OF BJP SINCE 1984

In 1980, when BJS resurrected itself from the ashes of the Janata Party, it became BJP. For our analytical purposes, therefore, BJP's emergence and evolution begins through 1980, when they fought for the first time as a party against Congress in many states during Vidhan Sabha elections. Their first Lok Sabha battle took place in 1984. Note that many other parties were splintered from the Janata Party, but today, 40 years later, BJP remains not only the 'chosen' one, but perhaps the 'only one' from amongst all those Janata Party offshoots.

It may be worthwhile to analyse how this party has been performing since its inception and see if there are regional variations over time.

A dominant narrative is that BJP is a party that appeals to, and is built on the support of, voters from Hindi-speaking states. This has many speculative reasons, but those are fairly commonplace now. Let us, therefore, focus on UP, Rajasthan, Bihar, Madhya Pradesh, Haryana, Himachal Pradesh, Gujarat and Delhi for a bit.

FIGURE 5.7 Seat share and vote share of BJP in UP

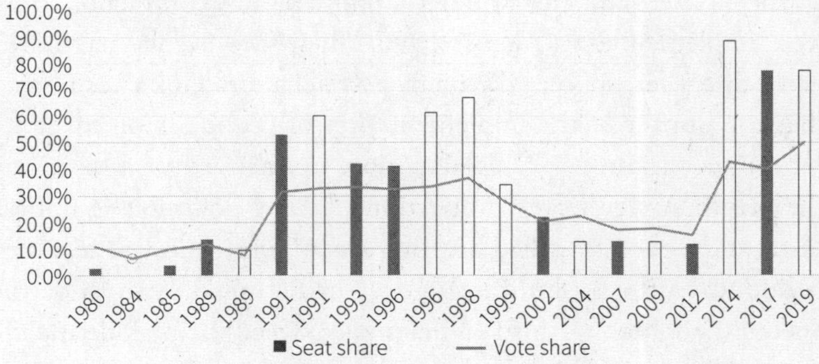

Note: Empty bars represent Lok Sabha and solid bars represent Vidhan Sabha

Figure 5.7 show a story that is unfamiliar to untrained eyes. UP is interesting for three reasons. First, the Lok Sabha has mostly drawn higher share of votes for BJP than the Vidhan Sabha here. This could either mean that local leaders of other parties did not carry the gravitas to take them to the national stage or because national politics and local politics were driven by separate agendas. One needs to probe further. Note that the vote share was higher than the seat share during 1980s and 2000s, indicating real competition and hard luck for BJP during these two decades. But during the 1990s and 2010s, BJP's vote share had been relatively far lower than the seat share, indicating that the margin of victory was thinner, and it was benefitted by swing vote shifts.

Interestingly, it can be seen that the link between Ayodhya and BJP is not as strong as it is suggested to be. There was a sudden rise in BJP's appeal between 1989 and 1991. But the Babri Masjid demolition took place only in December 1992, and in 1993, BJP's seats had, in fact, fallen (without impacting the vote share much). So, the real impactful period is 1989–91. This is prior to the mosque demolition. Two things had happened during this time: Advani's rath yatra took place in September–October 1990 and the Mandal Commission recommendations were implemented in August 1990. These two events may have had a direct impact on UP voters. Ramachandra Guha has noted that the impact of the implementation of Mandal Commission recommendations was felt much more in the north compared to the south. A significant proportion of UP's pollution is upper caste, and a good lot relied on government jobs. This was also the period when the Kashmir insurgency had erupted, with Rubaiya Sheikh (daughter of Mufti Mohammad Sayeed) being kidnapped by militants in 1989, and other events leading to direct rule from New Delhi being imposed in January 1990. We will discuss the events in UP and Ayodhya and the rath yatra issue later.

In Rajasthan, interestingly, as shown in Figure 5.8, BJP has performed almost in the same way in Lok Sabha and Vidhan Sabha elections before 2004. It was in 1990 that BJP secured power in the state for the first time, and it turned out to be short lived. Since then, Rajasthan has switched ruling parties in every assembly election, with the game of musical chairs where Ashok Gehlot replaces Vasundhara Raje and vice versa continuing till this day. But despite BJP's stronghold in the state, its vote share has remained relatively higher as compared to its seat share, suggesting that voting appeals are thinly distributed across the state, so high

FIGURE 5.8 Seat share and vote share of BJP in Rajasthan

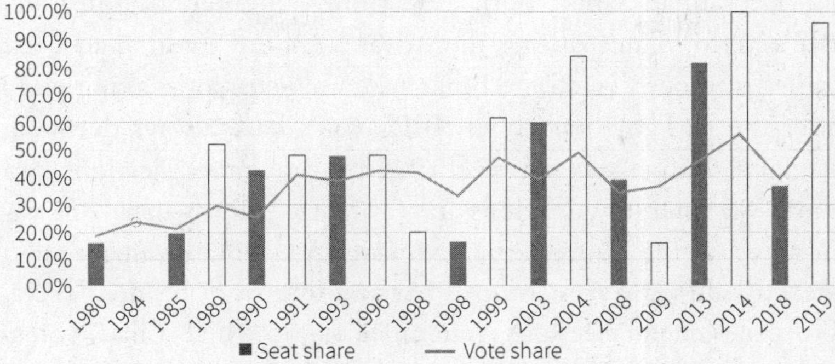

Note: Empty bars represent Lok Sabha and solid bars represent Vidhan Sabha

share of votes don't necessarily translate into seats. Note that even during BJP's worst years in the state (1997–98), it lost half of its seats without losing votes. Interestingly, the late 1980s and early 1990s witnessed BJP's swift rise, which plateaued for a while and picked up again recently. But note that it had firmly made its base in the state, before the mosque demolition in Ayodhya. Looks like Rajasthan did not really care as much about it anyway.

Figure 5.9 is about Bihar. Unlike UP or Rajasthan, Bihar has never given BJP more than 30 per cent votes, even as it has

FIGURE 5.9 Seat share and vote share of BJP in Bihar

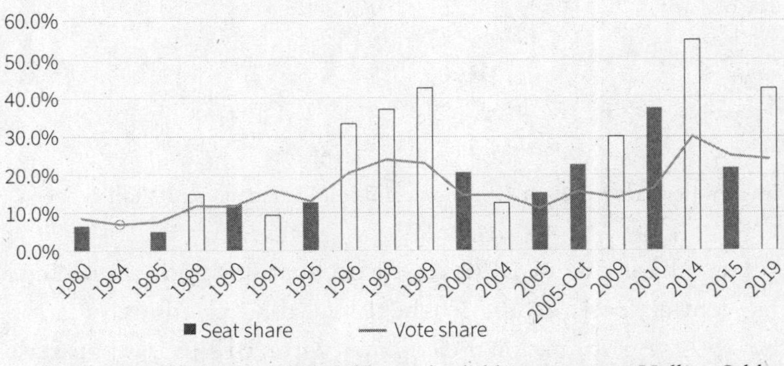

Note: Empty bars represent Lok Sabha and solid bars represent Vidhan Sabha

really contributed to BJP's seat share for Lok Sabha, although not for Vidhan Sabha. Both these things are interesting to note. BJP's performance during the Advani–Ayodhya years had been rather mediocre. In all the Bihar Assembly elections taking place after the parliamentary ones, BJP's votes have always declined. A major decline was between 1999 parliamentary elections and the 2000 assembly elections. In February 1999, when BJP was in power at the centre, Prime Minister Atal Bihari Vajpayee had sacked Lalu's government in Bihar and imposed president's rule. In April, general elections were called for, in which Bihari voters came out in large numbers in support of BJP. By then, Lalu Yadav had formed a new party called RJD, and just a year later, in the 2000 Vidhan Sabha elections, he won by a landslide. BJP suffered badly—a jolt it could not recover from, until recently. Bihari voters have never liked BJP within their state, but they admire it sitting in New Delhi.

FIGURE 5.10 Seat share and vote share of BJP in Haryana

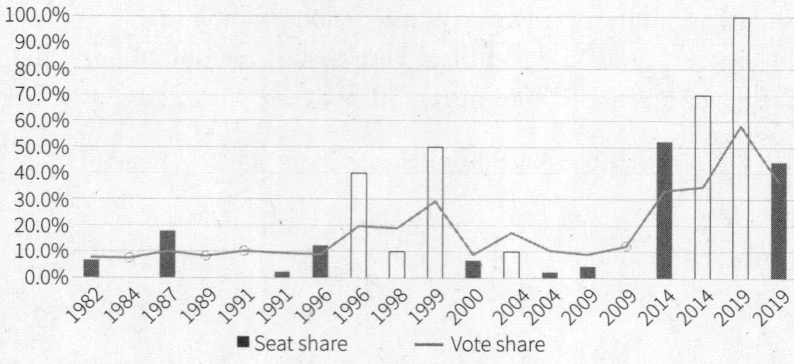

Note: Empty bars represent Lok Sabha and solid bars represent Vidhan Sabha

Haryana is one of BJP's recent occupations both at the state and central level, except in the Lok Sabha elections of 1996 and 1999. Again, national elections favour BJP more than state elections. Also note that Advani–Ayodhya hardly mattered in Haryana. And interestingly, the disparity in BJP's performance in Haryana during Lok Sabha and Vidhan Sabha elections is fascinatingly stark in 1996 and 1999 (see Figure 5.10).

The disparities are striking in New Delhi as well. But unlike Haryana, the vote share has not dramatically moved up or down in Delhi. So, a good 30–40 per cent Delhi voters have been voting for BJP, but the seat conversion has really happened in Lok Sabha, rather than Vidhan Sabha. The 2004 and 2009 Lok Sabha elections are interesting, with dismal performance by the party in terms of seats, but fairly admirable share of votes. See Figure 5.11. Delhi is one of the few places where BJP has had terrible luck. But one must also remember, Delhi witnessed a massive surge in BJP's base during Advani's rath yatra moment.

FIGURE 5.11 Seat share and vote share of BJP in Delhi

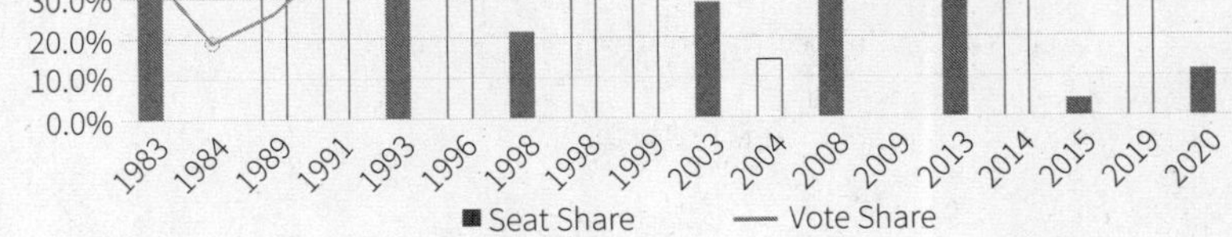

Note: Empty bars represent Lok Sabha and solid bars represent Vidhan Sabha

Let's look at Madhya Pradesh (Figure 5.12) and Gujarat (Figure 5.13). BJP's presence had a near-consistent vote share in Madhya Pradesh (hovering around 40–50 per cent), and interestingly, this consistency is also maintained in the seat share. The first major pick-up was, again, in 1989. This is seen in Gujarat as well, where the average vote share has not had either a sudden rise or drop. However, the last eight years in Gujarat have been remarkably different. Another notable difference is that BJP's rise in fortunes in Gujarat took place in 1989, much more steeply than in Madhya Pradesh. While in Madhya Pradesh, BJP already had a respectable voter base in the 1980s, it was not the case in Gujarat where it spiked up only in 1989. None of them exhibit a major rise post the 1992 mosque demolition and subsequent carnage.

FIGURE 5.12 Seat share and vote share of BJP in Madhya Pradesh

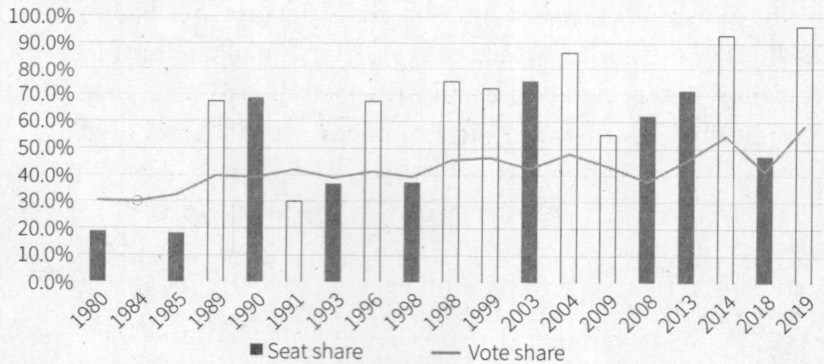

Note: Empty bars represent Lok Sabha and solid bars represent Vidhan Sabha

FIGURE 5.13 Seat share and vote share of BJP in Gujarat

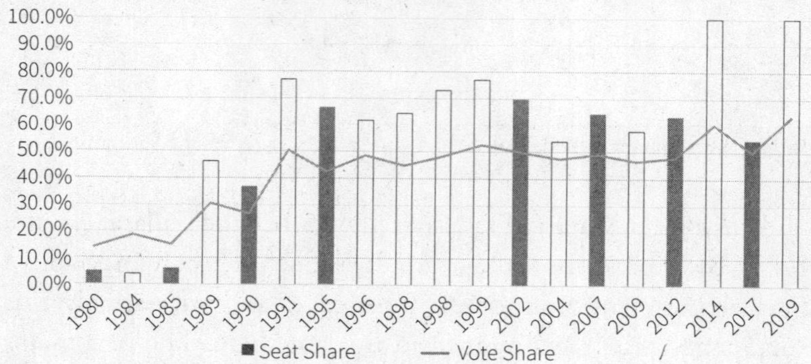

Note: Empty bars represent Lok Sabha and solid bars represent Vidhan Sabha

Finally, as shown in Figure 5.14, Himachal Pradesh also exhibits this consistency in vote share (hovering around the 40 per cent line). And here, the disparity in seat and vote share is huge. The year 1989, again, was the game-changer for the party here.

FIGURE 5.14 Seat share and vote share of BJP in Himachal Pradesh

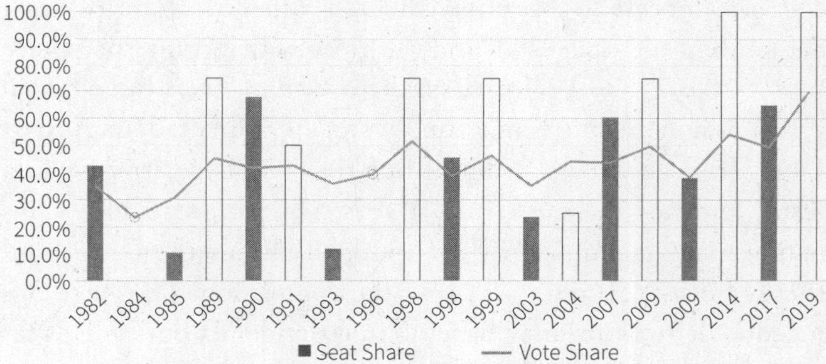

Note: Empty bars represent Lok Sabha and solid bars represent Vidhan Sabha

These are the states which we consider as prominently saffron today. If we were to look at large-scale insights, three things stand out. First, the rise in BJP's appeal really took place in 1989 in most cases and not right after the rath yatra post Ayodhya. Second, during the mid to late 1990s, BJP was far more preferred at the Centre than these states (this is also seen across the period, but was particularly pronounced during this phase). And third, in most cases, given the huge disparities between seat and vote shares, it looks like BJP's winning margins could not be huge, which reflects the importance of swinging votes.

Of these, the first inference is of peculiar interest. By 1989, the seats in UP had increased by four times (vote share hadn't increased by much though). In other words, BJP had already begun tasting success in UP in 1989. So, 1989 was actually a very important year for BJP. In fact, in states, barring Haryana, the remarkable rise in BJP's seats and votes really took place in the 1989 general elections. BJP's performance was dismal in the 1984 general elections and also in the assembly elections in 1985 in most places. But in 1989, it had emerged as a serious political force in the country.

The narratives that dominate today attribute BJP's electoral success to Ayodhya. But the rath yatra took place in September–October 1990 and the mosque demotion took place in 1992. BJP had begun rising before that. Even the Mandal Commission recommendations were implemented in August 1990. In other words, it looks like the Ayodhya dispute was a result and not the cause of BJP's rise. In fact, seats and votes had actually fallen slightly or remained almost the same in all these Hindi-speaking states after the demolition. The yatra and mosque demolition may have offered dividends but only as far as to not slow down the momentum which had already been set in motion in 1989. And interestingly, the 1989 poll results for BJP were strikingly similar in both Lok Sabha and Vidhan Sabha elections.

In fact, this pattern is also observed across the country even in non-Hindi speaking states. Let's look at the Lok Sabha elections and see BJP's performance, state-wise. We have picked up all the Lok Sabha elections from 1984, and examined BJP's seats and votes in the states until this date. For ease of representation, we have grouped the states into Central (Madhya Pradesh, Chhattisgarh and Jharkhand [Figures 5.15a and 5.15b]), Western (Gujarat and Maharashtra [Figures 5.16a and 5.16b]), Southern (Kerala, Tamil Nadu, Andhra Pradesh, Telangana and Karnataka [Figures 5.17a and 5.17b]), Eastern (Assam, Orissa and West Bengal [Figures 5.18a and 5.18b]), Himalayan (J&K, Himachal Pradesh and Uttarakhand [Figures 5.19a and 5.19b]), and two other groups, namely, UP–Bihar–Rajasthan (Figures 5.20a and 5.20b) and Delhi–Haryana–Punjab (Figures 5.21a and 5.21b).

FIGURE 5.15(a) BJP's seat share in Lok Sabha elections in Central India (Madhya Pradesh, Chhattisgarh, Jharkhand), 1984–2019

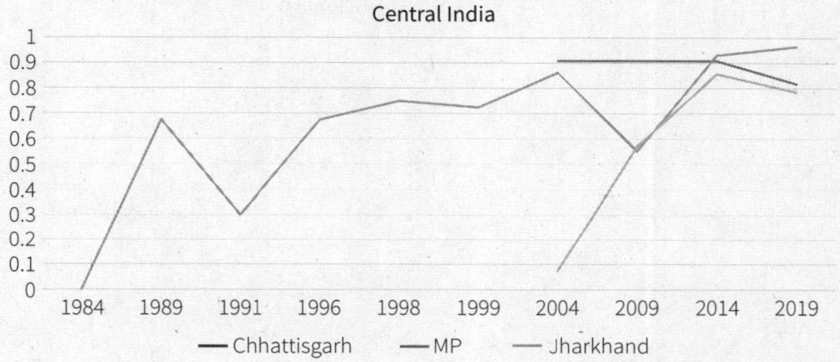

FIGURE 5.15(b) BJP's vote share in Lok Sabha elections in Central India (Madhya Pradesh, Chhattisgarh, Jharkhand), 1984–2019

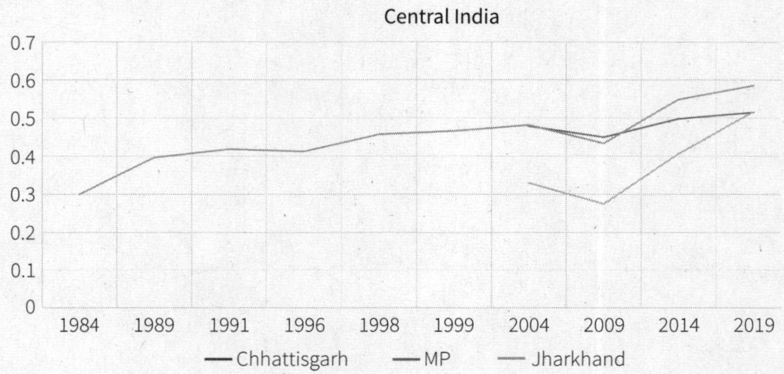

We have, for the purpose of this section, not considered the smaller north-eastern states and union territories. We wanted to get a large-scale picture and results may not change hugely even if we include them, because our subject of study is BJP, not the states. Also, this grouping has no particular logic or order. It is purely for ease of visualisation.

FIGURE 5.16(a) BJP's seat share in Lok Sabha elections in Western India (Maharashtra, Gujarat), 1984–2019

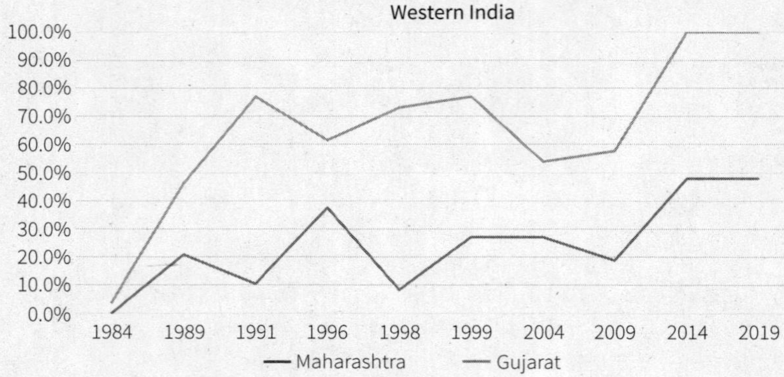

FIGURE 5.16(b) BJP's vote share in Lok Sabha elections in Western India (Rajasthan, Gujarat), 1984–2019

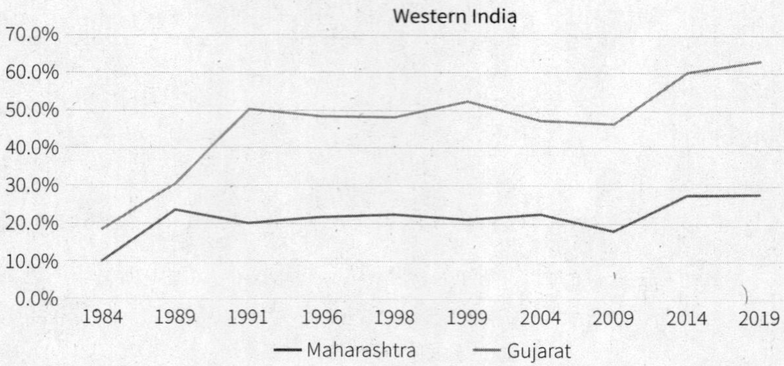

FIGURE 5.17(a) BJP's seat share in Lok Sabha elections in Southern India (Kerala, Tamil Nadu, Karnataka, Telangana, Andhra Pradesh), 1984–2019

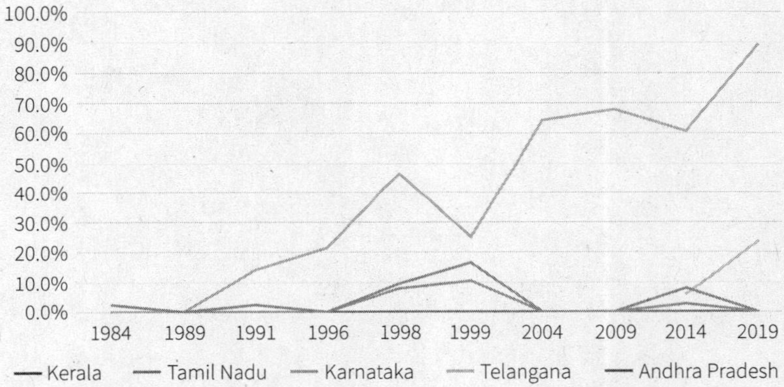

FIGURE 5.17(b) BJP's vote share in Lok Sabha elections in Southern India (Kerala, Tamil Nadu, Karnataka, Telangana, Andhra Pradesh), 1984–2019

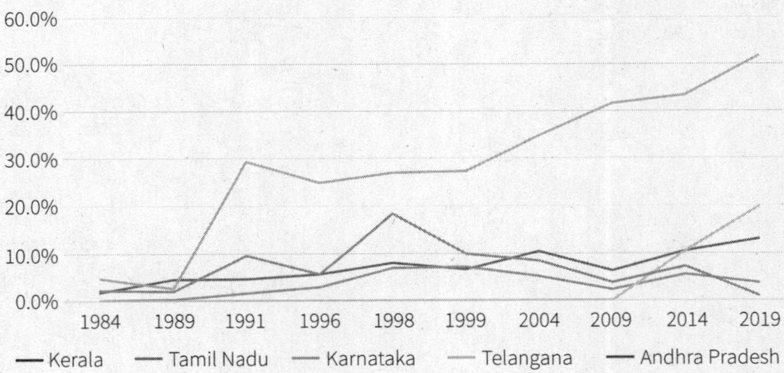

FIGURE 5.18(a) BJP's seat share in Lok Sabha elections in Eastern India (Assam, Orissa, West Bengal), 1984–2019

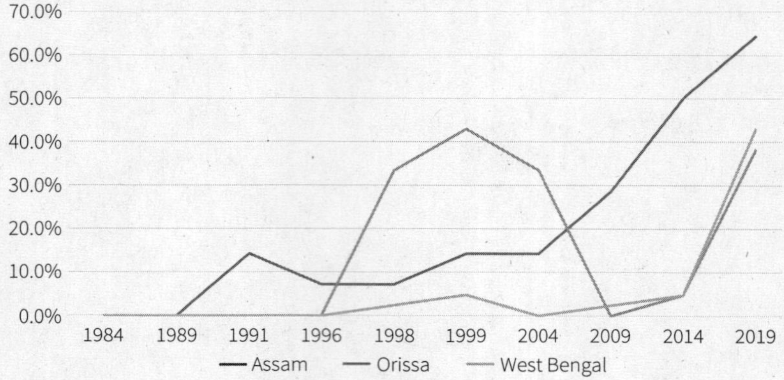

FIGURE 5.18(b) BJP's vote share in Lok Sabha elections in Eastern India (Assam, Orissa, West Bengal), 1984–2019

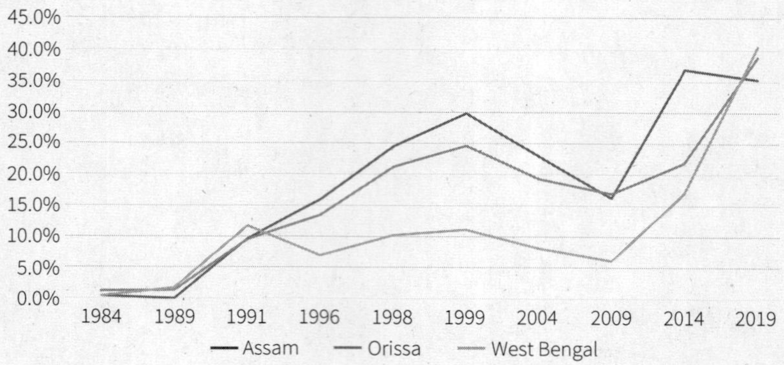

FIGURE 5.19(a) BJP's seat share in Lok Sabha elections in the Himalayan region (Jammu & Kashmir, Himachal Pradesh, Uttarakhand), 1984–2019

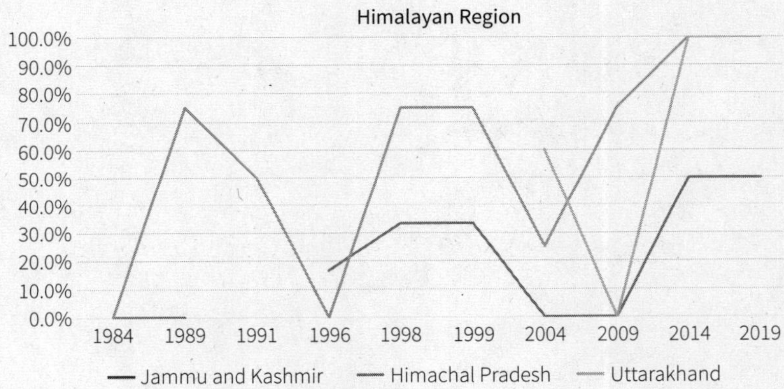

FIGURE 5.19(b) BJP's vote share in Lok Sabha elections in the Himalayan region (Jammu & Kashmir, Himachal Pradesh, Uttarakhand), 1984–2019

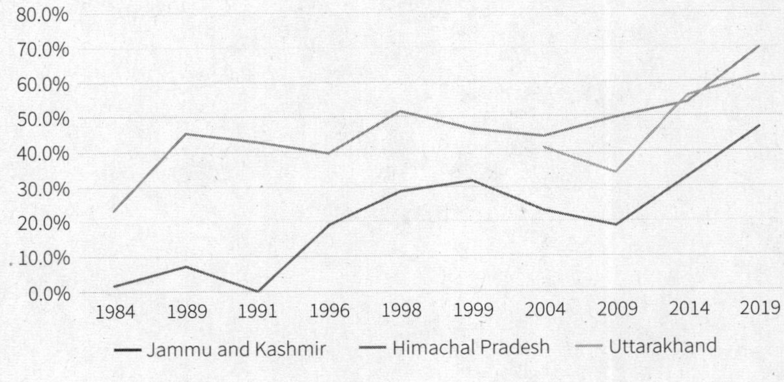

FIGURE 5.20(a) BJP's seat share in Lok Sabha elections in Uttar Pradesh, Rajasthan and Bihar, 1984–2019

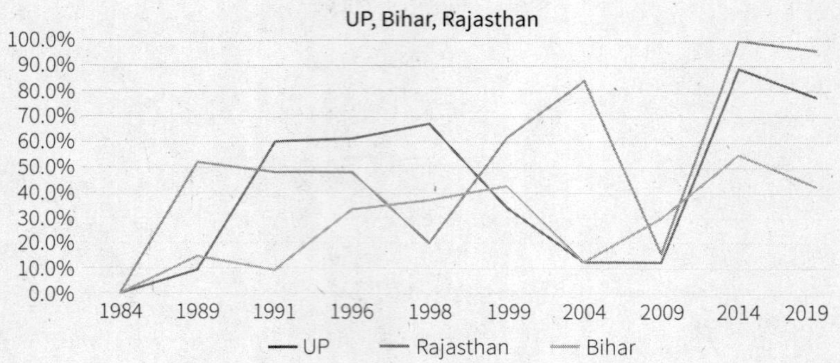

FIGURE 5.20(b) BJP's vote share in Lok Sabha elections in Uttar Pradesh, Rajasthan and Bihar, 1984–2019

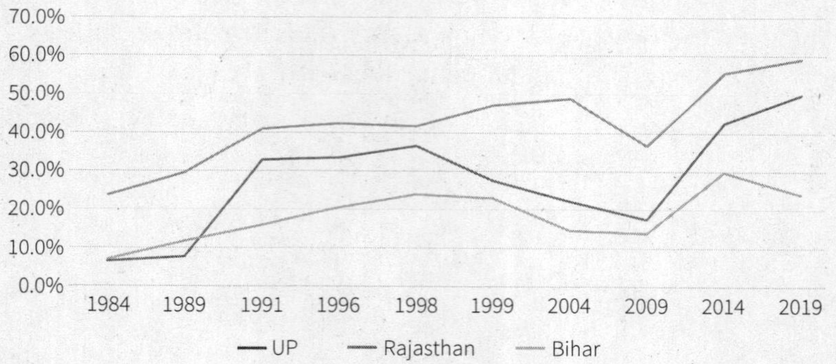

FIGURE 5.21(a) BJP's seat share in Lok Sabha elections in Delhi, Haryana and Punjab, 1984–2019

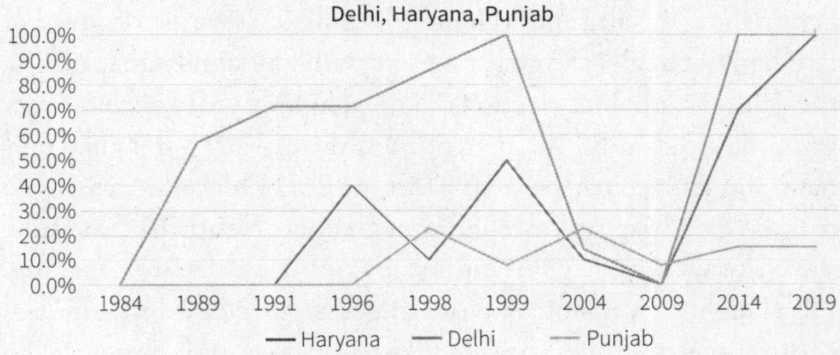

FIGURE 5.21(b) BJP's vote share in Lok Sabha elections in Delhi, Haryana and Punjab, 1984–2019

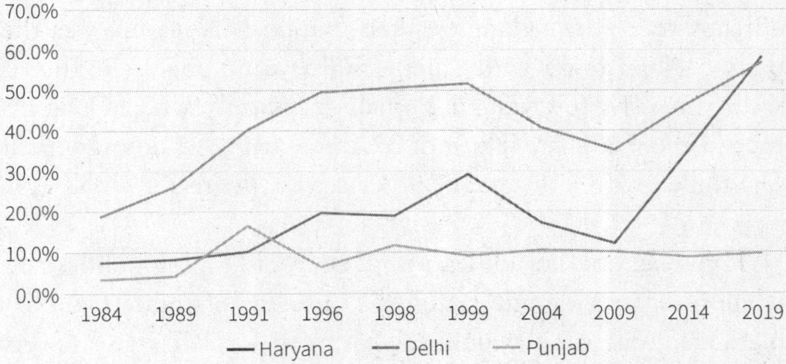

And what do we see? Literally everywhere, except a few states in the east and south, BJP's vote share shot up suddenly in 1989. And after that it followed the same path, flattening somewhat in the mid-1990s and picking up again recently. Seat shares also demonstrate the same story but with greater variations, attributed to the relative margins being low in many cases of wins. (We will come to this later.) But to understand BJP's rise and appeal, vote share is more important. And it is consistent with our 1985-to-1989-as-BJP's-turning-point story.

THE TURNING POINT: LOK SABHA OF 1989

We now recognise that BJP's rise in politics took place in 1989—before the rath yatra and Mandal Commission. We also know that BJP had not at all emerged as a party with any significance during the 1985 Lok Sabha elections. So, these four years become very important to study. What happened during 1985–89 that may have suddenly changed BJP's fortunes? The decade was surely marked by the entry of religion in politics. Nehru had carefully stayed away from religious influence on political decision-making. His daughter was not as wise. She was allegedly instrumental in installing a religious leader, Jarnail Singh Bhindranwale, to undermine the Akali Dal, her adversaries in Punjab. That, of course, through a series of events led to her assassination, and subsequent communal unrest across Punjab and Delhi. But this did not really dent Congress' mass support. Not only was the party back in power with Rajiv Gandhi's triumphant win, but it secured massive following in Punjab, specifically, where Congress topped the vote share list, with 32.1 per cent votes and the Akali Dal trailed with a distant 17.9 per cent. Congress' real fall was, again, in 1989.

Rajiv Gandhi did not learn the lesson of keeping politics and religion separate despite seeing the outcome of Indira Gandhi's blunders. And so, the political narrative for BJP's rise hovers around what emerged as the most important legal case of the decade and indeed of Rajiv Gandhi's career—the Shah Bano case of 1985. The case was concerned with the right of a divorced Muslim woman to alimony. The Supreme Court granted it, questioning the validity and competence of the Shariat court and its interpretation. Seeing the decision as a threat to their personal laws, Muslim clerics staged protests. Rajiv Gandhi began fearing an electoral backlash from Muslim communities, and his government passed the Muslim Women (Protection of Rights on

Divorce) Act, 1986, practically diluting the judgment. But this, in turn, created massive unrest among Hindu political circles. BJP was at the forefront, making a lot of noise, and mounting campaigns among urban Hindus against Congress. Desperate to pacify the Hindu anger, the government committed another blunder. They ordered the reopening of the Ram temple in Ayodhya, the gates of which had remained locked since 1948. This misstep was like planting a political landmine, explosions of which can still be heard in India.

Even amongst those who recognise that BJP's stars began shining in the late 1980s, people think that it was the Shah Bano judgment and its repercussions that explains BJP's rise. Our assessment challenges this notion. Let's go over it again. Popular accounts divide the story in three distinct steps. Step one: The Shah Bano judgment, which angered Muslim clerics. Step two: The Act was passed (which diluted the judgment) to appease Muslims, angering Hindus. Step three: The gates of the Ram Temple in Ayodhya opened up to appease Hindus.

Let's look at the dates now. The Shah Bano judgment came through in April 1985. The Act diluting the judgment was promulgated in May 1986. The gates of the temple were opened up in February 1986— between the judgment and the legislation, not after it.

This changes everything. The popular narrative misleads us to believe that BJP's rise was because of these events. This narrative must be complemented by another one which explains the rise of BJP better. Note that these events had their own impact surely. They led to an explicit political schism between religious priorities in Indian electoral politics. Muslim appeasement became a rallying cry for BJP workers after the Bill's enactment, and the gates of Ram Temple being opened up only fanned the fire. A religious fervour was let out of the box. Along with BJP's political cousin, the Vishwa Hindu Parishad's (VHP) aggressive campaigns to build the Ram Temple at the disputed site, BJP was able to reshape the imagination of middle-class Hindus who had earlier remained insignificant to electoral politics and had been loyal Congress voters.

The Ram Temple issue transformed India's political discourse, experts say. They connect it with slogans like 'Garv se kaho hum Hindu hain' which shook the masses who were getting involved in religious politics in India for the first time and who found BJP to be a valuable alternative.

Just when the Act was being promulgated in India, a newspaper in Sweden had uncovered a story about a recent, inflated arms purchase by India from a Swedish firm, Bofors. This purchase had been accompanied by massive kickbacks that Indian politicians under Rajiv Gandhi had received under the table. This story was going largely unnoticed. But then it was telecast on radio in 1987 and the nation was alerted.

In particular, it attracted one particular person—the then defence minister, V.P. Singh. By the time the scandal broke, he had become a champion of honesty and integrity in the murky waters of Indian politics. He had already been removed from his cabinet position as finance minister and given the defence portfolio perhaps on account of tax-evasion raids on industrial houses like Ambanis who allegedly had helped Rajiv Gandhi fight the 1984 elections. Following a major public outcry due to Bofors, and differences with Rajiv Gandhi, V.P. Singh resigned. The case shook India. It was perhaps the first politically distasteful experience that independent India went through. Bofors came to be synonymised as the symbol of crashed hopes for a promise that a new India emerging from the ashes of old political ideas and morality was looking forward to. There was widespread public anger against Congress. To make matters worse, it was also coupled with a stagnant, rather declining economy[4] with high unemployment and, consequently, a disgruntled youth. The voting age had come down from 21 to 18 in the 1989 elections. This additional brigade of youth, lacking a powerful institutional memory of the Congress Raj, may have seen it suitable to have India's future in the hands of anyone other than the 'dishonest' Rajiv Gandhi whose government had not affected daily lives, except pushing the nation into economic diseases and a moral pandemic.

This was still 1987 and elections were two more years away. The opening up of the gates of the Ram Temple coupled with the Shah Bano case could not have had a major impact in electoral preferences as we see in the dates that don't match. Also, the Bofors scandal was two years before the elections, and if the Indian electorate—often dubbed as forgetful—can forgive Indira Gandhi for the dreadful Emergency in three years, Bofors was perhaps not as horrific. The scandal reduced Rajiv Gandhi's popularity, but how does it relate to the rise in BJP's power?

Something unrelated was going on in India during 1987–88, an event of considerable importance to account for BJP's rise, and yet, it has simply escaped scholarly scrutiny. This was the first-ever public broadcast of the Hindu epic *Ramayana*![5]

Airing through January 1987 until July 1988, the series moved the country in ways unimaginable. A total of 78, 45-minute-long episodes aired on Sunday mornings were to become weekly rituals that lakhs of Indian homes ceremoniously indulged in, with great devotion and amazement. Streets would get deserted, buses and even trains would stop, and passengers would step out to watch the serial on TV in a roadside shop. At homes, people would bathe, garland the television, burn incense and kneel before the television as the show would begin. It was a like a spell no one could have imagined. Generations of families and neighbours would huddle together in the same room to watch the serial with unparalleled reverence and humanity's most ardent following for any soap opera ever broadcasted. The actors who played characters on the show became real-life gods for people.

Estimates suggest that around 65 crore people watched the show. The television revolution had only begun in India in the 1980s and the timing of the serial couldn't have been better. In 1983, India produced 8 lakh TV sets. This number had gone up to 30 lakh in 1986. During the eight years preceding the broadcasting of *Ramayana*, the number of TV sets had gone up by ten times, and the audience by six times. This was a revolution with a massive and long-lasting psychological impact. For the first time, people were able to view life and aspirations of fellow Indians. Serials like *Hum Log* and *Buniyaad* sensitised the masses to a 'way of living' that they could either relate to or aspired for. The normative understanding of Indianness as one nation (Benedict Anderson's *Imagined Communities* come to mind), and one way of thinking was triggered, and in a big way, constructed by television penetration in India. Note that despite low ownership rates, television viewership was high. One TV had so many viewers. They all huddled up around one television to watch it.

People in remote areas had now expanded their horizon of imagining India. And research shows that a strong node of this imagination had hinged around middle-class urban Hindu imagination. In one of the surveys of 1,170 people in Delhi, Pune and (then) Madras, conducted during the same period,[6] scholars discovered this centralising imagination. Eighty-five per cent of lower-caste TV viewers felt their needs and aspirations were not covered adequately in TV serials, 90 per cent of Muslim and Sikh respondents felt their religious customs and practices were not adequately portrayed, and over 90 per cent of labourers and artisans also felt their skills and knowledge were not properly depicted. Interestingly, 60 per cent of non-Hindi speaking population felt that their problems and difficulties were not being projected on Indian television. And yet, as a coordinating link that technology provides, the value judgments, traditions and customs appearing on TV were slowly acquiring the status of uniformity.

Let's try to connect all of these factors. Increasingly, high viewership of television had surfaced a singular imagination of who an Indian was, and how did they deal with everything that was India. As this benchmark was being established, Ramayana was telecast. It was impossible that it would not touch Indians deeply.

BJP was the biggest gainer. This doesn't mean that *Ramayana* was BJP's doing. Somehow when BJP was gaining ground, people received a sentimental religious dose every week, through 1987–88 in the form of *Ramayana*, and between 1988–90 through *Mahabharata*, which also drew a massive following (second only to *Ramayana*). This interweaving of political-real and religious-reel during 1987–90 provided a powerful recipe to mobilise the voters' minds into looking at BJP as a party that carries the emotions of India.

Hinduism is unlike any other religion, and, in fact, many question whether it is even a religion at all. It has a pagan character without a prescriptive text or a rulebook. It is, unlike the Abrahamic framework, not rooted in true and false gods, and therefore has innumerable deities. These deities and several varnas (loosely translated and collected into castes) are scattered across India, following their own rituals, religious symbols, rules and traditions which are customary to that group. There is no universal rule or text in Hinduism. It has a very flexible architecture, and shapes and reshapes itself over time. So, it evolves in a variety of ways, through people's own interpretation around customs. Many call it an open source religion (if one can call it religion in the first place). A.K. Ramanujam's essay, 'Three Hundred Ramayanas'—written for a conference to be held in 1987, the same year as *Ramayana*'s broadcast—is a valuable excursion of Ramayana's various 'tellings' across Asian societies over 2,500 years and presents the claim that there is no singular version of the Ramayana.

The 1987 broadcast of *Ramayana*, however, brought a singular consciousness of the Hindu epic to everyone in the country. Consider a nation suddenly realising that religion is becoming a more explicit tool in the hands of political leaders. Generations which evolved with Gandhian ideals were becoming irrelevant. Congress was failing to provide a sound economy; it was getting its hands dirty in corruption even in matters as important as national security, and was also pandering to religious minority interests. This India was scrambling for options when it came across BJP. Just when they noticed BJP's vision, television sets hooked them up to the epic. This India then began drawing inspiration and meaning of its own identity from the televised *Ramayana*.

While the seventh and eighth episodes of *Mahabharata* were being aired in November 1989, India was going out to cast its ballot once again. This time, they had an image of Lord Ram in their minds. And his birthplace.

Something else is important here—in the 1989 general elections, there was a pre-poll alliance between Janata Dal (JD) and BJP. And that may have been the reason for BJP's rise too, some may claim; perhaps BJP was piggybacking on JD's popularity. There was a huge anti-incumbency wave anyway. So, this is a fair point. In 1989, the two parties had a seat adjustment agreement, whereby they had agreed to put up a common candidate, so that they did not compete against each other. Since in many constituencies, only one common candidate was fielded on behalf of both these parties, how do we know where the vote went, really? For instance, if BJP had no candidate in constituency X, and JD did, it was possible that the votes going to this candidate may have actually been meant for BJP, but there is simply no way of finding out. Paul Brass,[7] for example, has suggested that BJP's reliance on the seat adjustment was very high in places like UP to gain a stronghold there.

But this may not necessarily be true. As Sreedharan[8] points out, BJP indeed had a strong base in places where they won. Gould[9] has also chimed in, suggesting that the anti-incumbency wave had swept the country during the 1989 elections. But the most important reason as to why it cannot be the partnership with JD that led to BJP's rise in 1989 comes from the assembly election results in 1989. Three months after the general elections of 1989, several states had assembly elections. In Rajasthan, Madhya Pradesh, Himachal Pradesh and Gujarat, BJP won with a resounding victory. Nothing particularly significant had taken place during the interim months, and BJP's victory was overwhelming. There is reason to believe that the magic of religious politics, in the background of *Ramayana–Mahabharata* consciousness, was working in favour of BJP. The actors who played the role of Sita (Deepika Chikhalia) and Ravana (Arvind Trivedi) in Ramayana, went on to become Members of Parliament (MPs) on BJP's tickets in the general elections of 1991, both from Gujarat.

JARIPATKA MANDAL

BJP has astounded political pundits globally. Its rise to power is of great intrigue. Numbers tell us invaluable stories. This chapter has three simple takeaways: first, BJP's performance in 2019 was less reliant on its saffron colour or the Hindi-speaking population than otherwise suggested. Second, it is the *Ramayana* and not Shah Bano or Ayodhya that really catapulted BJP in people's consciousness. Third, BJP preference in the Centre has to be looked differently from its performance in states. We hope this offers considerable fodder for future researchers.

Most people know that RSS, the parent body of BJP, was founded in 1925. But very few are aware that the organisation's name was decided later, in April 1926, during a meeting at

Hedgevar's (RSS' founder) home in Nagpur. There were four names that were floated and deliberated upon. They finally chose Rashtriya Swayamsevak Sangh. The other three names were, Hindu Swayamsevak Sangh, Bharat Uddharak Mandal and the last one, which is most interesting, Jaripatka Mandal.

Jaripatka may have signified either of the two things: the flag of the Maratha kingdom is called Jaripatka in Marathi. This is the saffron flag ending in two floating triangles joined together with the common base of the pole, often visible on top of Hindu temples. Also, Jaripatka is the name of an old neighbourhood in Nagpur.

It would have been poetic if the Sangh was named Jaripatka Mandal instead. Scholars often speculate that if the British had not colonized India, it would have been the Marathas who would have ruled over India. Jaripatka Mandal would have then sounded like the flag is laying its claim to its own land. If the name was derived from that of a neighbourhood in Nagpur, then, it would have indicated that the distance from the centre to the peripheries of India was a long journey of hundred years!

6

Coalition Politics in India

We began this book by imagining elections as a huge power-sucking motor. It draws power from crores of people and channels it into a few hundred contestants and their parties. This means that power convergence is taking place. Like a bunch of streams and tributaries combining into the mighty river. In principle, all tiny rivers must lead to this one main river, which enables the flow into the sea. Only one river is allowed into the political sea. And this must, therefore, be given all powers.

But suppose these streams, instead of converging, diverge into distributaries of power. That is, what if no one party secures a majority? Diffused power is of no use. It was as good as it was in the hands of the people anyway. Decision-making cannot happen with so many minds.

So, in case of a hung verdict, the simple answer is to organise elections again. This is unwise, because there is no guarantee that the new election will yield a strong mandate in favour of one party. Not to mention the high cost of conducting elections again. Another way is to force the smaller streams to join one of the larger streams to give one of them the minimum load needed to push them all to the sea. In other words, let smaller parties join hands with one of the big ones and add up their mandates algebraically. If the total reaches beyond a certain required number, then one of these organised parties forms the government. The resulting coalition politics saves the nation from an electoral iteration.

This looks pretty good as a procedure. And in a country as vast and diverse as India, coalition governments seem to reflect the interests, opinions and preferences of people better. But there are three fundamental issues inherent within this solution. One lies in the tussle between mathematics and ideology. While one party may want to join hands with another to fulfil the math behind electoral principles, they may not have similar ideologies or similar commitments towards public service. This means that since the value systems don't match, the political marriage may not last long. This ruptures the smooth running of the government. Secondly, small parties can become very powerful. Contributing a small (but necessary) share in the total seat tally, they can run major ministries and hold the ruling government for political ransom in many political or policy-based initiatives. While in practice it may not mean anything majorly disastrous, but in principle, parties that people hardly preferred get to run the show.

The third (and somewhat connected) issue is far more important from our point of view. And that is, the breach of trust that coalition governments may be a symbol of. Parties can engage in a pre-poll alliance or a post-poll coalition. In the former, they don't compete in the same constituencies and their voter base is aware in advance of the commitments they are making jointly, so the voters can make an informed choice. But in the latter, when parties join hands after election results are announced, as a voter, I may feel betrayed. When I vote for one candidate or a party, I want its ideologies and principles to reach the centre. But a coalition dilutes that desire from manifesting itself. I didn't like this party with who my preferred party is now forming a coalition, one may argue. And therefore, coalition distress in voters is most acute when coalitions are formed *after* elections.

Here, it is important to understand the dynamics of coalition governments in India. The focus of this chapter is primarily on national elections since 1967, when nationwide support to Congress first showed signs of dwindling. Since coalitions assume an indispensable role in the rising importance of regional parties and the occurrence of hung parliaments, no book on Indian politics can be complete without analysing coalitions. The problem is, coalitions are very complex to comprehend, because unlimited permutations can and have taken place on the Indian electoral battlefield. Consider, for instance, what would happen if two parties fight against each other in Lok Sabha polls but contest elections jointly in the Vidhan Sabha. General answers are hard to come by. The 1990s, for example, had portrayed coalition governments with a series of unstable governments. People had begun developing an utter distaste against coalition politics. But in the recent past, we have had four Lok Sabhas successfully completing their full terms with stable coalition parties, UPA and NDA.

THE DECLINE OF CONGRESS AND RISE OF COALITION POLITICS

Coalitional politics has a long history in independent India. Its roots can be traced to the first general elections in 1951–52, which were followed by a fragmented verdict in the state assembly of Kerala where no party could win a majority. It was the coalition of Congress and Travancore Tamil Nadu Congress in March 1952 that provided a short-lived government in Kerala. The coalition government fell soon due to internal tussles, and fresh elections were called for in 1954. Thus, the first experiment of a coalition government failed in no time.

The year 1967 was a watershed year in the political history of Congress as well as that of India. Even though Congress had failed to get an absolute majority in Madras, Orissa, Travancore–Cochin and Patiala and East Punjab States Union in 1952,[1] it was in 1967 that it lost badly. It was crushed in the assembly elections of as many as nine major states, namely Punjab, Haryana, UP, Madhya Pradesh, Bihar, Bengal, Orissa, Madras and Kerala. Interestingly, except Madras (where the Dravida Munnetra Kazhagam [DMK] formed the government), coalition governments were formed in all these states because of the fractured outcome.[2] Broadly speaking, these coalitions were formed by regional parties with a common anti-Congress thread binding them. In many of these states, Congress faced stiff competition from its own leaders who had quit the party in preceding years.

The subsequent parliamentary elections too didn't provide absolute reign to Congress either. But political scientists generally agree that the 1967 elections were the most remarkable ones from a pan-India perspective. It was an evident break from Congress dominance after almost two decades (1947–67) of independent India.

This outcome also had implications on the functioning of the federal polity of India because there was a new domain of tensions between state and national politics. The central government was formed by Congress and multiple state governments were formed by non-Congress parties. The year 1967 was also the last time when national and state elections were held simultaneously. With the early dissolution of the national government in 1970, the decoupling of state and national elections occurred. Congress returned with a majority at the national level, winning 352 seats the 1971 elections. However, this powerful avatar of Congress did not survive for long and the party lost badly in the 1977 elections held soon after the Emergency was lifted. This election result also gave India its first non-Congress government in Delhi.

THE FIRST COALITION GOVERNMENT AT THE CENTRE

The 1977 elections represent another benchmark in Indian politics because it was the first attempt to form a coalition government at the national level. This period is generally referred to as the Janata era, due to the unprecedented win of the Janata Party, which was a merger of Congress (O) (different from Congress), Jana Sangh, Bharatiya Lok Dal (BLD) and the Socialist Party. The Janata Party, with its supporters, won more than 300 seats.

The demise of Congress was so acute that even Indira Gandhi and Sanjay Gandhi lost elections. The party fared extremely poorly in the northern states. However, it still managed to get 154 seats across India with a decent vote share of 34.5 per cent. Its performance in the southern states saved it from a total wipeout. But it had lost its face. Noteworthy is the mention of Raj Narain, who won a famous legal battle of electoral malpractice against Indira Gandhi, while she was still the PM, which later triggered the Emergency in 1975. Raj Narain fought elections as a candidate of BLD and won against Indira Gandhi in the 1977 elections from the Rae Bareli constituency by a margin of more than 50,000 votes (nearly 17 per cent of the votes polled). Sanjay Gandhi too lost miserably from Amethi by a margin of nearly 76,000 votes, which was more than a quarter of all votes polled.

Unfortunately, this coalition government did not last long. To begin with, there was an internal quarrel over who would take up the position of the PM of the government. There were three contenders—Morarji Desai, Charan Singh and Jagjivan Ram. After interference from Jayaprakash Narayan and J.B. Kriplani, Morarji Desai was chosen. Later on, many other contentious issues arose that led to a split in 1979. The then President of India, Neelam Sanjiva Reddy, appointed Charan Singh as the PM of a minority government. However, Charan Singh could not find support from other parties and the government was dissolved.

Fresh elections in 1980 brought Congress back to the top. The party won 353 seats, with seat share of 67 per cent and a vote share of nearly 43 per cent. After the assassination of Prime Minister Indira Gandhi in 1984, Congress got its highest-ever success, winning 404 (79 per cent) seats, with a whopping vote share of 49 per cent. Most political commentators term this as the sympathy wave which resulted in the best-ever performance of Congress, both in terms of seats as well as votes. The 1984 general elections, however, were the last national elections where Congress had a majority on its own. Coalition politics reappeared at the national stage in the 1989 Lok Sabha elections. Since then, India has seen 11 coalition governments.

THE DECADE OF POLITICAL INSTABILITY AND EPHEMERAL COALITION EXPERIMENTS

Parties opposed to the Congress system came together again in 1989 to form the government through a coalition. A common minimum programme was devised to bring parties with little ideological symphony under a common platform of what was called the National Front (NF) government. V.P. Singh, the then defence minister, quit Congress in 1987. Of royal lineage, Singh was Indira Gandhi's minister, and also served as the CM of UP in 1980.

Rajiv made him the finance minister, and later in 1987, the minister of defence. There, Singh began opening up secrets from the world of defence procurement, and was supposedly very close to unearthing the scam in the Bofors purchase which could have exposed corruption even at the prime ministerial level. He was sacked.

The 1980s are often considered as the period of moral decline in Indian politics. The seeds had been sown when Indira Gandhi was in power. She was known to keep a band of loyalists close to herself and, as Paul Brass notes, gaining political mileage out of the misery of famine or riot victims.[3] She was succeeded by her son, Rajiv, who was not a sophisticated politician. With time, the moral decline became only more vulgar and open. Today, if a public servant wants to do something good and is soon transferred, there is little surprise expressed at it. We all go back to our living rooms, reading newspapers and sipping our chai the next morning like nothing happened. This complacency with waning public morality, a gift of Indira's Congress, only exacerbated during her son Rajiv's reign.

V.P. Singh resigned from Congress and in October 1988, he formed the Janata Dal (JD) with the merger of the Jan Morcha (which he founded in 1987), remnants of the Janata Party, Lok Dal and Congress (Socialist). JD became the main pillar for setting up the coalition government, the National Front (NF).

During the 1989 elections, Congress' seats had plummeted to a mere 197, with a vote share of around 39 per cent. JD won 143 seats with a vote share of approximately 18 per cent. With outside support from BJP (which had 85 seats) and left parties (with 52 seats), the NF formed the government swiftly. An interesting feature of this election was the pre-electoral arrangement of major anti-Congress parties where they had only one candidate against Congress candidates in each constituency.[4] This proved to be a successful strategy indeed.

By 1990–91, several big states had come under JD domination, helmed respectively by Om Prakash Chautala (Haryana), Chimanbhai Patel (Gujarat), Biju Patnaik (Orissa), Lalu Prasad Yadav (Bihar), Bhairon Singh Shekhawat (Rajasthan), E.K. Nayanar (Kerala) and Mulayam Singh Yadav (UP). NF had also taken up Andhra (N.T. Rama Rao) and Assam (Prafulla Mahanta). This was unprecedented. A non-Congress and non-BJP dominance of India during 1989–91 was a sight to behold.

Yet, coalition politics is difficult to sustain. In many ways, it bares open animal (read human) instincts for power. The ideas of mandate, electorate, preference, democracy, etc. take a back seat, if at all. With numbers on the lips and ego in the head, so-called leaders engage, disengage, debate, please and trade for seats. With coalitions, new types of leaders also emerge. The year 1989 was witness to all this. While V.P. Singh was one of the NF's choices to become the PM after the elections, it was not going to be as simple. Singh announced that he would like to nominate Devi Lal, the veteran leader from Haryana, to become the PM. Devi Lal, on the other hand, recommended he would rather see Singh as the PM while he would act as a senior mentor to the government. While Devi Lal was more receptive to everyone, his support for Singh frustrated another powerful player in the game—Chandra Shekhar.

In a coalition, all regional leaders come with their own elected supporters. Annoying one of them means annoying many, which, in turn, dries up your numbers. But suppressing the ego, particularly in a polity like India where hierarchy, patronage and subservience have become the fabric of society and politics, can only be done for so long. NF seemed well-balanced and strong in the beginning of its term, but the government was to face multiple problems in no time. While Singh was the PM, handling issues in Kashmir (the then Home Minister, Mufti Mohammad Sayeed's daughter had been kidnapped by militants), implementing the Mandal Commission report for reserving jobs for OBCs, tussling with Reliance, and dealing with a situation where Haryana's CM (Om Prakash Chautala) was being forced to resign due to his alleged involvement in election rigging meant he had to do a lot of firefighting. Chautala was the son of Devi Lal. The latter, being a principled, old-Congress leader, took moral responsibility and resigned as the deputy PM in the NF government.

The Mandal Commission in 1980 led to violent protests across India. Politically, it was a cause of trouble because it frustrated BJP, a major coalition partner. BJP had felt cheated with the Mandal Commission promulgation. But also, they were frustrated because L.K. Advani's famous rath yatra was stopped in 1990 by Lalu Yadav upon authority from V.P. Singh. BJP's exit led to the fall of the government. Chandra Shekhar had formed his own party in 1990, the Samajwadi Janata Party, and with the support of Rajiv Gandhi, he became the eighth PM of India.

This government too couldn't survive for long, although this time, in 1991, fresh elections were called for. The NF coalition fought elections against BJP and Congress. This year also saw the assassination of Rajiv Gandhi. In the end, Congress emerged as the largest party with 244 seats and approximately 36 per cent vote share. Janata Dal, which had 143 seats in previous elections, got merely 59 this time. BJP emerged as the second largest party this time. In 1989, it had 11 per cent votes and 85 seats. This time, it had 20 per cent votes and 120 seats. While it had really risen in 1989, it was in 1991 when its fate was really sealed. It had emerged as a powerful force that couldn't be ignored. Congress, after all, formed the government with support from the left parties, and ruled for a full term of five years.

In 1996, it was the turn of BJP with 161 seats. Funnily enough though, their vote share remained the same as in 1991, at around 20 per cent. Interestingly, Congress, the trailing party with 140 seats, had a higher vote share of 29 per cent!

Notice again, the seat–vote share dance in the first-past-the-post (FPTP) system. A difference of almost 9 percentage points in vote share where the vote-share winner lost in seat-share. Twenty-nine per cent people preferred Congress in 1996 while 20 per cent preferred BJP. Yet, BJP had higher seats. The vote base of BJP did not increase during 1991–96, but seats did. This may have been possible because the average win margin for BJP was rather thin. Congress was liked by more people but it most likely lost in several places by a thin margin. BJP was invited to form the government and prove majority in the House. In 1996, Atal

Bihari Vajpayee took the oath as the PM. However, BJP did not find enough support from others to sustain the government and failed to prove its majority. This government had a short life of just 13 days. Vajpayee, saddened by the failure to prove majority, ended his speech on that day with the words, '*Hum sankhya bal ke aage sar jhukate hain*,' translating into, 'We bow down before the strength of numbers.'

Coalition had become the order of the day. An alliance of roughly 15 parties, including JD, Samajwadi Party and the left parties, came together to form what was called the United Front (UF) government with support from Congress. The new coalition government was formed and surprisingly, the then Karnataka CM, H.D. Deva Gowda, became the PM. The UF government experienced multiple vacillations during this time, and Congress was not very happy about being sidelined. Another faction of the UF was later supported by Congress and Inder Kumar Gujral became the PM. He was chosen over Lalu Prasad Yadav and Mulayam Singh Yadav, who were probably seen as more powerful personalities.

In fact, the choice of Gowda and Gujral represented a fear in the ruling coalition and Congress in particular. In 1840, Thomas Carlyle had proposed the great man theory. He said one can understand history by looking at the impact of great men who had particular personalities to chart a course for society. Congress (and perhaps BJP as well) have bought this idea very well. In India, it is often said, people vote for faces, not ideas. Faceless contestations are useless. But what does one do, when one does not have a face?

After the demise of Rajiv Gandhi, the Nehru/Gandhi dynasty was bereft of that face. The confusion over who to hand over the baton of the Congress party to was matched only by the consistent and persuasive fear of the rise of BJP which had amassed the potential to form a single, powerful rival front to

Congress in India. And internal politics demanded that for as long as someone else was in power through their support, there shouldn't be the emergence of any parallel leader. Gowda and Gujral were seen as more low-profile leaders than the two Yadavs or Jyoti Basu, the unstoppable CM of Bengal. Congress remained an anxious party and withdrew its support to the second avatar of the UF government as well. This time, the reason was the Tamil party, DMK, which was said to have links with Tamil separatists in Sri Lanka who had taken responsibility for assassinating Rajiv Gandhi. Congress wanted it ousted from the UF, failing which, it withdrew its support. This brought down the coalition government in November 1997. (It is fascinating to note that in 2004, when government formation was again going through the coalition tug-of-war, Congress welcomed the very same DMK in its UPA pavilion with stretched arms.)

Anyway, back to 1998. Fresh snap polls were called for in February that year and the country was forced to go into election mode again. Once again, BJP came out as the largest party with 182 seats and approximately 26 per cent vote share. It formed another coalition government with the help of its regional partners. However, this was another short-lived government. The All India Anna Dravida Munnetra Kazhagam (AIADMK) withdrew its support from the coalition government and the government fell.

It is fascinating, yet again, to note that in 2004, BJP welcomed AIADMK in its NDA coalition. The same AIADMK which led to its downfall in 1998! Strange bedfellows indeed.

Imagine where the vote is, in all this circus of power and seats. Practically nowhere. Barring instances of pre-poll alliances, all these crazy designs reflect a miserable mockery of voters and their feebleness. We vote with some preference. And we get such different results. We choose our leaders and despite their popularity, we get someone else. The first-past-the-post (FPTP) system. You get to rule the country even without having a single vote cast in your favour. When Lal Bahadur Shastri died, Indira Gandhi was made the PM. Nobody voted for her, but she was the daughter of the party chief, Nehru. She was nominated into the Rajya Sabha and made the PM. Gowda and Gujral too became the PMs of India through Rajya Sabha nominations. Another two-time PM was nominated through the Rajya Sabha—Manmohan Singh. Not a single vote but sitting at the highest seat of power. In coalition, this blatant disregard for voter preferences is laid bare.

All in all, five Lok Sabha elections were organised during the ten-year period, 1989–98, and none of the elections in this period produced a stable government. This period also brought regional elements into national politics which persist until date. It also became clear that no individual party could control the politics of the whole of India. Players needed to coordinate with polar opposite parties to form governments. This, however, did not continue smoothly. Failure at multiple levels was a characteristic of this time period.

POST-ELECTION COALITIONS AND MOCKERY OF MANDATES

The real pain is that coalition-making in India has typically been characterised by post-poll alliances. For example, the first coalition government at the Centre came with the result of the 1977 elections with no single party having a majority. Essentially, coalition-making was not a desirable outcome by political parties, but it was an outcome of hung assemblies. It was also an imminent outcome of regionalisation of Indian politics and rise of local political leaders who commanded significant following in a specific region. In this way, power was rather decentralised in the wake of coalition governments.

What is even worse in Indian politics is the mockery of voters by changing of coalition partners *post elections* even when parties have formed a different pre-electoral coalition. An evidence of this behaviour was witnessed in the strange coalition of BJP and JD(U) in the state of Bihar following the 2015 state elections. BJP and JD(U) projected themselves as the main contenders in Bihar where BJP formed an alliance with its NDA partners in the state and JD(U) formed an alliance with Congress and RJD. The alliance of JD(U), Congress and RJD was called the Mahagathbandhan, the grand alliance. The alliance came to power.

What happened during the tenure of the Mahagathbandhan government was not foreseen by political experts, leave alone voters. The Mahagathbandhan broke down over a quarrel between JD(U) and RJD. And lo and behold—JD(U) formed a government with BJP, the very party which was its biggest rival during elections. That didn't matter. Both BJP and JD(U) had engaged in bitter battles during elections, and barely a year later, they joined hands to form the government. When it comes to coalition politics, a post-poll swapping of power decimates the value of the mandate given by voters in a trust-based relationship between voters and the parties. In simple words, this was a mockery of the voters of Bihar. As we prepare this manuscript, Nitish Kumar has pulled the plug from NDA, and rejoined the Mahagathbandhan!

Consider another story. Telegu Desam Party (TDP), soon after its birth in 1982, fought state elections in 1983 against Congress. It was essentially projected as the fight of 'Amma' (Indira Gandhi) and 'Anna' (N.T. Rama Rao or NTR), the cinema star from Andhra Pradesh, at the time. Congress fared badly, winning just 60 seats in an assembly of 294, while TDP won 197 seats and formed the government.[5] It was the first non-Congress government in the state. But the government ran into trouble due to the personal ambitions of another important TDP leader, Nadendla Bhaskara Rao (NBR). What followed was a cinema script playing itself out.

In 1984, NTR had to go to the US for his heart surgery. NBR saw an opportunity to become the CM in NTR's absence. He revolted against NTR and claimed the support of 91 TDP MLAs and 57 Congress MLAs to form government. The then governor of the state, Thakur Ramlal, who happened to be a former Congress CM, dismissed the NTR government and allowed NBR to take oath as the CM and prove majority for the newly formed coalition in one month. In the drama that ensued, NTR came back and NBR failed to prove majority. NTR formed the government again and proved majority, removing the month-old CM, NBR.

The moment was heavy on political India's conscience. A number of political parties staged protests against NBR's machinations done in collaboration with Congress, which was trying to topple NTR's government. When NTR returned, he went on a statewide yatra which he called Dharma Yuddham, a war for justice. The nation's collective conscience was shaken.

Consider what happened barely 11 years later in the same state, and the same family. When NBR was busy breaking up TDP and wooing the MLAs in the 1984 coup, one of NTR's sons-in-law was making all efforts to keep the MLAs together in NTR's group in his absence. When NTR was reinstated, he made this son-in-law the general secretary of the party. This same son-in-law revolted against NTR in 1995, and became the CM in almost the same way. His name is Chandrababu Naidu, the current president of TDP, who was the CM of Andhra Pradesh from 1995 to 2004 and later, during 2014–19. Morality in politics had withered away, perhaps irreversibly.

But nothing beats the injuries that voters of Karnataka went through in post-poll coalitions. There have been three dominant parties in Karnataka, Congress, BJP and JD(S), the last one headed by H.D. Deve Gowda, India's coalition PM of the late 1990s. In 2004, in the Karnataka Vidhan Sabha polls for 224 seats, BJP secured 79, Congress 65 and JD(S) 58. No one reached a majority figure of 112. To keep BJP out, JD(S) and Congress formed a post-poll alliance, with Dharam Singh from Congress and Siddharamiah from JD(S) becoming CM and deputy CM respectively. This went on smoothly for two years. Then suddenly, Deve Gowda's son, H.D. Kumaraswamy, who also belonged to JD(S), uneasy with the rising power of Siddharamiah, pulled out the support of 46 JD(S) MLAs and joined hands with BJP to form another coalition government in the state.

This government did not last long. But try and imagine the utter disrespect for people who voted. People went to poll booths trusting that their preference would reach Bengaluru and power would be accorded justly. Those who voted for JD(S) did not want to vote for Congress and BJP. And yet, their own party politicians made a joke of their mandate, supporting competing parties throughout.

In the next 2008 Vidhan Sabha elections, BJP secured 110 seats, but it was still short of majority by a few seats. Where did these seats come from? Independent candidates. People with merely one seat were able to be part of the ruling coalition and wielded far more power than major parties in the opposition.

The 2018 Vidhan Sabha formation was like a movie. BJP secured 104 seats, while Congress and JD(S) bagged 80 and 37. Congress, already wary of BJP's advance in south India, gave unconditional support to the same Kumaraswamy who had earlier betrayed them and supported BJP in 2004. Fearing that BJP would try and woo the MLAs of Congress and JD(S), these MLAs were packed off to resorts in Bengaluru, Kochi and Hyderabad so that BJP could not 'poach' them. By some accounts, their mobile phones were taken away from them as well, so that no one could contact and lure them. Kumaraswamy became the CM with merely 38 seats out of 224.

Taking MLAs to a tourist resort so that they remain unreachable to rival party leaders is an interesting phenomenon of Indian electoral politics. It also has a name—'resort politics'; the only way to ensure loyalty is to 'resort arrest' loyalists minus phones and internet until the confidence vote or coup is executed. Karnataka has been a leader in this type of political manoeuvring, with instances emerging from as early as 1983 (Ramakrishna Hegde's time). Even in the NTR case discussed earlier, during his move to recapture lost power, he had also taken his MLAs to a resort in Bangalore, and then to Delhi. The 1995 coup against him by N. Chandrababu Naidu also had loyal MLAs being taken to a hotel in Hyderabad. In 2017, Sasikala took her MLAs to a resort near Chennai, cordoning them off from Panneerselvam's loyalists. Vilasrao Deshmukh, Maharashtra's former CM, packed his MLAs off to a luxury resort near Bangalore, away from opposition members of BJP–Shiv Sena in 2002. In 2000, when Nitish Kumar was desperately seeking to win the trust vote, Congress and RJD's MLAs were sent off to a hotel in Patna (Nitish lost the vote after seven days). In Gujarat, driven by an internal rivalry within BJP, in 1995, Shankarsinh Vaghela took away 47 MLAs to some resort in Madhya Pradesh, locking them up for seven days until the then CM Keshubhai Patel was replaced. Numbers, not ideas, determine political entry and exit. Anyone can cohabit with anyone, and ideologies are the last thing that they need for persuasion.

These are disappointing stories. They cry out about the disregard our electoral design has for the people of this country, who, like mute and meek participants, go to polling booths thinking they are sending their mandates and that their considerations will have importance. Post-election coalitions almost always lead to breach of trust of voters. When there were no pre-electoral alliances, post-electoral alliances were essential for government formation in cases of hung assemblies and the Parliament. Many parties had begun making pre-electoral alliances at the national level in the 1989 elections. However, multiple cases of post-electoral trading of MPs and MLAs make a laughing stock of voters' political choices. So much so that the democratic practice of elections nowadays is dominantly viewed as an exercise to capture power, rather than understanding and respecting voters' opinions.

COALITIONS GETTING MATURE

Interestingly, the last 20 years have seen the emergence of stable coalition politics at the national level. All four governments were able to run for full terms, despite being heavily coalesced. In 1999, BJP formed a pre-poll coalition of parties called the National Democratic Alliance (NDA) with a combination of more than 20 parties. BJP led the elections with 32 per cent seats and 24 per cent votes. The trailing Congress had got more votes, 28 per cent, but it was able to secure only 21 per cent seats (again, an inconvenient truth of the FPTP system). But with its coalition partners, NDA took charge of the country this time. And as clear departure from the past, NDA ruled India without any deterring trouble from coalition partners for its entire term. One might say that the political class, which had been tasting the bitter nature of coalitions in the previous decade, had begun learning the art of maintaining them. By sheer numbers, BJP managed to organise a heavy list of partners for five years. One may not doubt the prowess of Atal Bihari Vajpayee as a statesman to have held it together carefully. (See Table 6.1 for the 1999 coalition matrix.)

But they were overconfident, buoyed by the rising sentiments of the Indian economy (which was in a boom mode during 2003–04, with a growth rate[6] of more than 8 per cent annually). With its victory in the state assembly elections of Rajasthan, Chhattisgarh and Madhya Pradesh, BJP became highly confident of its popularity. In stark similarity to the move made by Indira

Table 6.1 Seats won by parties in 1999 Lok Sabha elections

BJP and Allies	*Seats*	*Congress(I) and Allies*	*Seats*	*Left Parties*	*Seats*	*Others*	*Seats*
BJP	182	Congress (1)	114	CPI	4	BSP	14
BJD	10	AIADMK	10	CPI(M)	33	SP	26
DMK	12	KC(M)	1	FB	2	NC	4
HVC	1	ML	2	KC(J)	1	Independent and Others	21
Others	21	RJD	7	RSP	3		
INLD	5	RLD	2				
JD(U)	21						
LOKTANTRIK	2						
MDMK	4						
MGRADMK	1						
MSCP	1						
PMK	5						
SAD	2						
SS	15						
TRINAMOOL	8						
TDP	29						
IND.(Maneka)	1						
Total	299	Total	136	Total	43	Total	65

Source: N. Jose Chander, *Coalition Politics: The Indian Experience*

Gandhi, of dissolving the Lok Sabha earlier than the end of the term in 1971, BJP announced the elections six months ahead of schedule. However, unlike Congress in 1971, the NDA didn't have the fortune of forming the government again. Departing from predictions of political pundits and the expectations of its member parties, NDA lost the elections of 2004.

BJP, however, showed that coalition governments can be stable. This had been one of the reasons for them to mellow down the hardline stand they exhibited in the rath yatra phase of the early 1990s. Congress had learnt the art, but formed an alliance only after the election results of 2004 were announced. It thus reaffirmed the general trend of coalitional governments at the Centre since 1989. This was another example of the ever-rising importance of regional players. Congress formed a new post-poll alliance with regional parties calling it United Progressive Alliance (UPA).[7] It is important to note that Congress had entered into formal seat-sharing with some regional players from many states, notably in Andhra Pradesh, Tamil Nadu, Maharashtra, UP, J&K and Bihar. Except for UP, the performance of the alliance was encouraging. Congress contested on 414 of 543 seats from the Lok Sabha. This indicates Congress' acceptance of the strong influence of regional parties. Regional parties used this opportunity well in their favour. The UPA government worked under a common minimum programme and completed its full term. For the first time, instead of two national parties contesting each other, we now had two coalitions contesting each other. The two pavilions are shown in Table 6.2.

The UPA government came back to power after the 2009 elections. This outcome was exceptional because, for the first time since 1984, the incumbent government was re-elected. It is interesting to note that BJP performed quite well in many state elections in 2008 as against Congress, but lost in the national elections of 2009. In 2008 UPA faced its first confidence vote

TABLE 6.2 Seats won by parties in 2004 Lok Sabha elections

Parties	*Seats*	*Votes (%)*	*Parties*	*Seats*	*Votes (%)*	*Parties*	*Seats*	*Votes (%)*
Congress and allies	219	35.82	NDA	189	35.91	Left Front	61	8.34
Congress	145	26.69	BJP	138	22.16	CPI(M)	43	5.69
RJD	21	2.22	Shiv Sena	12	1.82	CPI	10	1.4
DMK	16	1.82	BJD	11	1.31	RSP	3	0.44
NCP	9	1.78	JD(U)	8	2.29	FBL	3	0.35
PMK	6	0.56	Akali Dal (B)	8	0.91	KEC	1	0.09
JMM	5	0.48	TDP	5	3.06	IND(LF)	1	0.08
THS	5	0.63	WBTC	2	2.08			
LJNP	4	0.72	MNF	1	0.05	Other Parties	70	19.93
MDMK	4	0.43	SDF	1	0.04	SP	36	4.33
PDP	1	0.08	IEDP	1	0.07	BSP	19	5.33
MUL	1	0.2	NDF	1	0.18	RLD	3	0.64
RPI(A)	1	0.09	IND (BJP)	1	0.18	JD(S)	3	1.48
IND(INC)	1	0.02	SJP(R)	1	0.09	AGP	2	0.53
						NC	2	0.13
						Other Independents	1	3.79
						NIP	1	0.09
						MIM	1	0.11
						Others	1	5.56

Source: The Hindu, 20 May 2004.

in the Lok Sabha. The reason for the confidence motion was the withdrawal of the left parties from the UPA government due to the latter's nuclear deal with the US. The general wave in the country and among many important parties during those times was in favour of the nuclear deal.[8] The UPA government won the confidence motion with 275 votes against 256 votes by the opposition. A year later, in 2009, UPA returned to power and successfully ran the government for its full term.

During 2009, the names of coalition became interesting. UPA was United Progressive Alliance and NDA was National Democratic Alliance. The keywords 'progressive' and 'democratic' were taken up. So, what was earlier called as the Left Front in 2004 became Third Front and Fourth Front in 2009. Quite funny actually—these parties had already relegated themselves to the third position, somewhat akin to many non-Western country scholars calling their own nations as third world countries.

Table 6.3 lists this down. Compare it with 2004. The Third Front, led by CPI(M), comprised many who were earlier part of UPA. The Fourth Front also had similar characteristics. The Fourth Front was interesting too—SP, RJD and LJP (Lok Janshakti Party) perhaps thought that they would strategically place themselves separately, and later, offer support to whoever won. In this way, even with tiny number of seats, they would still occupy positions in North and South Block. Coalition governments were the only governments out there, in some sense.

This is an important point to note. Voters do not think like this, and the emergence of coalitions and ambitions of regional parties operate at a very different scale, unconnected from the voters' preferences or emotions. Think of yourself as a mid-career politician, running for elections on a Congress ticket for a couple of decades already. Someone mighty in Congress circles leaves the party for a variety of reasons. This person is now making

TABLE 6.3 Seats won by parties in 2009 Lok Sabha elections

Parties	*Seats*	*Parties*	*Seats*	*Parties*	*Seats*	*Parties*	*Seats*
UPA	262	NDA	159	Third Front	80	Fourth Front	27
Congress	206	Bharatiya Janata Party	116	Bahujan Samaj Party	21	Samajwadi Party	23
Trinamool Congress	19	Janata Dal (United)	20	CPI-M	16	Rashtriya Janata Dal	4
DMK	18	Shiv Sena	11	Biju Janata Dal	14	Others	15
Nationalist Congress Party	9	Rashtriya Lok Dal	5	AIADMK	9	Independents	9
National Conference	3	Akali Dal	4	Telegu Desam Party	6	Assam United Democratic Front	1
Jharkhand Mukti Morcha	2	Telangana Rashtra Samithi	2	CPI	4	Bahujan Vikas Aaghadi	1
Muslim League Kerala State Committee	2	Asom Gana Parishad	1	Janata Dal-Secular	3	Swabhimani Paksha	1

Parties	*Seats*	*Parties*	*Seats*	*Parties*	*Seats*	*Parties*	*Seats*
All India Majlis-e-Ittehadul Muslimeen	1			Forward Bloc	2	Nagaland People's Front	1
Bodoland People's Front	1			Revolutionary Socialist Party	2	Sikkim Democratic Front	1
Kerala Congress (Mani)	1			MDMK	1	VCK	1
				Haryana Janhit Congress	1		
				Jharkhand Vikas Morcha (Prajatantrik)	1		

Source: *Hindustan Times*, 17 May 2009.

a new party. Would you defect from Congress and join them? Well, you make calculative assessments. If this person secures a good number of seats through their loyalists, they may well be a kingmaker in coalition politics era. They will have 2 per cent seats in Parliament, but perhaps just needed for the leading party to form a majority in the House. This 2 per cent is more valuable for the winning party than its own seats. With only their own seats, they are nothing. With 2 per cent more, they form the government. This arithmetic makes the person carrying the 2 per cent vote more important than all other long-serving loyalists in that party. If you think this leader has it in them, you will join them and later, as one of the important members of a small party whose support led to the formation of a government, you may get a chance to occupy positions in the capital. Numbers, and only numbers, matter.

The 2014 election changed the history of the country because it produced the strongest mandate 30 years later (the last election with such strong mandate was in 1984). Even though the victory went to the NDA alliance, BJP alone secured a clear majority and was capable of forming the government on its own. Interestingly, while the popularity of Narendra Modi helped BJP in north India, especially the Hindi-speaking belt, the performance of the party in the southern states was not so promising. For instance, BJP won 190 seats in the Hindi-speaking region with a strong 43.7 per cent vote share. However, its tally in the rest of India was merely 92 seats with a 22.3 per cent vote share.[9] Despite the rise of BJP's presence in non-Hindi speaking states in 2019 elections (as discussed in the previous chapter), it is hard to deny that regional parties and their popularities are here to stay, and coalitions cannot be done away with so easily.

WHAT ABOUT MY TRUST?

The rise of coalition governments, Christophe Jeffrelot argues, is attributed to increasing federalism and decentralisation, which make states more 'central' to the rise of regional parties. These parties claim huge number of votes even though lesser seats, and also result in the decline of national-level leaders and parties.[10] But within these parameters also lies an underlying worry about coalition politics as defining the nature of the Indian electoral results.

The tussle between ideologies fuels such worries. Consider what happened in J&K in 2014. BJP and PDP are so far apart from each other in their ideologies, and yet, they formed a coalition government. Before the government could complete its term, BJP pulled the plug, withdrawing its support to PDP, triggering a coalition circus and politicians playing trapeze artists, holding and leaving each other with their careers hanging in the air. In fact, of five coalition governments in J&K since 1975, only one (National Conference during 2009–14) was able to run for the full term.

Coalition governments destroy hard-earned faith in the electoral system. When we hire a lawyer, we expect that person to be governed by fiduciary duties. If my lawyer begins negotiating with the lawyer on the other side, and they deliberately delay the case for their private benefit, where will my faith go? The politicians who we vote for assume responsibilities with the same fiduciary duties as a lawyer. This political leader is my trustee. And if they engage in horse-trading, taking sides with competing parties who I did not vote for at all, what will my faith be relegated to? In time, I will not only lose faith in the party, but also in the institution of elections, or democracy itself.

APPENDIX

TABLE 6.4(a) NDA and UPA through elections, 1999–2009

Alliance	*1999* *Party*	*2004* *Party*	*2009* *Party*
NDA	Bharatiya Janta Party	Bharatiya Janta Party	Bharatiya Janta Party
	Telugu Desam	Shiv Sena	Shiv Sena
	Janata Dal (United)	Biju Janata Dal	Biju Janata Dal
	Shiv Sena	Shiromani Akali Dal	Shiromani Akali Dal
	Dravida Munetra Kazhagam	Janata Dal (United)	Janata Dal (United)
	Biju Janata Dal	Telugu Desam	Telugu Desam
	All India Trinamool Congress	All India Trinamool Congress	All India Trinamool Congress
	Pattali Makkal Katchi	Indian Federal Democratic Party	Indian Federal Democratic Party
	Indian National Lok Dal	Nagaland Peoples Front	Nagaland People's Front
	Marumalarchi Dravida Munnetra Kazhagam	Sikkim Democratic Front	Sikkim Democratic Front
	Shiromani Akali Dal	Mizo National Front	Mizo National Front
	Akhil Bhartiya Lok Tantrik Congress	Independents	Independents
	Independents	All India Anna Dravida Munnetra Kazhagam	All India Anna Dravida Munnetra Kazhagam
	M.G.R. Anna D.M. Kazhagam		

Alliance	*1999* *Party*	*2004* *Party*	*2009* *Party*
	Himachal Vikash Congress		
	Sikkim Democratic Front		
	Democratic Bahujan Samaj Morcha		
	Tamizhaga Rajiv Congress		
	Bihar People's Party		
	Arunachal Congress		
UPA	Indian National Congress	Indian National Congress	Indian National Congress
	All India Anna Dravida Munnetra Kazhagam	Rashtriya Janata Dal	Rashtriya Janata Dal
	Rashtriya Janata Dal	Dravida Munetra Kazhagam	Dravida Munetra Kazhagam
	Rashtriya Lok Dal	Nationalist Congress Party	Nationalist Congress Party
	Muslim League Kerala State Committee	Pattali Makkal Katchi	Pattali Makkal Katchi
	Bharipa Bahujan Mahasangh	Telangana Rashtra Samithi	Telangana Rashtra Samithi
	Kerala Congress(M)	Lok Jan Shakti Party	Lok Jan Shakti Party
	Communist Party of India	Jharkhand Mukti Morcha	Jharkhand Mukti Morcha
	Communist Party of India (Marxist)	Marumalarchi Dravida Munnetra Kazhagam	Marumalarchi Dravida Munnetra Kazhagam

Alliance	*1999* *Party*	*2004* *Party*	*2009* *Party*
	Republican Party of India	Communist Party of India (Marxist)	Communist Party of India (Marxist)
	Marxist Coordination	Communist Party of India	Communist Party of India
	All India Trinamool Congress	Muslim League Kerala State Committee	Muslim League Kerala State Committee
		Jammu & Kashmir Peoples Democratic Party	Jammu & Kashmir Peoples Democratic Party
		Republican Party of India (A)	Republican Party of India (A)
		Kerala Congress (M)	Kerala Congress (M)
		Janata Dal (Secular)	Janata Dal (Secular)
		Independents (Contested on 3 seats)	Independents
		Arunachal Congress	Arunachal Congress
		Republican Party of India	Republican Party of India
		Party for Democratic Socialism	Party for Democratic Socialism
		People's Republican Party	People's Republican Party

Source: Collated from www.indiavotes.com.

TABLE 6.4(b) NDA and UPA through elections, 2014 and 2019

	2014	
Alliance	*Party*	*Party*
BJP	Bharatiya Janta Party	Bharatiya Janta Party
	Shiv Sena	Shiv Sena
	Telugu Desam	Janata Dal (United)
	Lok Jan Shakti Party	Lok Jan Shakti Party
	Shiromani Akali Dal	Shiromani Akali Dal
	Rashtriya Lok Samta Party	Apna Dal (Soneylal)
	Apna Dal	All India Anna Dravida Munnetra Kazhagam
	Swabhimani Paksha	All Jharkhand Students Union
	Pattali Makkal Katchi	Nationalist Democratic Progressive Party
	All India N.R. Congress	Rashtriya Loktantrik Party
	Naga People's Front	All India N.R. Congress
	National People's Party	Bodoland Peoples Front
	Independents	Desiya Murpokku Dravida Kazhagam
	Revolutionary Socialist Party of Kerala (Bolshevik)	Pattali Makkal Katchi
	Desiya Murpokku Dravida Kazhagam	Asom Gana Parisad
	Republican Party of India (A)	Kerala Congress (Anti-merger Group)
	Marumalarchi Dravida Munnetra Kazhagam	Bharath Dharma Jana Sena
	Rashtriya Samaj Paksha	Tamil Maanila Congress (Moopanar)
	Haryana Janhit Congress (BL)	

	2014	
Alliance	*Party*	*Party*
UPA	Indian National Congress	Indian National Congress
	Nationalist Congress Party	Dravida Munetra Kazhagam
	Rashtriya Janata Dal	Nationalist Congress Party
	Jharkhand Mukti Morcha	Indian Union Muslim League
	Indian Union Muslim League	Communist Party of India
	Revolutionary Socialist Party	Janata Dal (Secular)
	Kerala Congress(M)	Kerala Congress(M)
	Communist Party of India	Revolutionary Socialist Party
	Bahujan Vikas Aaghadi	Jharkhand Mukti Morcha
	Bodoland People's Front	Viduthalai Chiruthaigal Katchi
	Rashtriya Lok Dal	Rashtriya Lok Samta Party
	Jammu & Kashmir National Conference	Vikassheel Insaan Party
	Mahan Dal	Jan Adhikar Party
	Socialist Janta (Democratic)	Hindustani Awam Morcha (Secular)
		Jharkhand Vikas Morcha (Prajatantrik)
		Rashtriya Janata Dal
		Bahujan Vikas Aaghadi
		Swabhimani Paksha
		Communist Party Of India (Marxist-Leninist) (Liberation)

Source: Collated from www.indiavotes.com.

7

Two Issues on Electoral Reforms

Francis Fukuyama, in his book *The Origins of Political Order*, compares Indian democracy with sausage making. He says the closer you get to it, the more repulsive it becomes![1] Think about it—34 per cent of MPs in the 2014 Lok Sabha elections had criminal cases against them, and those with serious criminal charges (murder, kidnapping, physical assault) made up 21 per cent of the House. These figures have been increasing, as Milan Vaishnav illustrates in his excellent work,[2] compiling data from the Association for Democratic Reforms. Numbers in state legislatures closely follow this statistic too. What's more, candidates with a criminal case against them have three times higher likelihood of winning the seat as compared to a clean candidate. As Vaishnav reminds us, headlines like 'In India's politics, jail is the badge of honour', 'India's jailbirds win elections', or for that matter, 'Criminals flourish in Indian elections' no longer surprise us.

And if criminalisation of politics is not enough, one needs to open the black box of party funds and campaign finance. Vaishnav's work is instructive indeed. Almost three-quarters of party funding comes from contestants who bring it from unidentified sources. No surprises then that MPs—by some estimates that came out in 2013—more than doubled their average wealth during their term. Eighty-two per cent of 2014 Lok Sabha members were crorepatis, with the average Congress

MP being worth ₹16 crores and BJP's, ₹11 crore. The total assets of 2019 Lok Sabha candidates was more than ₹27,000 crores. The 2019 Lok Sabha was 1,400 times richer than its people. India's per capita average monthly income is ₹12,000!

These are just some of the issues that make you repel from Indian democracy when seen up close. There is just so much more to derail our pride about the democratic freedom we have had in our independent history. While expectation of transparency, decriminalised politics, clean campaign finance, low rates of defection, and peaceful electoral experiences seem like hollow words in the context of today's politics, they are often at the top of most electoral reform voices. Santhanam Committee (1962), Wanchoo Direct Taxes Enquiry Commission (1970), Dinesh Goswami Committee (specifically on electoral reforms, 1990), Vohra Committee (on criminalisation of politics, 1993) have all made powerful sets of recommendations for electoral reforms. But much is left to be desired when it comes to the execution of many of those recommendations.

The prevailing discourse carries a contextual understanding. It converges mainly on money and crime. But a structural feature of our voting methods, electoral politics and arithmetic game—the bedrock on which corrupt practices flourish—is often ignored. Perhaps if we can redesign and restructure the fundamental design of our electoral method, we may see a marked reduction in the ills that originate as a by-product. These are closely connected issues that are woven into the fabric of electoral politics about voting as a method. And that is what we focus upon.

What happens to my vote after polling gets over, is a crucial black box that most of us trust blindly. How our votes are calculated and how our mandate is understood, is a fundamental design issue of our democracy. And to take this black box as given, without gauging its implication, is almost like missing out on the fundamental assumptions of our democracy at work. For instance, seat and vote share difference will determine, to a large extent, the emergence of the culture of horse-trading, rampant defection and sale–purchase of MPs/MLAs. Similarly, whether we elect our representatives directly or simply vote a party into power, which in turn elects its leader, will have far-reaching implications on the culture of political morality and types of governments we will inherit.

These issues are fundamental to electoral reforms and emerge directly from the nature of problems the book is concerned about. Must we have a presidential or a parliamentary democracy? Must we have a different type of representation rather than the first-past-the-post (FPTP) system that leaks mandates significantly? And if so, how could the new system(s) look like?

ISSUE ONE: PARLIAMENTARY OR PRESIDENTIAL?

Elections are to people's power what banks are to their money. A tiny amount of money which is of no immediate use to us can be hugely valuable collectively. What can hardly buy us monthly groceries, if collected over time, can build dams and launch satellites. Banks take small amounts of capital from each of us (deposits) and pump them into select individuals (loans) who can do things with that collective money. And as custodians of our power, banks are governed by rules, just like the Constitution sets out rules of governments and electoral games.

The Constitution spelled out the method. The Constituent Assembly members may have had a vision of politics, political association and leadership, in a somewhat Aristotelian sense (only in the epistemic sense, for Aristotle was not a fan of democracy!). The Indian freedom struggle had been far more than just a claim on geographical territory. It was a struggle for ideas, civilisational pursuit and competing versions of modernity and philosophies. That is why the debates of the Constituent

Assembly offer a rich tapestry of philosophical arguments, held most lucidly, thoughtfully and with profound level of collective camaraderie and politeness. The debates invoked a diverse range of perspectives from a diverse coterie of Indians from all corners. A group so committed and erudite that it puts the present-day Parliament to shame.

But the type of electoral method to be chosen for selecting our leaders, however, was also influenced by global affairs, methods followed in various countries and particularly the models set out by our colonisers. One cannot forget that Ambedkar and Nehru had gone to that very country to study. Nor can one ignore the influence of British promulgated laws and acts; most notably, the Government of India Act, 1935.

The Draft Constitution provided for a parliamentary form of government for India. This meant that the Constitution enabled conditions for a Britain-like parliamentary democracy to flourish. This type of government is characterised by an executive who is part and answerable to the legislature (Parliament). The executive branch of the government, vested in the PMs and their council of ministers, is part of the Parliament itself. Here, the voters elect their Parliament leaders from amongst several parties, and the party, in turn, chooses the head of the government. Also, here, the head of the state is different from head of the government (the President in India or monarchy in Britain represents the head of the state).

The model is a classic Westminster style, a method that the British had adopted historically for a variety of reasons, perhaps inspired from their unique experience of the relationship of their Parliament with the Crown, and from the events unfolding in the Glorious Revolution in 1688. Beginning as a consulting sounding board for the Crown through the twelfth and thirteenth centuries, Parliament in England was not a new affair, and was primarily called upon when the King needed money for wars. Fed up of these incessant and arbitrary demands, by the seventeenth century, the Parliament had begun revolting against the Crown. The Parliament won, but continued to have the Crown installed, after a series of credible commitments from the Crown to the public (through Parliament) were made.[3] Over time, the nominal order of the union was vested with the Crown, but the de facto power was lying in the Parliament (House of Commons). The de facto ruler, therefore, had to be chosen from within the House of Commons. India was not the only one. John Bright, the British politician, had remarked that England was the 'mother of parliaments' as early as 1865—manifested in parliaments set out across the world in almost all British colonies.

This was not the case with America. Americans wanted to ensure they didn't follow anything that their coloniser, Britain, was forcing them to. They reasoned why they would not adopt a parliamentary system of governments, but instead, a presidential model, built and inspired by the political philosophy of Montesquieu, whose ideas on the separation of executive, legislature and judiciary had profound influence on the administrative orders of the world. They have an independent executive, the President and their Cabinet, which remains separate from the legislature (Congress). While this increases the likelihood of authoritarianism since the executive is independent and is difficult to be removed (impeached), but on the same count, it makes the executive stable and decisive.

By the time India gained its independence, the story of the American war and the country's constitution had become old. Nation states in twentieth century had been experimenting with Westminster models, and this was something that the departing British had also been putting more faith into. Inspired by the ideas of federalism and parliamentary democracy, India's founding fathers and mothers scripted a similar algorithm for the political machine, much of it retaining the essence from the codes written by English colonisers. We cannot help but remind ourselves here of Ashis Nandy's brilliant weaving of an argument in his book *The Intimate Enemy*.[4] A nation does not colonise when it physically territorialises a region. It colonises when the colonised start thinking like the coloniser, and begin adopting the value system of the coloniser. India had been a real colony, in not just continuing with most of the codes, laws and by-laws that the British had drilled down through the last century, but also in the choice of the form of government. The new leadership, which was Indian in blood, remained English in thought. In fact, for a variety of reasons that are naturally observed in power-shifting epochs, here too, the elites retained much of the status quo. They did not want to risk the hard-earned power and expected peace in times of monumental change of institutions. Therefore, they perhaps felt safer in largely continuing with the existing models.

The Constituent Assembly debated many clauses indeed and surely there were some radical, imaginative departures. Of the total 7,000 plus amendments tabled, the committee deliberated, discussed and disposed of almost 2,500 of them.

Whether India is suitable for a parliamentary form of democracy was debated at some length as well. Not as much as one would have hoped today, though. A number of interventions during the Constituent Assembly debates were made, even as early as July 1947, when Syed Kazi Karimuddin from Maharashtra moved the House with a clause for a non-parliamentary executive that could not be removed by the Parliament in the fashionable no-confidence circus. In a prophetic vision, he outlined the possibility that future elections may not be able to yield vast majorities for one party and then, groupism would lead to favouritism and nepotism with ministers serving the party rather than the people of India. Mehboob Ali Baig from Madras explained how and why the British model had been largely a result of historical accidents and may not have the elements that would suit India. He was seriously concerned with the parliamentary form of democracy. He felt such a system would attract undemocratic selection of council of ministers within the Parliament, who would not be controlled by the electorate but by Parliament members. This, he highlighted, meant that the executive was not directly elected by the people even if the parliamentarians were. The executive, being comprised of party members, he feared, would form a cabinet serving the interest of the party, which also meant serving the interest of some people and some communities rather than Indians as a whole. Quite spot on today, one would say.

When Ambedkar moved the resolution to consider the Draft Constitution in November 1948, he gave an elaborate explanation for the choice of the parliamentary executive. He suggested that there were two competing qualities of any executive, namely stability and responsibility. But there was a trade-off between the two—one cannot coexist in the same degree as the other; you increase one and the other will decrease. He used the examples of America and Britain and explained how the US favours stability while Britain, responsibility to the legislature. The American President is not part of the legislature and does not need the legislature's support for its functioning, while the British PM is responsible to its Parliament and will depend on the majority for its sustenance. For India, he said, '… [t]he daily assessment of responsibility which is not available under the American system, it is felt far more effective than the periodic assessment and far more necessary in a country like India. The Draft Constitution in recommending the parliamentary system of executive has preferred more responsibility to more stability.' Ambedkar categorically departed from the idea of division of powers.

Karimuddin, in his vocal plea for an American style of government, reminded Ambedkar that Ambedkar himself, in his book *States and Minorities*, had mentioned that a non-parliamentary executive possessed greater advantage for protecting minority rights (in parliamentary system, the executive enjoys their position at the interest of their party members, who may not approve of protection of minorities that didn't vote for the party, and consequently may not allow executive orders to the benefit of minority). Ambedkar's design, therefore, could not have been thoughtless. As a man with utmost sense of righteousness and a sharp analytical mind, he would have carefully weighed in various competing ideas and chosen a parliamentary executive, he opined. Yet, the House was not convinced.

Baig, during the debates in 1948, continued his emphatic appeal about the high likelihood of corruption being seeded in such a parliamentary executive where party loyalty and not the interest of the nation was central for the executive. In explaining to the assembly as to how the executive in such a system lies at the 'mercy of hostile groups in their own party', he reminded them about the opinion of the Simon-Attlee Commission in which it was suggested that, '… the Ministry is so much engaged in cajoling, in satisfying its Parliament that there is hardly time to look after its administration or to put into effect its schemes.'[5]

In fact, the American example had constantly inspired these debates. Hussain Imam, another member, went into the details of the American system and said that '… [i]t is wrong to say that the executive in the US only comes in for a corrective after four years' term of the President. He is subject to day-to-day control and that control is far greater in the case of the Senate Committees and the House of Representatives than it is in the case of the British Parliament.'[6]

In arriving at the answer to what type of government would suit India, Ambedkar had relied on the structure more than the method. There is no doubt that barring a tiny episode in 1975–77, the constitutional aspiration of ensuring an executive that remains responsible to the legislature and does not turn authoritarian has remained fulfilled. But the idea that in being responsible to the legislature, the executive will remain responsible to the people may not have been so straightforward.

Think about a scenario. What if the Indian president was chosen through an election, rather than by an electoral college (which comprises the MPs and the MLAs) as is done today? This person, by virtue of being chosen by the people directly, will have direct accountability to the people of India, cutting across party lines and acting as the head of the nation, who is stable as well as responsible to the people of India directly rather than to any legislator.

K.T. Shah, the scholar and playwright politician within the Constituent Assembly (who moved one of the largest number of amendments during the debate), proposed the presidential system too. He said, in November 1948, that the president, '... must be in a position to command the confidence of the people, be they majority or minority ... [be] a real representative of the people, and one elected to function as the head of the State and as its representative.... After all, your Parliament is liable to be dissolved at any time... The local legislatures in the States may also be dissolved. The President, on the other hand, will be elected for a definite period. As such, he will be outside the turmoil of party passion, will be outside the momentary ups and downs, the vicissitudes of parliamentary fortunes; and will be much more likely to maintain balance, and to give a degree of stability to our Government which it may not have under party passions.'

Ambedkar dismissed this plea on two grounds. First, he raised the question of the crippling administrative costs and required machinery to conduct an election across the country with his estimate of 15.8 crore people queueing up for elections should president's elections be held. This size of the electorate, he said, 'forbids our adopting adult suffrage in the matter of the election of the President.' This response ignores that in the context of independent India, presidential elections in the manner K.T. Shah was proposing could have happened simultaneously with that of the Lok Sabha with little additional cost. But more importantly, at the level of principles, if we were deliberately choosing to have a less stable but a government more accountable to legislature, election costs are unlikely to have been weighing so prominently on anyone's mind.

Second, he reminded the House that the president in India was a nominal figurehead, and if anyone were to compare the American president with their Indian counterpart, it was the Indian PM and not the Indian president. Since people of India were electing their PM through their representatives anyway, getting the president of India elected was a futile exercise.

But the point of K.T. Shah's proposal was to address exactly this. We may understand the necessity of electing our president, not from the point of view of 'electing' alone, but from the point of view of electing the head of the state 'directly'! K.T. Shah was a firm believer of the separation of all three pillars of the government, and had tirelessly expressed the need for a non-parliamentary executive for India. This proposal was not approved (along with his proposal to make education an eligibility criterion to be an MP, and for candidates to disclose their wealth).

K.T. Shah's obituary published in the *Economic and Political Weekly*, poetically noted that he '... would have preferred to be a Don Quixote and tilt the windmills rather than deliberately choose to remain ineffective.' The leaders and assembly members of the time were men and women of character and spirit. During the debates in the winters of 1948, the assembly, in addition to paying homage to Mahatma Gandhi, also mourned the passing away of Jinnah. It sent its 'heartfelt sympathies to [its] brethren across the frontier', in an act of dignified conduct that has unfortunately become alien in the political discourse in the India of today. Many of us are not aware that Professor Shah was the runner-up in the election of the first president of India, which Rajendra Prasad won. That election was based on electoral college, not the way he had envisaged and proposed.

The Constitution was adopted, but the debate today has fresh colours. Scholars, commentators and the new opinionated generation of students are often found from their dinner tables to public forums, discussing whether a US-type presidential democracy is desirable for a country like India. Well, if the executive becomes independent, wouldn't that be almost like centralising power in the hands of one individual, which is a perfect recipe for authoritarianism, a dangerous place for a country with multiple ethnicities, religions and castes? But then, the arrest of the executive's power by the legislative does not help allay these fears—what if the party with strong majority in the parliament is the same to which the executive belongs? And if the party dominating the legislature is different from that of the executive's, then won't the legislature stall governance, leading to an administrative stalemate? Perhaps the even more difficult question is that of what, then, happens to state governments and chief ministers? Should they be directly elected and the executive then kept separate from the legislature?

Why not, those in favour of the presidential system of democracy would say. Not just the executive of the country, but also of the state, mayors and panchayat chiefs should all be elected directly by the people. Surely, the threat of authoritarianism remains, but that is not completely done away with in a parliamentary democracy either—think about the democracy-abortive steps taken by Indira Gandhi in the 1970s. But if we think about making it presidential across the board, we know that the power of New Delhi will be balanced by competing power centres in Lucknow, Guwahati, Bengaluru, Thiruvananthapuram, and so on, which would also have independent executives acting from there.

More importantly, in a parliamentary democracy, the legislature cannot really hold the executive accountable since the government has majority in the House. In such a system, the executive is responsible to the ruling party, not the people. Staying in power and toeing the party line becomes the focus of the leader, rather than governing the country because the latter may require taking decisions against party lines.

Also, in a presidential system, there is a higher level of efficiency since power is centralised. The leader would be in a position to cut across party lines and build issue-based coalition, making temporary alliances with the parliamentarians, rather than finding themselves locked in party-based monolithic oppositions to a bill. When we choose leaders directly, we are also able to view their performance closely and intimately, and can make an informed opinion. Parliamentary executive, particularly when the leader is not announced before the election, is like a black box—we vote for a candidate without knowing who will be the captain of the ship, and are often surprised at the chosen leader (think about Manmohan Singh in the 2004 Lok Sabha elections or Yogi Adityanath in the 2017 UP Vidhan Sabha elections!). Presidential form is an exercise of direct accountability. It also allows talent outside party politics to emerge. Outsiders who may be more capable than the insiders who seek rent, get a chance to demonstrate their leadership skills. This way, excellent administrators or leaders with humility and integrity, rather than old party loyalists, really get to run the affairs of the country.

Most of all, in the type of coalition governments that India has witnessed in the last three decades makes the cost of running governments rather high. The presidential form may reduce this massive cost by providing stability to the election process at national and state levels. This can be achieved rather simply, at least, logistically. The costs of organising elections are huge indeed, and therefore this must be accompanied by assembly elections to choose members of parliament or state assemblies.

Ambedkar was wary of election costs in India, and so was Nehru. Both of them had expressed their displeasure of holding elections frequently.

Sometimes, however, the debate feels like a burdensome exercise, because such a move may simply be practically not feasible. The parliamentary system of democracy is the basic structure of our Constitution. And any amendment to the basic structure of the Constitution is impossible.

Yet, if the Supreme Court takes a different view, and if this motion is discussed, when a directly elected leader who operates independent of the parliament is chosen, it fulfils the electoral philosophy at a more general level. As of today, we vote for our constituency leaders. But we vote keeping in mind our hopes and aspirations laid onto the central executive. Many of us truly vote for Naveen Patnaik or Narendra Modi, and not for the candidate contesting in Cuttack or Varanasi. In that, the voting system creates huge distortions. Many people, knowing their chosen candidate, will not be able to translate their victory in parliament because their party may not form the majority government, may not even be choosing to vote. It leads to a huge loss of electorate, given the psychological inaction this system brings with it.

Perhaps more difficult than having the Supreme Court of India change its view, is the retention of status quo by the elites today. Almost all political parties have elites that will want to hold onto their privileges. A presidential system may disrupt existing power equations and the game plan necessary to operate in the power corridors of India. They would rather stick to what they know and are comfortably enjoying the fruits of, than experiment with, a new system. The resistance to change is actually from the incumbent parties, who now get to choose their own leaders and run the system. Often, inefficient institutions get ossified in time because switching costs become too high (scholars call it 'path dependency'). And that is what may happen here. A strong political will is what we really need.

ISSUE TWO: PROPORTIONAL REPRESENTATION

An overarching scepticism that the book attempts to uncover is that of the FPTP system. This system considers the seats won by a party, not the votes. Whether one wins by one vote or 1 lakh votes doesn't matter. The winner will have the same power in parliament in both cases. We questioned if this seems to make sense from the perspective of fairness and objectivity of a democratic process in terms of preference aggregation.

Let's look at some facts. In 2014, BJP came to power, dominating the entire parliament with mere 31 per cent votes. This is the lowest vote share that has yielded Delhi to any party in India's history. Since not everyone comes out to vote, this translates into BJP coming to power with the support of 20 per cent eligible voters, which is 14 per cent of India's population. This is close to 17 crore people deciding the fate of more than 130 crores. And how many people did not vote for BJP? A whopping 55 crores! So, the number of people who did not want the BJP to come to power was three times the number of people who wanted it. This is just an example. The story will repeat for any other party in any other elections. Consider, for instance, the following:

In 2014, Congress' vote share was 19.3 per cent, with 44 seats.

In 2009, BJP's vote share was 18.5 per cent, with 116 seats.

Consider further, in 2014:

BSP's vote share in UP: 20 per cent. Seats: zero.

DMK's vote share in TN: 27 per cent. Seats: zero.

Congress' vote share in Orissa: 26 per cent. Seats: zero.

BJP's vote share in Bengal: 22 per cent. Seats: one.

Left Front's vote share in Bengal: 30 per cent. Seats: two.

These are major imbalances. The source of such leakages is the FPTP system. When every person's vote has the same value, and the focus is to discover the clear winner—not clear mandate—then the FPTP system serves its purpose. But what must be the aim of any election exercise? Should it be to find the winner or find aggregated preference? The book has highlighted the problem in some detail. The question is, how can this be rectified, or addressed?

Countries have adopted different types of electoral methods to build a fairer system of preference aggregation. Australia and Ireland, for instance, get their citizens to rank the candidates, rather than just select one of them. Despite its wide prevalence, including in India for electing our president, there is little that people know about it. Since this forms the backbone of most alternative voting methods in the world, in contrast with the FPTP system, it is important we discuss it at some length.

The method is called the instant runoff voting system (sometimes known as preferential voting method). Since the voters have mentioned their preferential ranks against each candidate, we know their order of preference. They don't necessarily need to choose one against all the rest. It offers a better competition of candidates. When voters have made their choices, we find the total number of times the candidate has secured the first choice. The candidate least preferred as the first choice is then removed from the table. The space thus emptying up is filled up by the next candidate preferred below the top choice by that voter. This process is repeated until we find the winner. Consider, for example, a family of eight members wanting to decide what to do on a Sunday, among the following options that they have: go to a zoo, a long drive, a movie theatre or perhaps simply rest. Let's say they decide to vote it all out through the preferential voting system. They all put their preferences on a paper and their final tally looks like this:

	Anu	*Leo*	*Sia*	*Mir*	*Mom*	*Dad*	*Grandpa*	*Grandma*
First preference	Zoo	Movie	Zoo	Drive	Drive	Rest	Rest	Zoo
Second preference	Drive	Drive	Rest	Movie	Movie	Drive	Movie	Drive
Third preference	Rest	Zoo	Drive	Rest	Rest	Movie	Drive	Rest
Fourth preference	Movie	Rest	Movie	Zoo	Zoo	Zoo	Zoo	Movie

What is the first impression that one gets from the table? Where should the family go? Anu, Sia and Grandma want to go to the zoo, while only Mir and Mom want to go for a drive and Dad and Grandpa want to rest. Only Leo wants to see the movie. But will zoo be a fair choice? Four voters (Mir, Mom, Dad and Grandpa) are putting it at the bottom of their lists, which means they hate going to the zoo. If zoo is chosen to be the Sunday spot, four (which is 50 per cent) of the voters will be extremely unhappy. Even Leo has indicated the zoo as his third choice. This would be akin to adopting a plurality system of voting, where the zoo will become the winner despite everyone else almost hating it.

Let's apply the instant runoff voting system here. The lowest number of first preferences is that of the movie (only Leo has it as his most preferred option). The new tally will look something like this (we have eliminated the movie from each column, and ranks of the options below will be pushed up). Here, now, for Leo, 'drive' will become first preference, 'zoo,' second and 'rest' the third.

	Anu	*Leo*	*Sia*	*Mir*	*Mom*	*Dad*	*Grandpa*	*Grandma*
First preference	Zoo		Zoo	Drive	Drive	Rest	Rest	Zoo
Second preference	Drive	Drive	Rest			Drive		Drive
Third preference	Rest	Zoo	Drive	Rest	Rest		Drive	Rest
Fourth preference		Rest		Zoo	Zoo	Zoo	Zoo	

We redraw this table by removing the next candidate set of lowest first choice options. Now, 'zoo' remains at three first choices, 'drive' also secures three first choices. 'Rest' has two voters supporting it as the first choice in this new table. We eliminate 'rest'.

	Anu	*Leo*	*Sia*	*Mir*	*Mom*	*Dad*	*Grandpa*	*Grandma*
First preference	Zoo		Zoo	Drive	Drive			Zoo
Second preference	Drive	Drive				Drive		Drive
Third preference		Zoo	Drive				Drive	
Fourth preference				Zoo	Zoo	Zoo	Zoo	

Finally, the competition is now between two candidates—zoo and drive. The votes of eliminated cells are readjusted for their next best choice. In this new table, Anu, Sia and Grandma prefer the 'zoo', but 'drive' is preferred by the remaining five members. Hence, the family goes for a drive.

Now, doesn't this seem fairer? This system ensures that the least hated emerges as the winner. Someone who has been rated as the best by few but placed at the bottom by everyone else is not better than a candidate who is placed at the second position by every voter, isn't it?

Instant runoff produced an interesting result in Ireland in 1990. There were three candidates: Brian Lenihan of the traditional Fianna Fail Party, Mary Robinson of the Labor Party and Austin Currie of Fine Gael. In the first preference voting, Mary got 38.9 per cent votes while Brian secured 43.8 per cent and Austin got 16.9 per cent. Under an FPTP system, Fianna Fail's Brian Lenihan would have formed the government. But since no party had a majority, Austin's 16.9 per cent votes were transferred to Mary and Brian, by reassigning Austin's votes to the next preference in each of those ballots. The results were dramatic. Mary's votes increased to 51.6 per cent while Brian's to 46.2 per cent. Take a look at Table 7.1.

TABLE 7.1 Votes tally in the 1990 elections of Ireland

Candidate	*Round 1*		*Round 2*	
Mary Robinson	6,12,265	38.90%	8,17,830	51.60%
Brian Lenihan	6,94,484	43.80%	7,31,273	46.20%
Austin Currie	2,67,902	16.90%	—	
Exhausted ballots	9,444	0.60%	34,992	2.20%
Total	15,84,095	100%	15,84,095	100%

This type of method is common in many smaller units around the world. Canada has tried it in municipal elections just like the US. Czech Republic uses it to find the winners of the Green Party, New Zealand for its mayoral elections, and even in the UK, where they call it alternative vote, it is used to select leaders of the party. In India too, the instant runoff method is used by various electoral colleges to elect the president of India or to elect members of Rajya Sabha or Vidhan Parishads (legislative councils) in various states. The method is indeed a brilliant solution to various charges levelled against the FPTP system. It tries to convert a forced binary choice of yes or no of the FPTP method to a more analogue choice architecture in which the voter is not forced to mention who they prefer but who they prefer relatively. This means that those at the top are not eliminated but those at the bottom are. This makes aggregation of preferences more comprehensive.

There are a variety of versions of instant runoff method that improvise on the original model. For instance, instead of ranking the candidates, voters can give marks or scores to the candidates.

These scores can be added up to see who has the highest. This is called as the Borda Count Method. We can either award a score or simply convert a ranked method of instant runoff with some weights applied to various ranks. We see this method more prevalent in private organisations, or in countries like Slovenia and Iceland.

Assessing the merits of these methods and playing with them are a delight for those who like to play with numbers. These methods are used to elect people with broad-based consensus rather than the ones which pick out those preferred by most people relatively and leave the rest. One of the benefits of the instant runoff method is that it doesn't let any vote go waste. Votes to disliked candidates are transferred to the next liked one, and so on. These methods are better for smaller parties and marginal communities to help advance their representative quotient. This is because, as mentioned, the votes going to small parties are not wasted. But there may be some gaps, too. Once ranking methods are introduced, concerns related to tactical voting may appear—manipulating the ranks to achieve a desired outcome (although instant runoff is less vulnerable to such manipulations as compared to Borda Count). There could be spoiler effect—presence of a third candidate who will predictably lose, or may alter the outcome of an election if the other two candidates are situated equivalently in the political battle. Although experts have claimed that instant runoff voting, in most cases, will actually be resistant to spoiler effects. Arguably, the real reasons for not using the instant runoff method are the costs and operational complexity associated with it. This not only increases administrative machinery's headache but may also lead to a high rate of invalid voting.

We do not intend to provide all forms of voting methods in this book, but one needs to be aware that there are so many other options outside FPTP. Think about the French presidential elections, for instance. Popularly known as a two-round system, the idea is simple. People vote for all the candidates in a classic FPTP system, and in the absence of absolute majority, the two most preferred candidates are selected for the next round. In the next round, the voting is reconducted for these two candidates. This means voters of the losing candidate now have to redecide who they should vote for, even if their preferred candidate is not in the final tally. This way, everyone takes part in a tight battle between two strongest contenders. The two-round system forces everyone, including the disgruntled voter whose preferred candidate did not make it to the top two, to make a choice between the two strong candidates. That way, the candidate with a more broad-based consensus and one who appeals to a larger cross section of people, wins.

This system would reduce the possibility of selecting candidates with extreme views. In 2002, for instance, something interesting happened in the French presidential elections. While prominent contenders were Jacques Chirac and Lionel Jospin, the campaign also witnessed the emergence of a far-right wing contender, Jean-Marie Le Pen. This was because the left vote was divided among a number of contenders. The final tally after the first round was:

Jacques Chirac (Centre-right, Gaullist): 19.88 per cent
Jean-Marie Le Pen (Far-right, National Front): 16.86 per cent
Lionel Jospin (Centre-left, Socialist): 16.18 per cent

In the absence of anyone securing absolute majority, the second (final) round was a battle between Chirac and Le Pen. In the second round, every voter had to re-select the President, between Chirac and Le Pen. Since Chirac was able to appeal to a broad range of voters and Le Pen, only to the far right, the winner was chosen with a massive margin.

Jacques Chirac (Centre-right, Gaullist): 82.21 per cent
Jean-Marie Le Pen (Far-right, National Front): 17.79 per cent

This system, being French, is used by a number of erstwhile French colonies in Africa, and several other countries. But again, the problem is its cost. Each election cycle consists of two elections in one go. So, the state needs to incur almost double the cost. But because this also keeps mindless candidates at bay, these costs are made up for by reduced expenses at an aggregate level.

It is due to the matter of costs that these methods have not been debated as much for their application in India, not to mention the complexity of the instant runoff. One wonders how will voters in India, of which a sizeable number come from backgrounds with limited educational or voting experience, be able to put their ranking orders in each electoral cycle. This, however, is by no means an impossible feat.

PROPORTIONAL REPRESENTATION FURTHER ILLUSTRATED

The proportional representation (PR) method is a way to ensure that votes contribute to the result. This is a different style. The 69 per cent votes that did not go to BJP in the 2014 Lok Sabha elections, for instance, or the 60 per cent votes that did not go to Congress in the 1967 Lok Sabha, are not rendered useless, because seats in the parliament will be offered in proportion to the share of votes that parties have got across the country/state. So here, seats don't come by allotment of victories in votes, but by how many votes one has received. The FPTP method will tend to reward the strongest party disproportionately, and punish weak parties harshly.

The PR system evens out these distortions. Parties in parliaments are as strong as their vote share on the ground is. It is embedded within the philosophy of representation. And primacy of representation is echoed in the Constituent Assembly debates as well. It was the bedrock of the trust that our founding fathers and mothers laid in universal adult suffrage offered to the largest electorate in the world. When H.V. Kamath, member of the Constituent Assembly, wanted to use the words, 'In the name of God', in the preface to the Preamble, his reasons were not because he was religious, or that he wished that the Constitution be framed by an act of faith, but it was because he felt that as representatives of the people of India, it was their duty to bring what may be the view of the Indians they all represented. He said, '[H]ere we are not individuals. Here we are the people of India. There is much difference between the two … we have come here as representatives of the people of India. Honesty demands that we should record what may be their view.' In fact, the reason this amendment was not accepted was not because the House disagreed with Kamath's view. It was because people's preferences would not be homogeneous, and in bringing in the words 'in the name of God', atheist Indians' view would not be represented![7]

Coming back to PR, the PR system, by account of Constituent Assembly debates, achieved representation better. The system has several versions, and all of them have been adopted widely, although some versions are more conducive to some regions and not the rest. The PR system works best for multi-member constituencies, which means more than one seat is being sought to be filled up. In such voting, the seats are allotted to parties based on the number of votes received by the party. So, if a party gets 20 per cent of votes in a 10-seat election, they get two seats in parliament. There are many ways of doing it, but a simple method of PR is the mixed-member proportional voting, often called as the two-vote system or the German system. Here, voters cast two votes, one for the candidate and the other for the party. So, let's imagine India is going to vote in 2024. The voter will do a two-step voting. First, she will vote for her most preferred candidate contesting for her constituency's MP seat. Next, she will choose a party that she wants to see as the leader in the Lok Sabha in New Delhi. Her vote for the MP counts towards securing her candidate in the Lok Sabha. But her vote for the party goes to the party's overall presence in the Lok Sabha. For instance, consider someone likes a candidate but not their party. Let's say, she chooses Congress to run the country. So, she will vote for Congress in one step when she is asked to choose her most preferred party. For her next vote for the constituency, she chooses the BJP candidate in her constituency. In such a case, while the BJP candidate has got one vote for her seat in the Lok Sabha, Congress has also got one vote for its seat in the Lok Sabha.

How are the two votes reconciled? Simple—half the parliament will be filled with candidates of various constituencies chosen by people directly, and the second half will be used to adjust the seats based on votes. For instance, if Congress has secured 40 per cent votes (first vote), and the total seats in parliament is 100, then Congress will occupy 40 seats. If Congress' candidates have won 28 seats already through their elected constituents (the next vote), then Congress will be asked to add 12 more candidates (40 – 28 = 12), in parliament to fill in its 40 seats.

This effectively means that we double (or halve) the size of our Lok Sabha or Vidhan Sabhas (or increase the weights of each seat accordingly). Fifty per cent of it will be filled by candidates chosen in the polls and the remaining 50 per cent will be used to ensure that the vote share is adequately reflected in parliament, and is used to correct the imbalance. So, the second 50 per cent is to be used to 'top-up' the seats of parties who had gotten more votes than seats. This 50 per cent corrects the imbalance by using the seats to adjust existing seats to bring proportionality.

Let's take, for instance, the 1982 Bengal Assembly elections. The seats and votes are actual values. Here is how the seat–vote share matrix looked like:

Congress' vote share: 35.7 per cent. Seats: 49.
CPI(M)'s vote share: 38.5 per cent. Seats: 174.

This imbalance is addressed by the mixed-member proportional voting type PR. The imbalance is shown in the fifth column. The sixth and seventh columns show shortages and surpluses of seats in the assembly and this can be readjusted. The extra 80.3 seats must be taken from the parties who have the surplus and be distributed among parties that have shortages algebraically. Parties can then decide which MLAs to let go of. Refer to Table 7.2.

If doubling is not an option, then the other way is to keep the strength of the house fixed, but change the weight ascribed to each of the seats, in relation to the new, adjusted seats. If we divide the deserved number of seats with the actual seats received, we will get how much a party is underloaded or overloaded with seats. This should be the weight to each MLA of that party in the assembly. So, let's say that CPI(M), in the above example, has secured 174 seats although vote share suggests that it deserved 113.2 seats only. This means the party is overloaded with seats. The weight ascribed to each of its 174 seats is therefore 0.65 (113.2 divided by 174). So, every time there is a bill or the House is put to vote, one vote of CPI(M) will be counted as 0.65 votes. This addresses the imbalance neatly. Not only do parties get represented, but they get representation based on how many people liked them rather than how many seats they have in parliament.

Another type of PR method is with a single transferable vote method (a version of the instant runoff method). Known as the Hare system, it has been used in Ireland, Malta, various cities of the US, and at the federal Senate level in Australia. In India, we use it to elect Rajya Sabha members, Vidhan Parishad members as well as to elect our President. It is, therefore, not at all alien to India, and has powerful merits over the FPTP system.

Here, just like instant runoff, you rank your preferences of candidates on the ballot paper. There is a threshold limit prescribed for the winner(s). After the voting, the total votes for each candidate are counted, where the candidate has been put as

TABLE 7.2 Results of the 1982 Vidhan Sabha of West Bengal

Parties	*Seats*	*Votes*	*Vote Share*	*Seats ought to be won based on vote proportion*	*Surplus*	*Shortfalls*
BJP	0	129994	0.6%	1.7		-1.7
CPI	7	407660	1.8%	5.3	1.7	
CPI-M	174	8655371	38.5%	113.2	60.8	
Congress (Socialist)	4	885535	3.9%	11.6		-7.6
Congress	49	8035272	35.7%	105.1		-56.1
Janata Party	0	187513	0.8%	2.5		-2.5
Lok Dal	0	22361	0.1%	0.3		-0.3
All India Forward Bloc	28	1327849	5.9%	17.4	10.6	
Muslim League	0	129116	0.6%	1.7		-1.7
Revolutionary Socialist Party	19	901723	4.0%	11.8	7.2	
Jharkhand Mukti Morcha	0	1268	0.0%	0.0	0.0	
Socialist Unity Centre of India	2	232573	1.0%	3.0		-1.0
Independents	11	1571101	7.0%	20.5		-9.5
Total	**294**	**22487336**	**100%**	**294**	**80.3**	**-80.3**

first preference. If the candidate reaches the quota, she is selected. If no candidate is able to reach the quota, then through instant runoff voting as described above, we eliminate the candidate with lowest first preference votes and allocate those votes to candidates who were given second preferences in those ballot papers. If no one still reaches the quota, we repeat the exercise. This way, no vote is wasted. Sometimes, we would not want to waste the votes of the candidate who has secured more than the quota, isn't it? In some systems, therefore, when there is a candidate who has secured more votes than the quota and, therefore, has a surplus of votes, her surplus votes are taken from her and allocated to the other 'needy' candidates based on instant runoff (taking the surplus votes to the second preferential candidate on the list).

One may imagine the single transferable vote in the following way. Imagine a class which is setting out to elect its prefect or class monitor.[8] Suppose four candidates stand in front of the class and two have to be elected. The rest of the class is asked to go and stand behind the candidate they prefer the most. The students form four queues behind their preferred candidates. They look at their own queue and the other queues. Those in the shortest queue realise that their candidate is losing anyway, so they shuffle themselves to other ones. This process of shuffling and iteration will continue until all votes clearly put out two winners. In effect, this is exactly how PR with a single transferable vote takes place.

This is a good form of representation for minorities. Why? Because the voting method is producing voter groups of equal sizes effectively, since surplus and shortfalls are all pushed towards the quota. Proportionality is implicit in this system. Interestingly, some bit of Constituent Assembly debates took up the issue of PR, and a large part of that debate was inspired by PR's ability to represent minorities in the government adequately. Karimuddin had made an emphatic plea to introduce PR as the electoral system in India since not only did PRs help in assuaging us from the 'tyranny of the majority', but also because the PR system was 'profoundly democratic' in its promise to make every vote count. Through this, he said, the PR system would enable representation to minorities in India. In fact, he did not want the reservation of seats based on religious grounds, because a better and more democratic representation accrues through PR.

Professor K.T. Shah was also in favour of PR. The same day, he remarked, 'I would only like to add, lest I should be misunderstood, that the principle of Proportional Representation is not intended so much to perpetuate communal minorities, as to reflect the various shades of political opinion which after all, should be reflected in your legislature, if you desire to be really a democratic government.'[9] His reference to the varying shades of political opinion can be considered, at the very least, prophetic. Such was his understanding of the PR system that he also proposed to have multi-member constituencies since PR would not work as effectively for single-member constituencies. Even Mahboob Ali Baig recommended the PR system, primarily because it 'enabled people, who held different views from the majority, to enter the legislature.'[10]

The move was not accepted. Ambedkar mentioned that implementing a PR system in general elections 'presupposes literacy on a large scale', and Indians then, with a tiny literacy rate, were not capable of marking numerals on a ballot paper. This seemed to be a fair point.

But he made another point. He said that the PR system would tend to fragment the legislature since even small parties would need to be represented, and that parties may not gain majority, and this would go against the basic tenet of how polity was being organised. The parliamentary system of democracy was to be the bedrock of our Constitution, and in such democracies, majority parties run the country. To bring a system which encouraged fractured mandates in the House would mean majorities would get diluted and the idea of a stable parliament will be eroded. Hence, the PR system, he said, '... is not suited to the form of government which this Constitution lays down ... [since] one of the disadvantages of proportional representation is the fragmentation of the legislature into a number of small groups ... [and therefore PR] would damage the stability of government.'

Ambedkar was intuitively referring to what would be known as Duverger's law in political science. Attributed to Maurice Duverger, a prominent twentieth-century sociologist who showed in his papers of the 1950s and 1960s that plurality rule elections through the FPTP system would tend to marginalise small parties, resulting in a two-party democracy, while proportional representation would create conditions for fostering a multi-party democracy. This is easy to understand. Since proportional representation allows for 'topping up' the seats of a party which has a significant voter base, even if it has secured a tiny number of seats, it will flourish in a multi-party system. The small parties will be rendered useless over time in an FPTP since FPTP penalises parties who do not secure seats, and seat winning is likely more for big parties than small ones.

The interesting thing is that for countries like India, Duverger's law does not hold. (It is not even a law, if one looks at it closely; rather a hypothesis. It was called a law by subsequent scholars and the name stuck.) In fact, many countries with plurality voting system have many parties. And new evidence has indicated that Duverger's law cannot be held without bringing the context in the picture.[11] In fact, perfect two-party democracies are found nowhere except in the US and some Caribbean nations. The UK, Canada, Australia and other major Westminster models have all yielded multi-party democracies. Look at India. The era of coalition governments is not new, and had begun a long time ago. The fragmented parliament is now considered to be so normal that 'stable government' has been a campaign promise in Indian electoral politics. A close look at the idea of India with its diverse cultural differences all rolled into one, necessitated emergence of regional, smaller parties attracting votes on a number of group-based loyalties and lines. This is exactly what we see today.

Ambedkar, with respect to representation of minorities, suggested that it could be better achieved through reserving seats rather than PR. In reserving the seat, however, the majority is also forced to vote for a minority candidate. This may not only distort the aim to aggregate the preferences of voters, but is also prone to political manipulation. PR could have been a better way of representation of minority party. Today, Muslim representation in Indian parliament is a cause of worry. The share of Muslims in the Lok Sabha has been consistently lower than their share in population by a significant amount. Refer to Figure 7.1.

FIGURE 7.1 Share of Muslims in Lok Sabha compared to their share in the population of India

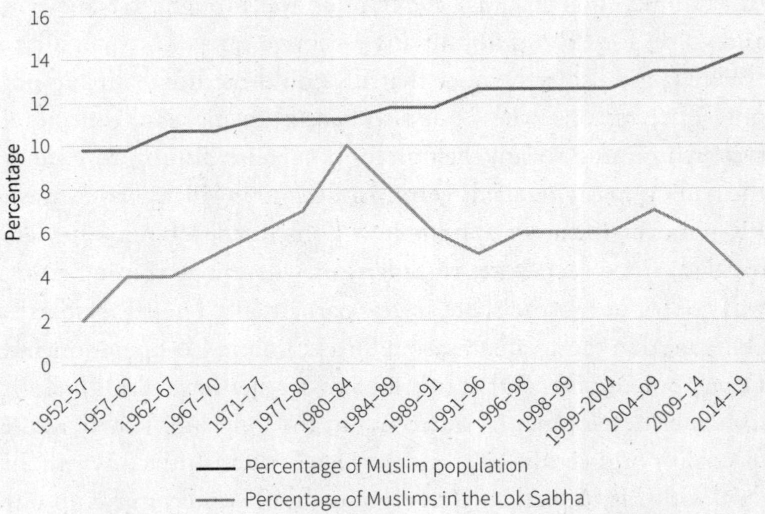

Source: Nasir Abdullah and Anuragini Priya, 'Debate: First Past the Post Means India is Only a Namesake Democracy', *The Wire*, 14 May 2018.

Z.H. Lari, another member of the assembly from UP, perhaps feared this. He passionately appealed for the adoption of PR, citing the interesting example of Ireland. Ireland's politics was divided on religious lines with two parties favouring Catholics and Protestants, but in places where the PR system was implemented, religious politics ceased to be the dividing line there, he claimed. He also connected the same argument for Switzerland's polity. Representation must be central to the vastness and diversity that is India, and that is what PR stood for.

Representation is a tricky matter after all. Must representation aim to reflect the preferences of people, or their interests?[12] And preferences and interest are not two sides of the same coin. What one prefers may not be in their interest. For most part, the idea of representation was driven by representation of preferences. But, in this, emerged another important issue, namely, must a true representative of Muslims be a Muslim person only? If yes, then the only way to achieve this was to establish separate electorates (for Hindus and Muslims). Reservation was thought to achieve it, and voices for PR did not hit any receptive ear.

We must also remember that PR could be more suitable not only in terms of fairness but also because it makes the electoral system immune to any delimitation exercise aiming to benefit the ruling party (called gerrymandering in many countries). PR removes the worry about how constituency boundaries are divided, since each vote, regardless of where it is coming from, will contribute to the share in the parliament. The PR system is being used in most Organisation for Economic Co-operation and Development (OECD) countries and studies have also linked it to higher developmental outcomes in the long run. It may result in coalition governments, but we have that in India anyway. In fact, with PR in place, a true representation would make up our polity in a way that fulfils not only the vision of our founding fathers, but also upholds the philosophical purpose of elections.

While the idea of an unexposed, illiterate population having to put their ranking orders makes sense, India is no longer that illiterate either. While we agree that PR with a single transferable vote may be tedious for the voters in India, the mixed-member proportional voting, or the German method, may be rather easy. Voters vote for the candidate in their constituency and then for the party at the centre. The vote share of the party then gets adjusted in Parliament based on how voters have voted.

Most of all, this is going to at least make voters heard in the formation of the dominant party at the helm of affairs in parliament. Today, we have no say in government formation, only in the nomination of our constituency representative. This way, we make central and state government formation closer to people's will. In some ways, isn't that the purpose of elections?

SOME THOUGHTS ON NOTA

Around 2 crore Indians reach voting age each year. Two crores! With every election cycle, we add more people on the voters' list than Germany's population. When memory is narrativised, it takes the shape of a solid mass. The young voters coming up to vote in elections must be carrying the heavy weight of a narrative of India's past which they have not constructed. These voters make sense of the India of the past through their aspiration about themselves and this country. Many of them will relate to it. Others would want to script their own connection and change these narratives for future.

Think about NOTA. An option called 'none of the above' is one of the choices you can now vote for in the elections. When people don't like any contestants, they simply push the button on NOTA. In the assembly elections in Gujarat, MP, Karnataka and Rajasthan, there were large number of instances where the number of people who preferred NOTA exceeded the victory margin. In Karnataka, NOTA votes were higher than the votes received by six parties, including national parties like CPI(M) and BSP! In MP, NOTA's vote share was 1.4 per cent, even though the vote share difference between the top two parties (Congress and BJP) was merely 0.1 per cent.

Commentators believe that it is young India which is the NOTA voter. In the 2014 Lok Sabha elections, A. Raja, the accused in the 2G scam, contested from the Nilgiris constituency. He lost by a huge margin there. NOTA was the third highest vote grosser there. Corruption affects the young more than the old. In attracting young and more voters, NOTA is said to have matured Indian democracy to some extent (although more data is needed to ascertain this).

It is in this sea of narratives that the youths' aspirations to see a new electoral politics will emerge. India is a vast country and it moves at a glacial pace sometimes. The aspiration of the youth, however, may add a new engine to it. And in that context, reformative ideas regarding presidential democracy and proportional representation may gain weight. It is also possible that the aspiration of youth may compete with (the now fossilised) drivers of our electoral designs. And that makes the idea of electoral reforms all the more important.

Epilogue

Bill Clinton, the former President of the United States, had famously said in the wake of results of the US elections in November 2000, 'The people have spoken; we're just not sure what they've said.'

Bush and Gore had a close battle that year. As election results kept on being declared, the uncertainty only increased. By the end, only Florida's results were left to be announced. When the results were announced, the difference was so low that laws required a recount. After the recount, Bush won Florida by 537 votes, which was a margin of 0.009 per cent. Bush ultimately got 271 electoral votes, one more than the required majority.

Soon, Bush was to preside over the devastating wars in Afghanistan and Iraq, spreading destruction and mayhem that the world is yet to recover from. With this ongoing war, he secured the White House once again in 2004, and this time, his policies oversaw the worst financial crises the world has seen since the Great Depression.

This is what 537 votes did to the world!

LIMITS OF DEMOCRATIC PROCESSES

Democratic processes and their designs are the very reasons why politicians love them. And perhaps they are also the reason why budding politicians hate them. Those who appreciate democracy, actually appreciate its principle, not necessarily structures and processes. They admire constitutional democracy, but perhaps not an electoral one. The principle is unwavering, which is that people should be able to decide their own leaders. In the romantic pursuit of our love to this principle, we slip over the processes over and over again. Like the moon that can't be seen during daylight, the power of democracy's principles gets eclipsed by these processes and structures.

The idea that people should decide their own leaders assumes that people know who one is voting for and what one means by leader. More importantly, is my leader a person or a party? And in case it is the latter, how is the party choosing the 'leader'? Do I know who they will choose, or will they only reveal it much later, after the results have been announced?

Consider the political rise of the current Indian PM, Narendra Modi. It is often attributed to his chief ministerial experience in Gujarat. In 2001, Modi became the CM of Gujarat without fighting any election. He was airdropped into Gandhinagar by BJP, replacing the incumbent CM. Modi was the new CM, a position he retained in 2007 and 2011. In 2014, these victories gave him a reason to be chosen as India's PM. Today, he governs a country of more than 138 crore people and even though he has won all subsequent elections, his first entry into politics was direct. In fact, it is not at all uncommon to have cabinet ministers who have otherwise lost elections in their respective constituencies.

Modi's predecessor, Manmohan Singh was the PM of India for ten years. How many elections did he fight in his overall career? One, in 1999, from the South Delhi constituency, which he lost by 30,000 votes. During his tenure as the PM, he remained a nominated member of Rajya Sabha.

We mentioned in the earlier chapter about how H.D. Deve Gowda and I.K. Gujral, who occupied the 'throne' in Delhi, were also Rajya Sabha members. Indira Gandhi, in 1966, was also let into the South Block as PM through the gates of Rajya Sabha.

The choice architecture of our leaders does not depend on the principle of democracy alone. It depends on structure. And this structure is predicated upon numbers. Democracy, therefore, becomes a mathematical performative, and everything else becomes secondary. Securing the seat is more important than representing people. And in securing the seat, numbers and campaign performances matter more than the trust of people.

METHOD OF ELECTIONS

Let's speak of numbers first. Numbers explain, first of all, that no voting method will be perfect. None, whatsoever. It's like Churchill, as is frequently claimed, famously said, 'democracy is the worst form of government, except for all others.' Whatever these words mean, there is some mathematical reality to this idea. When we think about elections, we are thinking about finding a way to aggregate preferences. This makes the idea of elections applicable across the board; whether it's a family with a bunch of kids planning to decide where to go on a Sunday, a school deciding upon its next educational tour, decision-making in a corporate boardroom or in an international organisation (think about European Parliament). Choice of a leader can range from electing class prefects in a school to someone in your municipality, province, state or even the country. People may want different things, but only one of those is to be selected. So, consider elections like a Russian roulette. Many of the slots are preferred by different people but the ball will rest on one of them alone. Which one should it be? The game will induce maximum total happiness if it stops at a slot preferred by most people who are betting.

Rules can be different in different societies or at different levels. For instance, while proportional representation is used for electing the president of India, but the first-past-the-post (FPTP) system is used for electing the PM. Or for that matter, in the US, people elect their top leaders directly, while in India, we do so indirectly—we vote for the party and the party selects its leader. Many-a-times, the method used to fulfil democratic principles is simply locked in time and the coordination costs associated with switching it are too high to even be considered.

If methods can, and do, differ, how does one believe that each method is adequately fulfilling the fundamental guiding principle? Well, the only test for the method to be appropriate (or better still, not be grossly inappropriate) is that it should be fair and should be applied to every contestant equivalently. So, everyone participating in the elections believes in it, and agrees to the rules of the game.

You may have heard of search engine optimisation (SEO). Google has an algorithm with which it sorts out which webpages will appear first, and which ones later. Various companies employ SEO professionals who try to understand the algorithm behind Google, and customise their website in such a way that the algorithm picks their website on its first page. This enhances the visibility of the websites. In many ways, SEO professionals work out the Google algorithm and play with it. One may think this is manipulation. Someone's webpage may not deserve to appear on the first page of Google results, but if they have understood how Google ranks pages, they can make use of this understanding to jack up their visibility even though it replaces some really useful webpage. Some say this is not a manipulation because SEO is a difficult game to win. If a company can hire smart people who can win this game, it must be a smart (and, therefore, maybe deserving) company to appear on the first page anyway. This way, undeserving candidates will be weeded out.

But there's another catch. Google keeps changing its algorithm; so, a manipulating company cannot always have an advantage. Google adopts a principle to rank pages in its search machine.

The principle remains the same, but the method to reach there can change. Google keeps changing it and outsmarts the manipulating companies. So, everyone tries to catch up. In time, this system makes the entire network more efficient and better.

Now if people outsmart Google, it is one thing. If they outsmart our election machinery that helps elect our leaders, it will be disastrous, isn't it? Once we understand the method to elections, we can out-trick the method, often times at the peril of missing out on the principle. And, unlike Google, the method to election doesn't change so easily. In most cases, it has never changed. So, all we need to do is to capitalise on the method's weaknesses.

That's what politicians and political parties do. They keep outsmarting election methods. We discussed briefly in the first chapter about how, after the introduction of voting machines, we now have access to booth-level data. With some feet on the ground, the booth-level data can tell a candidate which households are likely to have really voted for her and which ones would not have. This (coupled with hyperlocal marketing applications, including Google Maps, which has phone numbers of many establishments on it) allows one to do hyperlocal campaigns within those booths (or avoid spending money on booths where one knows there will be no conversion). All of this makes the data analysts often very important in elections.

In time, when the method is outsmarted by everyone, there is a big case for changing the method, to ensure that the sanctity of the principle remains. Just like Google keeps changing its algorithm, so should we, with changing times. After all, democracy is at stake here.

IMPOSSIBILITY OF FAIRNESS

Kenneth Arrow was one of the most brilliant minds of the last century. The youngest Nobel Prize winner in Economics, he developed ideas on wide-ranging topics, from general equilibrium, economics of information, and endogenous growth theory, among others. Many of his students went on to win the Nobel Prize later, and his work inspired several scholars of the time, including Amartya Sen (armed with Arrow's ideas, he came up with what we call the liberal paradox, in which he argued that no social system that respects individual freedom can be Pareto optimal. Pareto optimality is achieved when you cannot make anyone better off without making someone worse off). Perhaps Arrow's most profound contribution has been in building what is called as the 'impossibility theorem'.

Preference aggregation is a difficult compromise to achieve. This should be evident from this book. Perhaps people may not agree on which preference is to be finally selected, but they would all agree on the method with which the preference selection is made. They will all agree if the method seems fair to everyone.

What is fair, then? How do we know whether a particular preference aggregation method is fair?

Well, we can have fairness criteria, and we should test the election method against each of those criteria. If it fulfils all of them, we have arrived at the fair system of elections. One may say that such criteria should be based on principles of equality and freedom, and follow general rules which everyone will agree upon. For instance, if every voter prefers A to B, then the group preference should also remain as A over B. Mathematicians who work on social choice have come up with a small list of such fairness conditions which must be satisfied in any election method. Most important of them are three.

Arrow was able to demonstrate that the only way to hold these three fairness conditions is to have a dictator. That by definition is not allowed, since dictatorial leadership is unfair. Mathematically, therefore, regardless of whichever voting method you find, you will always run the risk of disrupting one of the fairness conditions. In other words, it is impossible to design a voting method which is fair by all counts, except if a dictator comes to power! Intriguing and disappointing at the same time, right?

The book doesn't allow us to go into the mathematics of it, but we must recognise that there is no harm in changing the rules of elections since there is no one rule which is fairest of all.

DOES OUR METHOD NEED A RETHINK?

Armed with some scepticism, let us recapitulate what the book tells us about our own elections. The first one concerns with how vote shares don't matter, but seat shares do. Does this seem to be fair? Must we elect the party which will head our state or country based on how many seats they won or based on how many votes they received?

Winners in each constituency, regardless of their victory margins, become representatives in parliament—even if they have received rather small number of votes, just more than the second highest. So, in a constituency with 1,000 people, if there are five equally strong contenders contesting, and if all get almost the same number of votes, then someone with just around 201 votes will win and represent even those who had not voted for her. This seems unfair at many levels. When number of parties increase, the number of contestants increases as well. If competition is tough, perhaps no one will get a majority vote.

In athletics, this makes sense. She who reaches the post first is the fastest. That's because in athletics, we are looking to find the fastest, even if the second fastest is almost as fast. In politics, there is no race taking place. There is a preference contest taking place. Who do we consider most preferred? One who is liked by most or disliked by least? In any constituency following FPTP, it doesn't matter if the elected wins by margin of 1 per cent or of 99 per cent votes. The winner is the one above the next best. Winning by 99 per cent votes means that the winner was preferred by 99 per cent of the people, and disliked by merely 1 per cent. But winning by a margin of just 1 per cent means that almost half the voters disliked the winning candidate.

This means numbers are all that matter. And the disturbing aspect of this is that you don't need to persuade everyone in the constituency. As long as you get the required plurality numbers on your side, your job is done, however small that number is. To do this, voter calculations are done through groups, also called as vote banks. The aim is to collect groups (vote banks) on your side, because each group contains many voters. The group will vote based on what the group leaders dictate. This grouping can happen on any line—caste, region, religion, class, gender, age, political preferences and so on. But most of these groups will have their own group leaders. If you can't 'buy out' the group, you can buy out the leader(s) of the group. Party politics is then geared to attract community leaders somehow. You can get the leader using various means—either the person believes in you and your party, or you have promised her benefits, money, position and so on. Her words will matter to her group. You do your calculations based on how many voters you have secured. As long as you secure more than what others may have secured, you are done. You don't need majority, just plurality.

How does this system militate against the principles of electoral democracy? Let us give you a personal example.

A PERSONAL ANECDOTE

One college that one of the authors went to had a state-wise admissions quota. Here, not just merit but national integration too was amongst the aspirations of the college's value system. Although we never appreciated such a system much, it makes sense now when we look back. One argument was that since merit may be dependent upon various other characteristics, including presence of good schools or coaching institutions in a particular state, it is unfair for someone to be declined admission on exam scores alone because the person may not have had access to a good college or coaching institute. A more important reason, however, was to have representation from around the country. This led to the campus harbouring a mini India. It was incredible, since we had friends from every part of the country, sitting in the same class. A cultural immersion of this type goes a long way in building sensitivity among citizens for the future. At least, so was the intention. The campus was a melting pot of languages, culture and distinct lifestyles, all together. Very few colleges are able to achieve this.

The admission quota for each state was decided as a proportion of the state's population with one exception—the home state. The college had 50 per cent seats reserved for students of the home state, and the remaining 50 per cent was divided up across all Indian states as a ratio of the states' population. That means the highest representation in the student body was from Gujarat, if we are talking about a college in Gujarat. Populous states like UP, Bihar, Maharashtra, Madhya Pradesh and Andhra Pradesh had large student bodies. Smaller states also had their students but in smaller numbers.

The moment you have these groups collected, with whatever noble intentions you may have, you see them gravitating towards their own kinds. Think about why Hindus are more Hindu in the US than in India, or Bengalis are more Bengali outside Bengal. In the college, various states made their own associations, fondly called Assos (lot of fondness, right!). So, there was a UP Asso, Karnataka Asso, Rajasthan Asso and so on. Students didn't have a choice as to which Asso they were joining. If you came from a state, it meant you belonged to that Asso. Somehow or the other, everyone was aligned to some group. Some brave souls who decided not to be part of any Asso, rebelling against their seniors, ended up being in a group themselves that one would call Nonasso Asso. Those whose parents were first-generation migrants into a state they came from were allowed to choose their Asso based on where they think they are 'originally' from (often decided by the languages they spoke or preferred). Interesting, isn't it?

What was the point of being in an Asso? Well, first, you could be ragged ('ragging' or 'hazing' has been common in many Indian colleges definitely at the time we went to college) only by your Asso seniors, not anyone else. This was a code of conduct. Second, your seniors would act as your mentors (whatever that would mean) in many ways. Third, and most important, Assos would become politically very relevant in college elections. Because usually, you would vote for who your Asso was voting for.

The last one is an interesting point. We are talking about a premier higher education institution of the country, where the top 1 per cent of students in the country study. Very well capable of harbouring independent views, motivations and actions, these students cannot be brainwashed into something. Voting for the college general secretary was by a secret ballot, and one would expect a literate, empowered mass to vote based on the candidate's skills and qualifications.

Interestingly, most of their votes went en masse to the candidate their Asso has decided to side with, regardless of the candidate's personality or skills. Such strange loyalty to a totally flimsy fabrication of a group, in the minds of educated young people for whom politics is not even a matter of career or a matter of securing entitlements, is interesting indeed. There are various psychological and evolutionary biology-based explanations for in-group affinity but we keep them aside. Group loyalty is often strong and, in many ways, may not need any hard association with the group.

Be as that may, voting means numbers became important. The total number of people in an Asso were easily countable. Assos follow a lineage, so all your juniors were also in your Asso. To be able to win, you only needed more than the next best candidate. So basic calculations began. There was an 'Asso President' of each Asso in the final year. Some president friends would form an informal political loyalty around one candidate. Those who were on your side would be on your side perhaps because you guys had been friends, or because you gave them another elected post (it was mostly a him) or their people.

Once we analogise Assos as parties, the way FPTP works becomes clear, more so in a scenario of patronage politics. The difference is, entitlements are really in the hands of parties, unlike in a college where, regardless of the Asso you belong to, the college treats you equally.

So, the basic deal is how many Assos would have made a pre-poll coalition. The calculation ends when you have the requisite number of expected Assos (which means voters) by your side. There are speeches and promises but as far as persuasions are concerned, only Asso presidents matter. It's a season of high-pitched drama and electrifying vibrancy in the campus, with several days of campaigning, building a political beehive out of a college campus. It's a sight to behold indeed, and we would not be wrong if we can generalise these scenarios for any other college campus in India. But all of that goes into getting the group leaders, until the time when your party is expecting just as much votes as the possible next best party.

Let's take a step back and remind ourselves what the primary reason for conducting elections was. We needed an ethical leader who could represent our views and concerns to the university administration and organise college events. This required everyone to consider and think about these qualities of every contestant, and whether they were in line with these expectations from them. True, the candidates were chosen keeping in mind these considerations by the Assos, but voting hardly happened on the basis of that. Electoral method convoluted linear thinking. People were voting based on who the Asso was supporting. This would mean that Asso presidents and other influential leaders might have supported candidates simply because they were being promised favours of some kind (position or money), and not remotely close to the skillset expected from the candidate. But who cared!

Switch to national politics and you find the same process copied on a large scale.

THE GOOD POLITICS

Milan Vaishnav tells the tale of 2008, when UPA was going through its litmus test in parliament—vote of no confidence due to withdrawal of left parties from the coalition on account of the nuclear deal—and Congress was anxiously making phone calls to garner support from elected MPs. Six of these phone calls went to six lawmakers lodged in jails, collectively facing more than a hundred cases of kidnapping, murder, arson and extortion.[1]

The question needs a further dig. Why do we have political elections? Very simply stated—to elect our leaders. But what must we seek in a leader?

This is a fundamental question, bearing the load of centuries of political thought. Aristotle, in many ways, had answered it rather profoundly.

For Aristotle, the highest offices and political honours had to go to the person greatest in civic and moral virtues. This person had to have an honourable character of the highest ethical conduct, and display civic excellence in their actions and deeds, and one who was the most virtuous amongst them all. Expertise in economics or international affairs is not what one must aspire in political leadership, since for that, we have professional experts. The leader must have the ability to inspire citizens to be virtuous citizens.

Aristotle came to this conclusion by answering the question: what is politics or a political association for? What ought we seek when we associate ourselves with a particular party or political group, either actively or passively, by voting for it quietly? In other words, the Aristotelian question is normative, focusing on what ought to, rather than what we do. Not about what our preferences are, but what they should be. And he answers the question going to his Holy Grail idea that puts 'telos' in the centre.

Telos is a Greek word for purposiveness. It is the reason or purpose for something; an end or a goal of something's existence or an effort. Justice, like anything else, is teleological, as Michael Sandel explains in his famous book *Justice*. For justice, one ought to look at the purpose of the issue at hand, and make that the central idea around which debates are tied up. Amartya Sen had posed a famous flute problem in his book *The Idea of Justice*. If three kids are fighting for a flute, who will you give it to? Should Anne get it, because she knows how to play it, or Bob because he is poor and has no toys. Or should you give it to Carla, who actually made the flute? You will all have a different logic to your choice. The libertarian amongst you may go for Carla, utilitarian for Anne and perhaps a Rawlsian/Kantian will choose Bob. Aristotle, who predated this Western scholarship by 2,000 years, had categorised the centrality of 'purpose'. One may well argue that he would have wanted us to look at the telos of the flute. The very purpose of the flute was to be played well; flutes are not meant to address redistributive justice (Bob), nor are they produced so that they can incentivise their higher production (Carla). In fact, they are also not made to enhance greater happiness for greater number of people as a utilitarian might say. But they are made to be played well. That is it. End of debate. Therefore, it must go to Anne.

This formulation is powerfully simple and elegant. It puts 'why' before 'how'.

Similarly, it is pertinent to ask: what is the telos of politics and political association?

Picture some of the political leaders (dead or alive) you would revere and vote for. Do Gandhi, Mandela, Lincoln, Anna Hazare come to your mind, or Bush, Obama, Manmohan Singh and Modi come to your mind?

Why is our mind tuned already to look for morality in politics? Because that is what public leadership is all about, at its root. For Aristotle, too, politics aimed to form good citizens and good character. Removing all the technical chaff of rights and frameworks, at the core of it, politics serves a purpose, which is to build a moral and ethical society. He had said, '[A]ny polis which is truly so called, and is not merely one in name, must devote itself to the end of encouraging goodness. Otherwise, a political association sinks into a mere alliance.... Otherwise too, law becomes ... a guarantor of men's rights against one another– instead of being, as it should be, a rule of life such as will make the members of a polis good and just.'[2] Political association exists to cultivate the highest number of virtues in citizenry, to inspire them to be good, civic and virtuous individuals. For everything else, we have experts and professionals. Politics is to cultivate leaders, not administrators.

A simple test of who and how should you choose a leader comes from a tiny experiment. If you can idolise some politician to your children, she is the honourable politician. If you can tell your five-year-old, 'Be like him/her....' then you know the telos of politics or political office. You are looking for a leader, not an administrator.

Although it is important to recognise that in a world order predicated on power, power may also become a virtue important in a leader. Game theory tells us that repeat interaction between aggressive and docile kingdoms over time will end up in an equilibrium with aggressive groups everywhere.

FETISH FOR DEMOCRACY

Democracy enjoys a high level of legitimacy in India. Surveys, popular opinion and commentaries often celebrate our democratic polity. Yet, through arguments in the book, we question the worshipping ritual of democracy, manifested in electoral politics. India spends considerable energies in executing elections. So high is our fervour for elections that a country where administrative machinery most efficiently delivers polling booths and voter ID cards to every citizen, fails to prevent lakhs of deaths on account of proper sanitation services, food or even safe drinking water. Lloyd and Susan Rudolph famously called it the paradox of a 'weak-strong' state.[3] This would have been a better place if our kamikaze-type loyalty to voting matched even halfway with our commitments to basic services that the state promises its citizens.

And yet, the way in which vote is played and worked around, it loses its sanctity, at least in some way. A poignant reminder of this was the 2017 Bollywood movie *Newton*. Setting up a polling booth in the middle of the forests in Jharkhand, the movie portrayed the Sisyphus-type democratic process of election, its meaninglessness to the local population matched only by the cosmetic appreciation by international journalists yelling to the camera about how Indian democracy runs deep; and all this where the state has failed to send anything except military in the last several decades. The protagonist's adherence to the procedural code runs against the substance of elections in that part of India. It is a stark reminder to us about whatever happened to the essence of voting.

And part of our endeavour in writing this book has been to emphasise this reminder. Our fetish for democracy assumes election processes and voting methods to be a tick-mark bureaucratic exercise in the larger aim of ensuring a government for the people, of the people and by the people. Voting methods are not a tick-mark exercise. Within them is the load of the entire democratic institution itself.

In 1952, when the first elections were being envisaged, it was a mammoth task. Guha calls it, 'an act of faith'.[4] Sukumar Sen, the first Election Commissioner of India, executed it out of a tight budget and limited manpower under pressures from Nehru to organise it as soon as possible. Sen built the Herculean edifice from practically nothing. During that time, an average constituency had around 4,00,000 voters. In 2019, more than 90 crore eligible voters came out to elect their leader. Can you imagine the collective emotions and 'acts of faith' these elections represent! All of them blindly believing that our democracy is at work.

Be that as it may, and whatever form democracy has taken here in India, it is truly a miraculous one with lots of fanfare. Ashutosh Varshney cites the work of Adam Przeworksi to show how improbable a democracy India is. Studies have shown that income is the best predictor of democracy, and India is one of the few instances where this prediction fails. On the low-income side, India is the biggest surprise to have remained a democracy.[5] Amartya Sen has written about the argumentative traditions of India through history, and how our sustained democracy is hinged on this pluralistic and ancient culture of public debates in India. We are a talkative people, and that fuels our democratic values.[6] We are surprisingly, uniquely and indeed celebratorily democratic. In fact we may need to understand the Indian way of thinking about democracy, in which election rituals play such a pivotal and participatory role. For many of us, electoral democracy is the democracy to cling to. If nothing else, it is a lot of fun.

S.N. Balagangadhara's work contrasts Indian knowledge systems, which are empirical in nature, with the theory-driven, Western ones.[7] For the Abrahamic cultures, practices must be preceded by belief (theory) while for pagan Indic ones, ancestral practices and customs are ends in themselves. There is hardly any need for a doctrine to justify a practice here. Maybe this is the reason why the love for procedures and rituals of elections can be preserved with such vigour, without a corresponding concern about what is happening to 'democracy' at large (again, the movie *Newton* comes to mind). Although one must say, it is this very design of empiric-based knowledge system which may be the reason for sustenance of democracy here. And in that sense, there is a need to unpack and understand the very nature of the Indian democracy.

MOVING THE MOVEMENT

We often ask students in our classes to take a guess at India's population. Students, well-informed and well-read, often come up with figures close to the accurate one. Some say, it's 125 crores; some 130 crores. Others peg it at 135 crores. And then we ask them to consider the following: their tolerance and measure of error in population estimates itself is bigger than so many countries, like Colombia, South Korea, Spain, Argentina, Iraq, Canada or Kenya.

The size makes this country wondrous. Because there is no theory. There is no rule that can predict anything. As many people have said, whatever you say about India, the exactly opposite could also be true. The number of smartphone users in this country rose from 15 crores in 2014 to 50 crores in 2019–20. People claim smartphones will win elections this time. But around 40 crore people are also eligible to vote who won't have any smartphone or internet. While Facebook/Twitter battlegrounds will be occupied, parallel battles offline will have equal power to determine election results.

The excitement will continue unabated. The election motor will keep its pumps on. Again, political power will be sucked from all of us and offered to some. And again, many of us will feel cheated. Sometime, however, it will be good if we dig and find out, where is my vote taking my political power. What happened to it after it was cast? This is my movement. And they keep on moving it! For this may be a small journey over, but there are longer voyages ahead.

As a sequel to his famous work *Blindness*, the Nobel Prize winning Portuguese author José Saramago wrote another book, *Seeing*. Here, in the same unnamed democratic country as in the previous book, Saramago tells us the story of a parliamentary election gone horribly wrong. On the day of voting, a storm hits the capital. During the first few hours, no one shows up at the polling booths. The storm subsides and by 4 p.m., people begin showing up in large numbers. The state is happy in moments of democracy celebrations. When the results are announced, it surprises everyone—more than 70 per cent votes were blank! The government is shocked, and returns to the Constitution to seek advice. They announce new elections on the coming Sunday, hoping for people to show up and cast their votes. This happens to be a clear day, and voting goes on as usual with no abstentions. This time, the results are even more shocking—83 per cent blank votes. The government is flabbergasted, accusing the voters of having struck a 'brutal blow against the democratic normality'.

The rest of the story explains the dethroned government's embarrassment turning into desperation. It imposes an emergency, and orders strikes, bombings, stasi-type espionage and killings. It sets out to destroy this non-movement movement of the people.

Non-movement movement.

Notes

Prologue

1. Stéphanie Tawa Lama-Rewal, 'Studying Elections in India: Scientific and Political Debates', *South Asia Multidisciplinary Academic*, vol. 3 (2009).
2. Niraja Gopal Jayal, 'Introduction', in *Democracy in India*, edited by Niraja Gopal Jayal (Delhi: Oxford University Press, 2001), pp. 1–49.
3. Wendy Singer, *A Constituency Suitable for Ladies and Other Social Histories of Indian Elections* (New Delhi: Oxford University Press, 2007).
4. Ramashray Roy and Paul Wallace, *Indian Politics and the 1998 Election: Regionalism, Hindutva and State Politics* (New Delhi, Thousand Oaks, London: Sage Publications).
5. Christophe Jaffrelot, 'The Class Element in the 2014 Indian Election and the BJP's Success with Special Reference to the Hindi Belt', *Studies in Indian Politics*, vol. 3, no. 1 (2015): 19–38.
6. David Butler, Ashok Lahiri and Prannoy Roy, *India Decides: Elections 1952–1995* (New Delhi: Books & Things, 1995).
7. S. Nihal Singh, 'India Decides: Unique Study of Elections' (book review of *India Decides: Elections 1952–1989* by David Butler, Ashok Lahiri and Prannoy Roy), *India Today*, 31 October 1989.
8. Center for the Study of Developing Societies, *India National Election Study 2009* (New Delhi: CSDS, 2009).
9. Niraja Gopal Jayal, 'Introduction', in *Democracy in India*, edited by Niraja Gopal Jayal (Delhi: Oxford University Press 2001), pp. 1–49.
10. Stéphanie Tawa Lama-Rewal, 'Studying Elections in India: Scientific and Political Debates', *South Asia Multidisciplinary Academic*, vol. 3 (2009).

11. Myron Weiner, *India at the Polls: The Parliamentary Elections of 1977* (Washington, DC: American Enterprise Institute for Public Policy Research, 1978).
12. Paul R. Brass, *Caste, Faction and Party in Indian Politics, Volume Two: Election Studies* (Delhi: Chanakya Publications, 1985).
13. Paul R. Brass, *Theft of an Idol: Text and Context in the Representation of Collective Violence* (Princeton University Press, 1997).
14. James Michael Lyngdoh, *Chronicle of an Impossible Election: The Election Commission and the 2002 Jammu and Kashmir Assembly Elections* (Delhi: Penguin/Viking, 2004).
15. Mukulika Banerjee, 'Sacred Elections', *Economic and Political Weekly*, vol. 42, no. 17 (28 April 2007): 1556–1562.
16. Javier Auyero, 'Introductory Note to Politics under the Microscope: Special Issue on Political Ethnography I', *Qualitative Sociology*, vol. 2 (2006): 257–259.
17. Benedict Anderson, *Imagined Communities: Reflections on the Origin and Spread of Nationalism* (London: Verso Books, 2006).
18. Christopher Alan Bayly, *Rulers, Townsmen, and Bazaars: North Indian Society in the Age of British Expansion, 1770–1870* (Cambridge: Cambridge University Press, 1983).
19. John Berger, *Ways of Seeing* (London: Penguin Books, 2008).

Chapter 1. Digging through the Lok Sabha

1. 'From 6 paise to Rs 46: Poll Expense Per Elector', *Economic Times*, https://economictimes.indiatimes.com/news/elections/lok-sabha/india/from-6-paise-to-rs-46-poll-expense-per-elector/articleshow/68847287.cms?from=mdr, last updated on 12 April 2019.
2. Azman Usmani, 'In Charts: India's Election Becomes The World's Most Expensive', https://www.bloombergquint.com/elections/india-election-expenditure-2019-lok-sabha-elections-was-the-worlds-costliest, last updated on 4 June 2019.
3. Milan Vaishnav and Reedy Swanson, 'Does Good Economics Make for Good Politics? Evidence from Indian States', *India Review*, vol. 14, no. 3 (2015): 279–311.
4. Kanchan Chandra, 'Hardly the End of Dynastic Rule', *Economic and Political Weekly*, vol. 49, no. 28 (July 2014): 25–28.

5. Rukmini S., 'They Have Politics in Their DNA', *Hindu*, 9 June 2014, www.thehindu.com/news/national/they-have-politics-in-their-dna/article6095560.ec
6. Sanjay Kumar, Shreyas Sardesai and Pranav Gupta, 'The Weakening of Electoral Anti-Incumbency', *Economic and Political Weekly*, vol. 48, no. 13 (March 2013): 128–131.
7. The formula for these steps is given as $ENP = [\Sigma_{j\varepsilon P}(\frac{s_j}{\Sigma k\varepsilon P s_k})^2]^{-1}$ where s_j denotes the seat share of the j-th party and P is the set of political parties. See Markku Laakso and Rein Taagepera, '"Effective" Number of Parties: A Measure with Application to West Europe', *Comparative Political Studies*, vol. 12, no. 1 (1979): 3–27. See also, P. Chhibber, and I. Nooruddin, 'Do Party Systems Count? The Number of Parties and Government Performance in the Indian States', *Comparative Political Studies*, vol. 37, no. 2 (2004): 152–187; B. Bortolotti and P. Pinotti, 'Delayed Privatisation', *Public Choice*, vol. 136, no. 3–4 (2008): 331–335.
8. The formula for ENP_v is exactly the same as ENP, except that here, instead of seat share, we use vote share. $ENP_v = [\Sigma_{j\varepsilon P}(\frac{v_j}{\Sigma k\varepsilon P v_k})^2]^{-1}$ where v_j denotes the number of seats won by the j-th party and P is the set of political parties.
9. Michael Gallagher, 'Proportionality, Disproportionality and Electoral Systems', *Electoral Studies*, vol. 10, no. 1(1991): 33–51. The formula, where s_j denotes the number of seats of political party *j* in the elected body, v_j, denotes the number of votes received by the *j*-th political party and *P* denotes the set of political parties contested, is

$$\text{DISP} = 100\sqrt{\frac{1}{2}\sum_{j\varepsilon P}[(\frac{s_j}{\Sigma k\varepsilon P\, s_k}) - (\frac{v_j}{\Sigma k\varepsilon P\, v_k})]^2}$$

10. Sacha Kapoor and Arvind Magesan, 'Independent Candidates and Political Representation in India', *American Political Science Review*, vol. 112, no. 3(2018): 678–697.
11. Francis Fukuyama, *The Origins of Political Order: From Prehuman Times to the French Revolution* (Farrar, Straus and Giroux, 2011).
12. Abdurashid Solijonov, 'Voter Turnout Trends around the World', *IDEA*, 2016, https://www.idea.int/sites/default/files/publications/voter-turnout-trends-around-the-world.pdf.
13. Lori Beaman, Raghabendra Chattopadhyay, Esther Duflo, Rohini Pande and Petia Topalova, 'Powerful Women: Does Exposure Reduce

Bias?', *The Quarterly Journal of Economics,* vol. 124, no. 4 (November 2009): 1497–1540.

14. Lori Beaman, Esther Duflo, Rohini Pande and Petia Topalova, 'Female Leadership Raises Aspirations and Educational Attainment for Girls: A Policy Experiment in India', *Science Magazine*, vol. 335, no. 6068 (3 February 2012): 582–586.
15. Raghabendra Chattopadhyay and Esther Duflo, 'Women as Policy Makers: Evidence from a Randomized Policy Experiment in India', *Econometrica*, vol. 72, no. 5 (September 2004): 1406–1443.
16. Thushyanthan Baskaran, Sonia Bhalotra, Brian Min and Yogesh Uppal, 'Women Legislators and Economic Performance', *United Nations University World Institute for Development Economics Research*, 47 (May 2018).
17. Bhanupriya Rao, 'Women MPs in Lok Sabha: How have the Numbers Changed?', *Factly*, 2019, https://factly.in/women-in-parliament-where-does-india-figure-among-the-rest-world/.
18. Mudit Kapoor and Shamika Ravi, 'Why So Few Women in Politics? Evidence from India', Working Paper, Brookings, 2014. See also, F.R. Jensenius, (2016). 'Competing Inequalities? On the Intersection of Gender and Ethnicity in Candidate Nominations in Indian Elections', *Government and Opposition*, 51(3), pp. 440–463.
19. Laura Alfaro and Anusha Chari, 'India Transformed: Insights from the Firm Level 1988–2007', *India Policy Forum*, vol. 6 (2009): 153–224.

Chapter 2. Bihar

1. S. Kumar, M.S. Alam and D. Joshi, 'Caste Dynamics and Political Processes in Bihar', *Journal of Indian School of Political Thought*, vol. 20, no. 1/2 (2008): 1–32.
2. F.T. Jannuzi, *Agrarian Crisis in India: The Case of Bihar* (New Delhi: Sangam Books, 1974).
3. Christophe Jaffrelot, *India's Silent Revolution: The Rise of the Lower Castes in North* India, London: C Hurst & Co. (2003). See also, Yogendra Yadav. 'Electoral Politics in the Time of Change: India's Third Electoral System, 1989–99', *Economic & Political Weekly*, Vol. 34, No. 34–35 (1999): 2393–2399.

4. Bipan Chandra, *In the Name of Democracy* (Delhi: Penguin Random House, 2003).
5. Ibid.
6. Arvind N. Das, *The Republic of Bihar* (Delhi: Penguin Books, 1992).
7. Farzand Ahmed and Ajay Kumar, 'Root Cause of Almost All Rural Conflicts in Bihar Attributed to Land', *India Today*, 31 December 1986, https://www.indiatoday.in/magazine/special-report/story/19861231-root-cause-of-almost-all-rural-conflicts-in-bihar-attributed-to-land-801564-1986-12-31.
8. Santosh Mathew and Mick Moore, 'State Incapacity by Design: Understanding the Bihar Story', IDS Working Paper 366 (University of Sussex: Institute of Development Studies, 2011).
9. Subrata K. Mitra, *The Puzzle of India's Governance: Culture, Context and Comparative Theory* (London: Routledge, 2006), p. 103.
10. Sankersan Thakur, *The Making of Laloo Yadav: The Unmaking of Bihar* (New Delhi: HarperCollins 2000), p. 77.
11. S. Kumar, M.S. Alam and D. Joshi (2008), 'Caste Dynamics and Political Processes in Bihar', *Journal of Indian School of Political Thought*, Vol. 20, No. 1–2, pp. 1–32.
12. Sanjay Kumar, Mohammad Sanjeer Alam and Dhananjai Joshi, 'Caste Dynamics and Political Process in Bihar', *Journal of Indian School of Political Economy*, vol. 20, no. 1&2 (2008): 1–32.

Chapter 3. Uttar Pradesh

1. Vazira Fazila-Yacoobali Zamindar, *The Long Partition and the Making of Modern South Asia: Refugees, Boundaries, Histories* (New York: Columbia University Press, 2007).
2. See, for example, Ian Talbot, 'The Growth of the Muslim League in the Punjab, 1937–1946', *Journal of Commonwealth & Comparative Politics*, vol. 20, no. 1 (1982): 5–24.
3. Saeed Naqvi, *Being the Other: Muslim in India* (Delhi: Aleph Book Company, 2016).
4. Paul R. Brass, *Forms of Collective Violence: Riots, Pogroms, and Genocide in Modern India* (Three Essays Collective, 2006).
5. Raghuram G. Rajan, 'Is There a Threat of Oligarchy in India?', speech to the Bombay Chamber of Commerce on its Founders Day

celebration (2008), http://faculty.chicagobooth.edu/raghuram.rajan/research/papers/is%20there%20a%20threat%20of%20oligarchy%20in%20india.pdf.

Chapter 4. Bengal and Kerala

1. John Harris and Olle Törnquist, 'Comparative Notes on Indian Experiences of Social Democracy: Kerala and West Bengal', *Simons Papers in Security and Development*, no. 39 (2015).
2. Patrick K. Heller, 'Kerala: Deepening a Radical Social Democracy', in Richard Sandbrook, Marc Edelmann, Patrick Heller and Judith Teichman (eds), *Social Democracy in the Global Periphery: Origins, Challenges, and Prospects* (Cambridge: Cambridge University Press, 2006), pp. 65–92; Dilip M. Menon, *Caste, Nationalism, and Communism in South India: Malabar, 1900–1948* (Cambridge: Cambridge University Press, 1994).
3. S. Basu and A. Majumdar, 'Dilemmas of Parliamentary Communism: The Rise and Fall of the Left in West Bengal', *Critical Asian Studies*, vol. 45, no. 2 (2013): 167–200; A. Kohli, in F. Frankel and M.S.A. Rao (eds), *Dominance and State Power in Modern India Volume II* (Delhi: Oxford University Press, 1990).
4. Manali Desai, 'Party Formation, Political Power, and the Capacity for Reform: Comparing Left Parties in Kerala and West Bengal', *Social Forces*, vol. 80, no. 1 (2001): 37–60.
5. Coomi Kapoor, *The Emergency: A Personal History* (Delhi: Penguin, 2016).
6. B. Chakrabarty, 'The 2011 State Assembly Election in West Bengal: The Left Front Washed-out!', *Journal of South Asian Development*, vol. 6, no. 2 (2011): 143–167; B. Chakrabarty, 'The Left Front's 2009 Lok Sabha Poll Debacle in West Bengal, India', *Asian Survey*, vol. 51, no. 2 (2011): 290–310; J. Chatterjee and S. Basu, 'West Bengal: Mandate for Change', *Economic and Political Weekly*, vol. 44, no. 39 (2009): 152–156; P. Bardhan, D. Mookherjee and A. Nath, 'Changing Voting Patterns in Rural West Bengal', *Economic and Political Weekly*, vol. 49, no. 11 (2014): 55.
7. P. Radhakrishnan, *Peasant Struggles, Land Reforms and Social Change: Malabar 1836–1982* (New Delhi: Sage Publications, 1989).

8. Thomas Johnson Nossiter, *Communism in Kerala: A Study in Political Adaptation* (California: University of California Press, 1982).
9. Cithara Paul, 'EVMs: First Ever Trial Had Gone Wrong in Kerala in 1982', *The Week*, 15 March 2017, https://www.theweek.in/content/archival/news/india/electronic-voting-machines-controversy.html.
10. Robin Jeffrey, *Politics, Women and Well Being: How Kerala Became a 'Model'* (Delhi: Oxford University Press, 2003).
11. Govindan Parayil, *Kerala: The Development Experience: Reflections on Sustainability and Replicability* (London: Zed Books, 2000).
12. Moni Nag, 'Political Awareness as a Factor in Accessibility of Health Services: A Case Study of Rural Kerala and West Bengal', *Economic and Political Weekly*, 24, no. 8 (1989): 417–426.
13. Patrick Heller, K.N. Harilal and Shubham Chaudhuri, 'Building Local Democracy: Evaluating the Impact of Decentralization in Kerala, India', *World Development*, vol. 35, no. 4 (2007): 626–648.
14. Anna Lindberg, *Experience and Identity: A Historical Account of Class, Caste and Gender among the Cashew Workers of Kerala, 1930–2000* (Lund: Department of History, University of Lund, 2001); Ashwini Deshpande, 'Does Caste Still Define Disparity? A Look at Inequality in Kerala, India', *American Economic Review*, vol. 90, no. 2 (2000): 322–325; J. Devika, 'Egalitarian Developmentalism, Communist Mobilization, and the Question of Caste in Kerala State, India', *Journal of Asian Studies*, vol. 69, no. 3 (2010): 799–820.
15. Moni Nag, 'Impact of Social and Economic Development on Mortality: Comparative Study of Kerala and West Bengal', *Economic and Political Weekly*, vol. 18, nos. 19–21 (1983): 877–900.
16. Manali Desai, 'Party Formation, Political Power, and the Capacity for Reform: Comparing Left Parties in Kerala and West Bengal', *Social Forces*, vol. 80, no. 1 (2001): 37–60.
17. John Harriss, 'Renewing Development and Deepening Democracy', *Frontline*, vol. 17, no. 13 (19 August–1 September 2000).
18. Ross Mallick, *Development Policy of a Communist Government* (Cambridge, UK: Cambridge University Press, 1993).
19. Here, n is the number of constituencies in which party f won, denoted by t; v_f is the number of votes secured by the first party f; v_s is the number of votes received by party s, which is second to party f. Just like above, $f\varepsilon P$ and $s\varepsilon P$. $AMS = \frac{100}{n} \sum_{t=1}^{t=n} \left[\frac{(v_f - v_s)}{v_f}\right]_t$.

20. D. Battacharyya, 'Left in the Lurch: The Demise of the World's Longest Elected Regime?', *Economic and Political Weekly*, vol. XLV, no. 3 (2010): 51–59.
21. A. Chattopadhyay, 'Distributive Impact of Agricultural Growth in Rural West Bengal', *Economic and Political Weekly*, vol. XL, no. 53 (2005): 5601–5610.
22. K. Beg, 'Red Bengal's Rise and Fall', *New Left Review*, vol. 70 (2011): 69–98.
23. P. Bardhan, S. Mitra, D. Mookherjee and A. Sarkar, 'Local Democracy and Clientelism: Implications for Political Stability in Rural West Bengal', *Economic and Political Weekly*, vol. 44, no. 9 (2009): 46–58; A. Ruud, 'From Untouchable to Communist: Wealth, Power and Status among Supporters of the Communist Party (Marxist) in Rural West Bengal', in B. Rogaly, B. Harriss-White and S. Bose (eds), *Agricultural Growth and Agrarian Change in West Bengal and Bangladesh* (New Delhi: Sage Publications and London: Thousand Oaks 1999).
24. D. Battacharyya, 'Left in the Lurch: The Demise of the World's Longest Elected Regime?', *Economic and Political Weekly*, vol. XLV, no. 3 (2010): 51–59.
25. K. Beg, 'Red Bengal's Rise and Fall', *New Left Review*, vol. 70 (2011): 69–98.
26. Patrick Heller, 'Reinventing Public Power in the Age of Globalization: The Transformation of Movement Politics in Kerala', in Raka Ray and Mary Katzenstein (eds), *Social Movements in India: Poverty, Power and Politics* (New York: Rowman and Littlefield Publishers Inc., 2005).
27. John Harris and Olle Törnquist, *Comparative Notes on Indian Experiences of Social Democracy: Kerala and West Bengal*, Simons Papers in Security and Development No. 39, 2015.
28. Aditya Nigam, 'The Changing Faces of Political Violence in West Bengal', *The Wire*, 2018, https://thewire.in/politics/west-bengal-political-violence.
29. Biplab Dasgupta, 'The 1972 Election in West Bengal', *Economic and Political Weekly*, vol. 7, no. 16 (1972): 804–808.
30. Partha Sarathi Banerjee, 'Party, Power and Political Violence in West Bengal', *Economic and Political Weekly*, vol. 46, no. 6 (2011): 16–18.
31. Adrija Roychowdhury, 'Politics of Violence in West Bengal: When History Keeps Repeating Itself', *Indian Express*, 6 June 2018, https://

indianexpress.com/article/research/politics-of-violence-in-west-bengal-when-history-keeps-repeating-itself-5205222/.

32. Ashwani Kumar, *Community Warriors: State, Peasants and Caste Armies in Bihar* (London: Anthem Press, 2008).
33. Partha Chatterjee, 'The Coming Crisis in West Bengal', *Economic and Political Weekly*, vol. 44, no. 9 (2009): 42–45.
34. Ibid.
35. Myron Weiner, 'Changing Patterns of Political Leadership in West Bengal', *Pacific Affairs*, vol. 32, no. 3 (1959): 277–287.
36. Ibid.
37. Jan Breman, *Patronage and Exploitation: Changing Agrarian Relations in South Gujarat, India* (California, University of California Press, 1974).
38. Atul Kohli, *Democracy and Discontent* (Cambridge: University of Cambridge Press); James Manor, 'Changing State, Changing Society in India', *South Asia: Journal of South Asian Studies*, vol. 25, no. 2 (2002): 231–256.
39. Patrick K. Heller, 'Kerala: Deepening a Radical Social Democracy', in Richard Sandbrook, Marc Edelmann, Patrick Heller and Judith Teichman (eds), *Social Democracy in the Global Periphery: Origins, Challenges, and Prospects* (Cambridge: Cambridge University Press, 2006), 65–92; Dilip M. Menon, *Caste, Nationalism, and Communism in South India: Malabar, 1900–1948* (Cambridge: Cambridge University Press, 1994).
40. D.P. Bhattacharya, 'Mahatma Gandhi's Autobiography Has More Readers in Kerala than His Home State Gujarat', *The Economic Times*, 23 November 2018, https://economictimes.indiatimes.com/news/politics-and-nation/mahatma-gandhis-autobiography-has-more-readers-in-kerala-than-his-home-state-gujarat/articleshow/66777536.cms.

Chapter 5. The Rise of BJP

1. Christophe Jaffrelot, *Hindu Nationalism: A Reader* (Princeton: Princeton University Press, 2007).
2. The data source in these figures come from www.chanakyya.com
3. Ragamalika Karthikeyan, 'Understanding Azaadi: Why South Indians Need to Care More about Kashmir', *The News Minute*, 13 July 2016,

https://www.thenewsminute.com/article/understanding-azaadi-why-south-indians-need-care-more-about-kashmir-46433.

4. K.P. Kannan and G. Raveendran, 'Growth Sans Employment: A Quarter Century of Jobless Growth in India's Organised Manufacturing', *Economic and Political Weekly*, vol. 44, no. 10 (7–13 March 2009), pp. 80–91.
5. Arvind Rajagopal tries to make these connections in his book, *Politics after Television: Religious Nationalism and the Reshaping of the Indian Public* (Cambridge: Cambridge University Press, 2001).
6. Arvind Singhal, J.K. Doshi, Everett M. Rogers and S. Adnan Rahman, 'The Diffusion of Television in India', *Media Asia*, vol. 15, no. 4 (1988): 222–229.
7. Paul Brass, 'Caste, Class and Community in the Ninth General Elections for the Lok Sabha in Uttar Pradesh', in Harold A. Gould and Sumit Ganguly, *India Votes: Alliance Politics and Minority Governments in the Ninth and Tenth General Elections* (New York: Routledge, 1993), pp. 109–11.
8. E. Sridharan, 'Coalition Strategies and the BJP's Expansion, 1989–2004', *Commonwealth & Comparative Politics*, vol. 43(2005): 194–221.
9. Harold A. Gould, 'Patterns of Political Mobilization in the Parliamentary and Assembly Elections of 1989 and 1990', in *India Votes: Alliance Politics and Minority Governments in the Ninth and Tenth General Elections* (New York: Routledge, 1993), p. 20.

Chapter 6. Coalition Politics in India

1. For an extensive analysis of Indian politics during 1952–1970, refer to Rajni Kothari, *Politics in India* (Boston: Little Brown, 1970).
2. For a detailed analysis on coalition politics in India, see Bidyut Chakraborty, *Forging Power: Coalition Politics in India* (New Delhi: Oxford University Press, 2006).
3. Paul R. Brass, *Theft of an Idol: Text and Context in the Representation of Collective Violence* (Princeton: Princeton University Press, 1997). Brass tells us how Indira Gandhi gave rise to populist outreach by visiting the families of the bereaved in villages, creating an outstanding display of service, triggering a race in which every political party subsequently participated. And they continue to do so.

4. Atul Kohli, *India's Democracy: An Analysis of Changing State-Society Relations* (New Delhi: Orient Longman, 1991).
5. K.N. Rao and D.S. Ram, 'Political Developments in Andhra Pradesh 1978-1989: A study', *The Indian Journal of Political Science*, vol. 5, no. 14 (1990): 540–564.
6. The Gross Domestic Product (GDP) revised estimates for 2003-04 were 8.52 per cent per annum. The comparative figure for GDP growth rates can be found at https://community.data.gov.in/gdp-growth-rate-of-india-constant-prices-during-2001-02-to-2013-14/.
7. E. Sridharan, 'Electoral Coalitions in 2004 General Elections: Theory and Evidence', *Economic and Political Weekly*, vol. 39, no. 51 (2004): 5418–5425.
8. Bidyut Chakrabarty and Sugato Hazra, *Winning the Mandate* (New Delhi: Sage Publications, 2016).
9. P. Chhibber and R. Verma, 'The BJP's 2014 "Modi Wave"', *Economic and Political Weekly*, vol. 49, no. 39 (2014): 50–56.
10. Christophe Jaffrelot and Frederic Grare, 'The Regionalization of Indian Politics and the Challenge of Coalition-building', Carnegie Endowment for International Peace, 8 November 2012, http://carnegieendowment.org/2012/11/08/regionalization-of-indian-politics-and-challenge-of-coalition-building/eaq5.

Chapter 7. Two Issues on Electoral Reforms

1. Francis Fukuyama, *The Origins of Political Order: From Prehuman Times to the French Revolution* (New York: Farrar, Straus and Giroux, 2011).
2. Milan Vaishnav, 'Understanding the Indian Voter', Carnegie Endowment for International Peace, 2015, https://carnegieendowment.org/2015/06/23/understanding-indian-voter-pub-60416.
3. See, Douglass North and Barry Weingast, 'Constitutions and Commitment: The Evolution of Institutions Governing Public Choice in Seventeenth-century England', *The Journal of Economic History*, vol. 49, no. 4 (1989): 803–832.
4. Ashis Nandy, *The Intimate Enemy: Loss and Recovery of Self Under Colonialism* (Delhi: Oxford University Press, 1989).
5. The proceedings of the Constituent Assembly debates are available at https://www.constitutionofindia.net/. The specific statement was

made during the debate on 8 November 1948, available in l. VII of the Proceedings, available at https://www.constitutionofindia.net/constitution_assembly_debates/volume/7/1948-11-08.

6. Ibid.
7. Shefali Jha, 'Representation and Its Epiphanies: A Reading of Constituent Assembly Debates', *Economic and Political Weekly*, vol. 39, no. 39 (2004): 4357–4360.
8. Phill Elder and Alvin Finkel, 'Back to the Future: Proportional Representation in Alberta and Canada', *Alberta Democratic Renewal Project*, http://www.assembly.pe.ca/photos/original/leg_ws6abdemrnw.pdf.
9. The specific statement was made during the debate on 4 January 1949, available in vol. VII of the Proceedings, available at https://www.constitutionofindia.net/constitution_assembly_debates/volume/7/1949-01-04
10. Ibid.
11. Patrick Dunleavy and Rekha Diwakar, 'Analysing Multiparty Competition in Plurality Rule Elections', *Party Politics*, vol. 19, no. 6 (2013): 855–86, http://eprints.lse.ac.uk/38452/1/Dunleavy_Analysing%20multiparty_2014_author.pdf.
12. Shefali Jha, 'Representation and Its Epiphanies: A Reading of Constituent Assembly Debates', *Economic and Political Weekly*, vol. 39, no. 39 (2004): 4357–4360.

Epilogue

1. Milan Vaishnav, 'Understanding the Indian Voter', Carnegie Endowment for International Peace, 2015, https://carnegieendowment.org/2015/06/23/understanding-indian-voter-pub-60416.
2. Aristotle, *Politics: Book III*, Chapter IX.
3. Lloyd Rudolph and Susanne Hoeber Rudolph, *In Pursuit of Lakshmi: The Political Economy of the Indian State* (Chicago: University of Chicago Press, 1987).
4. Ramachandra Guha, *India after Gandhi: The History of the World's Largest Democracy* (Pan Macmillan, 2017).
5. Ashutosh Varshney, *Battles Half Won: India's Improbable Democracy* (UK: Penguin, 2014).

6. Amartya Sen, *The Argumentative Indian* (New Delhi: Penguin, 2012).
7. S.N. Balagangadhara, *Reconceptualising India Studies* (New Delhi: Oxford University Press 2012). See also, S.N. Balagangadhara, *The Heathen in his Blindness* (Leiden, New York and Cologne: E.J. Brill, 1994).

Index

Acknowledgements

Writing a book is like a journey of mind through ideas. This journey, like most others, cannot be accomplished alone. We are thankful to a number of people who made it possible for us to navigate and indeed propel us through the whirlwind of ideas that the voyage encountered. We mention some of them here.

We began conceptualising the ideas present in the book several years ago, and we thank Varun Rana and Raghu Karnad to see the value in these ideas, and encourage us to take it up as a book project. We were extremely fortunate to work with Karthika V.K., our editor at Westland. She helped us in structuring the argument and planning the blueprint of this work. Her ideas on how to make the book accessible to general audience were invaluable. We also thank her colleague Sonia Madan, who is an excellent editor any writer would wish for, not only for her meticulous reading and incisive comments, but also a great deal of patience.

We have gained significantly from our discussions with various scholars and professionals in diverse fields of inquiry. Rupayan Pal has been a mentor to us for a very long time and we thank him for his efforts in shaping our thoughts early on. We express sincere gratitude to Shivprasad Swaminathan, Deepanshu Mohan, Aseem Prakash, Mohsin Raza Khan, Brajesh Ranjan, Katherine Hunt, Sushant Chandra, Rahul Jayaram for reading and commenting on an earlier version of the chapters in the manuscript. In addition, we would like to thank Anup Kumar, Amrit Raj, Partha Pratim Das, Pramod Shrotriya, Vinayak Pachalag, Shardul Manurkar, Samta Arora, Dwarika Uniyal, Ranjan Ghosh, Sonal Shah, Snigdha Poonam, Shivakumar Jolad and Santosh Kudtakar, for helping us understand the deeper contexts of politics in India. We think all of them—and many more—have added so many points of view and enriched the ways in which we look at the world.

This book would not have been possible had it not been for our brilliant student researchers. We would particularly like to thank Tanay Puneet Manaktala, Nirali Shekhwa, Harnoor Kaur, Madhumita Suresh, Veni Kothari, Paavani Pegatraju, Sakshi Chindaliya, Taarika Peres, Vidhi Khaitan and Gauri Kundalia.

The intellectual ecosystem, research culture and amazing sets of colleagues at both O.P. Jindal Global University and FLAME University deserve a special mention too. The two new-age, global universities of India offer a rich promise for knowledge creation in India, and their recognition of impactful research goes a long way in cultivating projects like ours.

Finally, the enormous support and patience that our families gave us particularly during the intense research and writing period has been incalculable. Our parents and siblings Vinod Kaushik, Praveen Kaushik, V.K. Goyal, and Manju Goyal were our unending inspirations. We thank our wives, Prerna Kaushik and Harini Shah, for patiently listening to our chapters and the many stories that came from our research. And especially Arun's three-year-old, Rihan, the wonder in whose eyes kept our excitement alive through this project.